CONSUL ZEPHYR ZODIAC EXECUTIVE

CONSUL ZEPHYR ZODIAC EXECUTIVE

MICHAEL ALLEN

MOTOR RACING PUBLICATIONS LTD
Unit 6, The Pilton Estate, 46 Pitlake, Croydon CR0 3RY, England

ISBN 0 947981 42 X

First published as *CONSUL, ZEPHYR, ZODIAC: The Big Fifties Fords*, 1983

Second edition, revised and extended, 1990

Printed in Great Britain by The Amadeus Press Ltd
Huddersfield, West Yorkshire

Contents

Acknowledgements

Piecing together the history of this long-running series of large cars from Ford of Britain and amassing an appropriate collection of illustrations would not have been possible without the help and encouragement of many people, and therefore I must express my gratitude to the following: Ford Corporate History Manager David Burgess-Wise, for the generous provision of company archive material; Steve Clark and Sheila Knapman, of Ford Photographic Services: Ford Personnel Supervisor, D.J. Pasterfield; former senior Ford employees, engineers Fred Hart, George Halford and Les Geary, and also Ted Rawlinson of Ford's Body Division; Product Planners Maurice Sury and Dacre Harvey, and former Senior Stylist Charles Thompson; Bob Murray, editor of *Autocar & Motor*, former editors Ray Hutton and Tony Curtis, and also Simon Taylor of Haymarket Publications; the Australian motoring magazines *Wheels* and *Cars Today*; A.H. Leake, of Laycock Engineering; J.N. Green, of Servais Silencers; Major A.P.R. Rolt and John Braithwaite, of FF Developments Ltd; J.S. Graham, Assistant Chief Clerk, The Royal Mews, and R.S. French, Public Enterprise Manager, Sandringham Estate; Police Chief Superintendent J. Smith, of the Home Office, Superintendent Westwood, of West Yorkshire Police, police officers John Charlton and Dave Sowden, and police mechanic Peter Tindall; fellow Ford enthusiasts Dave Barry, Dick Barry, Ian Carey, Howard Foottit, Peter Scott, Keith Roe, Paul Boothby, Paul Jarvis and John Glaysher; fellow writer and Ford devotee Martin Rawbone, who kindly gave me access to his large collection of Ford material.

Motorsport played a considerable part in the story of the big Fords, and for their kind response with reminiscences of those adventurous days I'm most grateful to Anne Hall, Jeff Uren, Gerry Burgess, Edward and John Harrison, Denis Scott, Ken Armstrong, Maurice Gatsonides, Eric Jackson, Dacre Harvey, Jack Reiss, Barry Lee, and Lionel Sangster; also Mike Wilds of the BRSCC.

Acknowledging the help willingly given to me by former Ford Competitions Manager Edgy Fabris and competition department mechanic Norman Masters is now unfortunately tinged with sadness, as both these gentlemen have since passed away. Their contribution to the Ford Zephyr's sporting successes however will not be forgotten.

Michael G.D. Allen

CHAPTER 1

Dagenham after the War

Anglia, Prefect and Pilot

As the Second World War receded into the past, the British motor industry, which had worked so hard throughout the period of hostilities turning out an amazing variety of armaments and military vehicles, was able to turn its attention once again to the production of passenger cars. Almost inevitably, all its early offerings were nothing more than thinly disguised versions of the manufacturers' respective prewar models, hastily re-introduced with the minimum of revision to either the styling or the mechanical specification, and intended only to fill in the time that it would take for the design and engineering teams to come up with something entirely new.

So by the end of the 1940s a steady stream of new models was emerging from the factories of most of the major manufacturers, often featuring overhead-valve engines, independent front suspension and, in some cases, monocoque construction that did away with a separate chassis-frame, and all displaying styling features which immediately rendered visually obsolete their prewar-inspired predecessors. Meanwhile, to the surprise of many people, the production lines at Dagenham continued to turn out what were barely facelifted prewar Fords, and it appeared that the Ford Motor Company, who had so often been the market leaders in the past, were now being left well and truly behind.

At the economy end of the range, the familiar 8hp 933cc two-door Anglia and the 10hp 1,172cc four-door Prefect were selling well, their 1930s ancestry allowing the Ford Motor Company to list them in 1948 at £293 and £352, respectively, and so fully uphold the Ford tradition of value for money.

The first serious opposition to the small Fords came in October 1948 with the introduction of the Morris Minor, a model that set entirely new standards of road behaviour for this class of car, and was also extremely competitive at a price of £358. It was, however, let down somewhat at this stage by the rather surprising use of a prewar side-valve engine that itself had Ford connections. When, in 1932, Dagenham had introduced the all-new 8hp Y type Ford and, at a stroke, rendered obsolete such opposition as the contemporary Morris Minor and Austin 7, Morris Motors had purchased an example of the new Ford, taken it to pieces, carefully measuring the components as they went along, and then proceeded to produce a remarkably similar version of the engine for their own new car,

which had been announced in 1934 as the Morris 8. It was a developed version of the engine from this car that was used to power the otherwise completely new 1948 Morris Minor.

Other than the Minor there was little opposition to the small Fords at this time, as the other rival manufacturers had been concentrating their efforts on new models in the medium-size category, and so it was considered at Dagenham that with their firmly established following, coupled with the low prices at which they were being offered, the Anglia and Prefect could soldier on into the 1950s.

Above the Prefect, however, there was a considerable gap in the Ford range, and those motorists who wished for something in the $1\frac{1}{4}$- to $1\frac{1}{2}$-litre category, with a modern appearance and an up-to-date mechanical specification, were placing their orders for the recently introduced Austin Devon and Dorset, Morris Oxford, Hillman Minx and Vauxhall Wyvern, models that were well suited to satisfy the demands of what was to prove a rapidly expanding sector of the car buying public, which was not being catered for at all by Ford at that time.

Ford of Dagenham's flagship for the late 1940s was the big, V8-engined Pilot. A fast, roomy and very well appointed car, it could be regarded as the logical conclusion of a sturdy theme whose origins could be traced back to 1932, when Henry Ford had triumphantly announced to the world the first Ford V8. With its cylinder block cast in one piece, this engine had been regarded by many contemporary observers as something of an engineering miracle.

Priced at £764, the Pilot, like its smaller stablemates, represented typical Ford value. The 3.6-litre side-valve V8 engine propelled the 30cwt car with remarkable ease, giving a maximum speed of more than 80mph under favourable conditions, whilst at the other end of the scale allowing a driver to retain top gear right down to below 10mph and still be able to pull away from this speed smoothly and quite rapidly. Contemporary road test reports published in the popular motoring press revealed that the Pilot had the ability to reach 70mph from a standing start in around 30 seconds if full use was made of the three-speed gearbox. By the standards of the day all this was, of course, very definitely 'high performance', but the price was a

The 1949 American Ford on which the styling of Dagenham's Consul and Zephyr Six was based.

fuel consumption that could be as high as 14mpg in heavy traffic conditions, and even if a feather-footed technique was adopted whilst driving on the open road, the result was unlikely to be anything better than 19-20mpg. This was less than satisfactory in the austerity of those early postwar years.

The suspension, with its transverse leaf springs front and rear, was very much 'traditional' Ford. Aided by the excellent seats, it would give the occupants of the Pilot a very comfortable ride, but in terms of handling, the big Ford could not hope to match the agility of some of the more recent offerings from rival manufacturers with their newly-adopted independent front suspension systems. The design showed its age, too, in the use of a braking system with hydraulic operation for the front brakes only, whilst the rear shoes were activated mechanically, resulting in high pedal pressures being called for, particularly if an emergency stop was required.

A close examination of the fittings and furnishings of the Pilot would reveal a high degree of quality and good workmanship, and in this respect particularly, the Pilot was a product of which Dagenham could be justifiably proud. But with large separately-mounted headlamps and wide running boards accentuating its typically 1930s styling, as well as its dated mechanical specification, it was obvious that it could not hope to compete for long in the postwar market place.

Clearly, if Dagenham were to take a lead in the 1950s, they urgently needed a new car that would not only replace the big V8 and perpetuate its high performance with a new-found economy, but would also fill that important gap in the middle of the range. In addition to all this it would have to be sufficiently advanced in both style and engineering to ensure a lengthy production run and, of course, bearing the name of Ford, it would have to sell at a bargain price.

CHAPTER 2

The Five Star Cars

Mk 1 Consul, Zephyr and Zodiac

Ever since the assembly lines at Dagenham had first come into operation in October 1931, the cars which emerged from the Thameside factory had shown a strong American influence. The diminutive 8hp Y type of 1932 had been wholly designed in Dearborn, and the big V8 models that had culminated in the postwar Pilot could be regarded as little other than right-hand-drive versions of a typical late 1930s full-size American Ford.

In the United States, passenger car production was sanctioned once again by the Government soon after VE day and, characteristically, it was the Ford assembly lines at Dearborn that were the first to roll. On July 3, 1945 the first postwar Ford, a Tudor (two-door) Super De Luxe left the line and was personally delivered by Henry Ford II, grandson of the famous founder, to US President Harry S. Truman.

Owing to the untimely death of his father, Edsel Ford, young Henry had been 'thrown in at the deep end' and had had little time to gain the experience necessary to hold down the Presidency of an industrial giant such as the Ford Motor Company. Wisely, he looked around for outside help, and in 1946 he recruited Ernest R. Breech, former President of the Bendix Aviation Company, to be his Executive Vice-President at Ford.

As was the case at Dagenham, the new cars being assembled at Dearborn were virtually identical with the last of the prewar models, and Breech decided that an all-new model would be needed quickly if Ford were to re-establish their position as leaders in the low-price field. With the full agreement of Henry Ford II, he set the engineers to work on a completely new chassis which would do away with the traditional Ford running gear that had its origins in the famed model T. In order to ensure that the new car would also have a completely new image, an outside styling consultant, George Walker, was brought in to produce the mock-ups for the body. The new car that was soon taking shape as a result of these decisions was appreciably bigger and heavier than Dearborn's previous products, and although the chassis was to feature entirely new running gear with wishbone-type independent front suspension and longitudinally mounted leaf springs at the rear, the car would still be powered by the venerable side-valve V8 engine and, surprisingly, would continue to utilize a 6-volt electrical system.

In 1948, a team of engineers from Dagenham visited the parent company in Dearborn to discuss plans and proposals for a new British

Ford. It was obvious from the outset that the new car nearing completion at Dearborn would be far too big and heavy, and therefore also too thirsty, to stand a chance of significant sales in postwar Britain or Europe, or in the many other world markets in which Dagenham competed so successfully, and so a right-hand-drive version of this particular car for Britain was never under serious consideration. It was important, however, that the new image that was being created by stylist George Walker should be a feature of the Dagenham product if at all possible, and fortunately the final shape which had evolved at Dearborn lent itself well to the scaled-down dimensions that would be acceptable in Europe.

Executive engineer George Halford was a member of the Dagenham team, and he recalled later that the 'joint consultations' which took place with their American hosts went very smoothly, with no serious areas of disagreement, and as a result of these talks, the team returned to England with plans for a car that would be technically far in advance of the new American Fords. A completely new four-door bodyshell, incorporating a large glass area and of monocoque construction, had been decided upon. Development of this new body was to be in conjunction with long-time suppliers of Ford bodywork, Briggs Motor Bodies, whose subsidiary at Dagenham had been established in the 1930s at the suggestion of Henry Ford in order to enable them to supply his English operation. Briggs had already some experience of monocoque construction, as the parent company had supplied prototype unitary bodies of their own design to the Lincoln Division of the Ford Motor Company for the 1935 Lincoln Zephyr.

Whilst featuring quite substantial chassis-type members welded into its

Consul and Zephyr Six, the 'Five Star Cars'. According to the brochure, the five star features were: OHV 'oversquare' engines; 'centre slung' within-the-wheelbase seating; independent front suspension; all-steel integral body/chassis construction; hydraulic brakes all round. Although produced by Ford of Britain, the new model was designed at Ford of America in Dearborn, with the assistance of a British team headed by George Halford. Also heavily involved in engineering the new range at Dagenham were Fred Hart and Briggs Motor Bodies man Andy Cox.

lower regions, the new bodyshell would also use its large side frames, the front scuttle/toeboard bulkhead and, through the windscreen pillars, the roof pressing in combination with each other to provide a structure of immense strength and rigidity without excess weight. The rear extension of the bodyshell formed an unusually large full-width luggage compartment, under the floor of which was situated a 9-gallon fuel tank, protected at the sides by the chassis rails and at the rear by the bumper bar, the mountings of which were themselves extensions of the chassis members. The upper halves of the rear wings were part of the integral construction, whilst the lower halves were unstressed bolt-on panels. Forward of the windscreen the bodyshell consisted of sturdy inner wing panels, and across the front end joining these together was another welded-in bulkhead featuring a large central aperture into which the radiator would be bolted. Additional bracing of the front end structure was by struts welded into the inner wings at the point where the suspension upper mounting was situated and running diagonally across the engine compartment to be welded into the scuttle beneath the windscreen. The whole front end structure differed in length according to which of the four- or six-cylinder engine options that had been decided upon for the new cars was to be installed. The front wings, which contained the lamp units, were bolted on, as was a separate front panel. This latter section varied to accommodate the different grilles that would identify the four- or six-cylinder model.

One of the factors that led the design team to choose monocoque construction for the new cars was that one of the American Ford engineers, Earle MacPherson, had recently schemed out a brilliantly simple independent front suspension system for use with an integrally-constructed body. This front suspension, which eventually became known universally as the MacPherson strut and would also, after the Ford patents on its design had exceeded their time limits, be widely adopted throughout the motor industry, was built up around what was in effect a very long

Ford Consul and Zephyr Six MacPherson-strut front suspension, looking forward. The utilization of the track control arms and forward-pointing anti-roll bar to form a wishbone lower location can be seen. The tubular crossmember in the centre bolts to the chassis rails along the lower edges of the inner wings. When installed, the steering box is situated just above the track rods (lower right in this picture) and is thus behind the axle line and well protected in the event of a frontal impact. Even if the box were displaced, its position and the angle of the steering column are such that the steering wheel would move forward away from the driver, a valuable safety feature.

kingpin, the upper part of which was in the form of a telescopic shock absorber. This section was surrounded by a coil spring and was mounted at the top to the inner front wing, and so, as the inner wing was an integral part of the whole shell, the stress was widely spread, with the front scuttle/ bulkhead, the floor and, via the windscreen pillars, the roof, all combining to take the load. By utilizing the strongest part of the car in this way, the MacPherson strut offered substantial savings in both cost and weight over the conventional subframe-mounted double-wishbone installation. At the bottom, a track control arm linked the suspension strut to the front bodywork crossmember, and was thus effectively one half of a lower wishbone, the other half of which was the swept-back end of a transverse anti-roll bar.

This was, of course, the first application of the MacPherson strut, and trouble was experienced with too much friction in the system in the early prototype cars, although, according to engineer George Halford, this was successfully overcome before the production stage was reached by very careful attention to detail. At the rear the car was supported by longitudinally-mounted leaf springs, on which was carried the rear axle, controlled by lever-arm shock absorbers. The steering gear chosen utilized a Burman worm-and-peg type steering box, which, in company with the new front suspension, gave the cars a far more accurate degree of control than on any previous Dagenham product.

The braking system was by Girling, and consisted of 9in diameter drums all round, those at the front being of the two-leading-shoe arrangement. The total lining area was 121sq in, and the system was activated hydraulically from a master cylinder mounted high up on the scuttle above the toeboard, operated by a pendant brake pedal. The mechanically-operated handbrake activated the rear shoes only, controlled by a pull-out lever under the dashboard.

The 13in diameter road wheels were shod with 5.90 x 13 tyres on the four-cylinder car, running at a recommended pressure of 28psi, and on the six-cylinder model the very amply sized 6.40 x 13 on $\frac{1}{2}$in wider rims, running at 24psi pressure. The track was 4ft 2in at the front and 4ft 1in at the rear, whilst the wheelbase was 8ft 4in and 8ft 8in, respectively, for the four- and six-cylinder models.

It was in order to achieve both the performance and the economy levels that would appeal to the widest possible sector of the buying public that two engine capacities had been decided upon for the new range. An in-line or 'straight' six-cylinder engine was chosen for the high-performance model, as six cylinders in this configuration, driving a three-plane crankshaft, offer outstanding mechanical smoothness accompanied by a very worthwhile saving in cost and weight in comparison with a V8 engine, and can in addition be very conveniently reduced in length to four cylinders, and so provide another engine of two-thirds the capacity with the maximum of interchangeability of internal moving parts between the two units. The abolition of the 'horsepower' tax in Great Britain in 1947 had been very timely as far as the Ford engineers were concerned. This tax, which was calculated on the area of the piston crown, had forced engine designers to use narrow-bore engines with a long piston stroke in order to be in the lowest practicable taxation class with any given cubic capacity, and had thus hampered engine development for many years. This narrow-bore, long-stroke arrangement was undesirable as it resulted in very high piston speeds at relatively low rpm, and also required a long-throw crankshaft, which can be lacking in rigidity. Freed from these constraints, the Dagenham engineers were able to adopt wider bore, shorter stroke dimensions, and produce what was to become known as an 'oversquare' engine, 'square' being the term used when the bore and stroke dimensions are identical.

The weight-saving process with the six-cylinder version was apparently taken too far at first as, according to George Halford, the original prototype cylinder blocks proved to be too thin, and a new block with considerably more 'meat' was introduced early in the development programme. To ensure even cooling, the water jacketing circled around each individual cylinder, and this, coupled with the large bore, resulted in a somewhat long engine in six-cylinder form. The cylinder dimensions chosen, 79.37mm bore x 76.2mm stroke, (3.125in x 3.00in) gave a capacity of 1,508cc (92cu in) and 2,262cc (138cu in), respectively, for the four- and six-cylinder units. This short piston stroke required only a very

Cutaway view of the left-hand side of a Zephyr Six engine. Water jacketing around each cylinder in a large-bore 'six' results in a long engine, but ensures even cooling and freedom from distortion problems. The cutaway of the right-hand side of the engine shows camshaft and pushrod details. The air cleaner is the oil bath type fitted for certain export markets where dusty conditions prevailed. A sump guard and a four-bladed fan were also available in certain territories.

short-throw crankshaft in comparison with earlier designs, and with a crankpin journal diameter of 1.93in allied to a main bearing journal diameter of 2.25in, the cast-alloy steel shaft was an extremely rigid affair even in its comparatively long six-cylinder form. Fully counterbalanced, the crankshaft ran in either three or four main bearings depending upon the four- or six-cylinder application. These bearings, along with those of the connecting rod big-ends, were steel-backed with a white-metal lining, and were of the replaceable shell type.

Overhead valve gear, Zephyr Six. The pipe to the centre of the rocker shaft is the oil feed. The three studs are for rocker cover fixing.

Zephyr Six crankshaft in both original cast state and fully machined. The extremely short throw, allied to wide bearing journal diameters, can be appreciated in this view.

Zephyr Six engine, showing the simple exhaust manifold.

Consul engine with standard, home-market air filter. The tube from the side cover is the crankcase breather. Note the gearbox dipstick which is reached from inside the car by pulling back the floor covering and removing a small plate in the transmission tunnel.

Aluminium alloy pistons of the controlled-expansion 'autothermic' type were used, with two compression and one oil control ring all above the gudgeon pin. The connecting rods were steel forgings of I-section. Lubrication was by a gear-type pump situated in the sump and driven from the camshaft; a full-flow oil filter with a large replaceable element was incorporated in the system. Overhead valves were another innovation for Ford, and were operated by what could be described then as the 'conventional' arrangement of pushrods and rockers. The valves opened into wedge-shaped combustion chambers in the cast-iron cylinder head, which featured siamesed inlet ports and gave a necessarily low compression ratio of 6.8:1 in order to cope with the very low octane petrol of the period.

A camshaft-driven AC mechanical fuel pump supplied petrol to a single Zenith carburettor in both cases. The cast aluminium inlet manifold had very carefully thought out internal passages on the six-cylinder application, designed to swirl the mixture and so ensure that each cylinder would receive an equal amount of fuel despite the engine's length. In contrast, the exhaust manifold seemed a particularly primitive affair, consisting of a pipe simply clamped to the side of the cylinder head and designed to take the gases to the front of the engine before curving back into the downpipe and thence into the silencer. The cooling system, pressurized to 4psi by the

Classic layout. An excellent illustration of the straightforward simplicity of the 'Five Star Cars'. These models exhibited a combination of features which would eventually be copied by many other major car manufacturers.

radiator cap, was pump-assisted and of $16\frac{1}{2}$ pints or 22 pints capacity according to the engine size.

The four-cylinder engine developed 47bhp at 4,400rpm and 74lb/ft torque at 2,400rpm. The corresponding figures for the six-cylinder unit were 68bhp at 4,000rpm and 108lb/ft at 2,000rpm. With the low piston speed of 500ft/min/1,000rpm these engines had a built-in capacity for sustained hard work coupled with long life.

The 8in diameter clutch was hydraulically operated for the first time on a Dagenham car, its master cylinder being situated alongside that of the braking system, operated by a similar pendant pedal and sharing the same fluid reservoir. This reservoir had an internal division, so that a leak in either circuit would not affect the operation of the other. The bhp and torque characteristics of the new engines were well suited to a three-speed gearbox, and so by retaining this traditional Ford layout, complete with an unsynchronized first gear, worthwhile savings could be made in the overall development costs of the new models. The gears were selected by a steering column-mounted lever which was chosen in order to allow unrestricted access to the front bench seat. An open propeller shaft replaced Ford's previous torque tube arrangement, and transmitted the power to a new hypoid-bevel final-drive assembly. The final-drive ratios chosen, of 4.625:1 and 4.375:1, respectively, for the four- and six-cylinder models, gave relatively low overall gearing that would endow the cars with exceptionally good top gear acceleration and, because of the short-stroke engine's willingness to rev freely, would still allow useful maximum speeds of around 73-74mph and 80-81mph, respectively, at approximately 5,000rpm, but at only 2,500ft/min piston speed. Typical rival designs of similar engine capacities, but of the then-normal long-stroke arrangement would reach these piston speeds at around 60-65mph or, in a few cases, even less than this. So, by comparison, the new Ford engines would be operating under far less stress, even when being driven at maximum speed.

A 12-volt electrical system was another departure from previous Ford practice, although in spite of this, and the provision of a very ample battery, the windscreen wipers were still vacuum-operated from the inlet manifold in the time-honoured Ford tradition. These wipers did, however, have the advantage of a vacuum booster pump which was incorporated in the base of the fuel pump, and if the wiper control was set towards the slow end of the motor's variable speed range, the booster pump ensured that the previously annoying tendency of the wipers to stop under wide throttle openings was largely overcome.

During the early development the new cars were known only by their factory designations, EOTA and EOTTA for the four- and six-cylinder versions, respectively. Before the production stage was reached, the name Consul was applied to the four-cylinder car and, as the Lincoln Division of the Ford Motor Company in America had decided to phase out their low-priced Zephyr model in order to concentrate on the luxury Continental, Dagenham adopted the Zephyr name for the six-cylinder model. The Lincoln Zephyr had always been powered by a V12 engine, and in order to avoid any possible confusion with that unit, the full title 'Zephyr Six' was to appear on the Dagenham car.

As the rear seat was well within the wheelbase, a good, level ride was assured, and with a width of 50in and 53in for the front and rear bench seats, a six-seater claim was entirely justified. Access to the interior was excellent through the wide-opening front-hinged doors. Rather in keeping with what was Dagenham's established image, the interior appointments were not particularly lavish in the new cars, the designers having gone for a simple, functional durability at this stage. Upholstery was in PVC, although leather would be available as an optional extra, and both front and rear seats were devoid of a central armrest. Both cars featured swivelling quarter-lights in the front door windows. The Zephyr Six had padded armrest-cum-doorpulls on all four doors, but these were omitted from the Consul, the floor of which was covered by a moulded rubber mat, whereas the Zephyr Six featured fully fitted carpets with bound edges. Both cars had cloth roof linings, and the twin sun visors were covered in the same material. The interior light, mounted centrally in the roof, was not automatically illuminated by opening the doors. Two powerful horns were sounded by means of a chrome-plated full-circle horn ring attached to the T-spoked steering wheel on the Zephyr Six; the Consul's single horn was operated by a button in the wheel centre. Also mounted centrally in the steering wheel boss was the self-cancelling switch for the semaphore-type direction indicators. Facing the occupants was a simply-styled flat dashboard incorporating, in front of the driver, a speedometer with total mileage recorder, ammeter and fuel contents gauge. Warning lights were provided for ignition and low oil pressure. In front of the passenger was a small lidded compartment which matched in shape the instrument surround, and mounted centrally along the lower edge of the dash panel were the choke knob and the switches for the starter, ignition and lights, panel light and wipers. These switches, along with the gear lever knob, were

1951 Consul with optional radio. When fitted by the factory or a Ford dealership, the radio aerial was always placed in the position shown, which allowed it to be extended by the driver without leaving the driving seat.

of an attractive 'see through' design. A fresh-air heater and demister unit, complete with a booster fan, was an optional extra, and when fitted its controls were situated beneath the dashboard panel in a central position.

The spare wheel was housed in an upright position in the offside of the luggage boot and could be extracted without having first to remove any luggage that was being carried. Of 15cu ft capacity, the boot was very conveniently shaped, and the fully counterbalanced lid was a nice finishing touch. At the front, the large bonnet was held in the open position by a ratchet-type stay, and accessibility for routine maintenance was excellent; the dipstick, oil filler, hydraulic reservoir, distributor and battery were all ready to hand. In contrast, the fuel filter was rather difficult to reach as it was incorporated in the fuel pump body, which was mounted low down on the side of the engine and was partially obscured by the optional heater unit, which few Consuls or Zephyrs, in fact, seemed to be without.

Exterior chromium ornamentation was confined to the grille, bumpers, hub caps, door handles, lamp surrounds, wiper arms and name badges on the Consul. In addition to these items the Zephyr Six featured chrome-plated bumper overriders, window surrounds, bonnet motif, front wing flashes and rear number-plate lamp cover. For easy identification the Consul grille was oblong in shape with vertical bars, whilst that on the Zephyr Six featured a raised centre section and horizontal bars. A chrome/enamel badge — a lion rampant and three swords — was mounted on the central bar of the Consul's grille, and a 'winged' version of this was positioned just above the grille on the Zephyr Six and repeated on the boot lid at the rear. A small range of paint colours was offered, which included, in addition to the inevitable Black, Bristol Fawn, Edinburgh Green, Canterbury Green, Winchester Blue and Dorchester Grey. A very subtle pale blue, named Opal, was an additional colour for export only.

The overall measurements were a compact 13ft 6½in and 14ft 3¾in, respectively for the four- and six-cylinder models, with a width of 5ft 4in. The overall height was given as 5ft 0¾in in both cases, despite the difference in tyre sizes, although this difference was apparent in the listed ground clearances of 6½in and 7in. In relation to these dimensions the unladen weights of 21.77cwt and 23.1cwt indicated a particularly sturdy overall design.

Although production was still some weeks away, prototypes which represented the production specification were ready in time for the 1950 Motor Show at Earls Court, and on opening day, October 18, the Consul and Zephyr Six were unveiled. Billed as the 'Five Star Cars', the new models received tremendous acclaim from both the public and the motoring press and, indeed, in the opinion of many people, they were the stars at Earls Court that year. The stylists had produced a very well-balanced scale-down of the 'three-box' shape devised in Dearborn, and this, coupled with the monocoque construction, oversquare engines, MacPherson struts and pendant pedals, was a revolutionary combination in 1950, although 20 years later it would be the norm for medium/large quantity production saloons. So Dagenham had produced, probably quite unwittingly, by far the most significant postwar car that had yet appeared from a British manufacturer.

At a tax-paid price of £532, the Consul was competing against cars like the smaller 1.2-litre Austin Devon at £537 and 1¼-litre side-valve Hillman Minx at £543, and the similarly-sized 1½-litre side-valve Morris Oxford at £573. The Zephyr Six at £608 had to contend with the 2.1-litre four-cylinder Standard Vanguard at £703, the 2.2-litre four-cylinder Austin

Nearside view of a 1951 Zephyr Six. These early, flat-dashboard Zephyrs were a rare sight, as Ford at first largely ignored the demand for their new six-cylinder car and concentrated much of their production capacity on the more economical Consul, which was also of course in great demand, and the little 8 and 10hp Anglia and Prefect models.

Hereford at £738 and the 2.2-litre six-cylinder Morris Six at £718. Although similarly priced, at £531 and £601, Vauxhall's Wyvern and Velox were still hastily revamped prewar models, a fact evident in both their appearance and their performance, and so were not serious contenders for the time being.

After studying the specification and examining the cars at close quarters, the question uppermost in the minds of many of the 475,326 visitors to Earls Court was 'How can Ford do it at the price?'. The answer to this question lay in the completely new manufacturing and assembly techniques which had been devised at Dagenham hand in hand with the development of the new models. New machining processes that were in advance of anything used in the world before had been introduced. To illustrate this point it is necessary to explain that in machining a cylinder block, for example, the practice up to that time had been to break the process down into separate stages with a machine tool and operator at

The prewar styling of the bottom-of-the-range Anglia, later to be adopted almost unchanged for the Popular, contrasts sharply with the Zephyr Six in 1951.

The lack of stowage space in the original flat dashboard is evident in this shot.

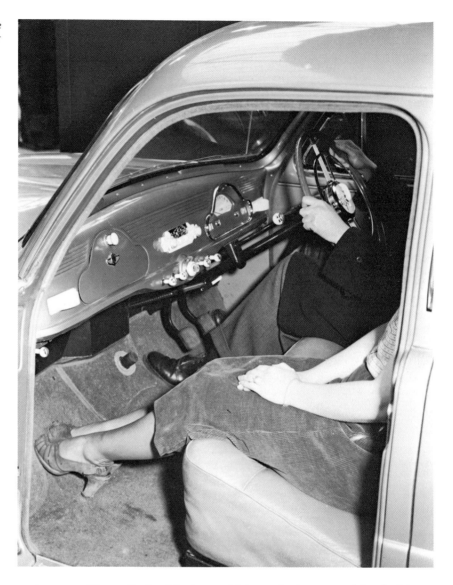

each stage. The cylinder block would have to be moved by hoist, or sometimes even manhandled, to the next machine tool after each operation. The new line of machines that was producing the Consul and Zephyr cylinder blocks at Dagenham was known as a 'transfer' or 'process through' line, and eliminated the handling of the block between operations by employing a series of mechanical/electrical/hydraulic sequences to move the block from one stage to the next. The separate machine tools on this new type of line were arranged in 'tunnel' formation on each side of a central rail on which the cylinder block was mounted. At the press of a button, the block would be moved on the rail to the first stage, where it would be automatically clamped in position for the machining operation. This pressbutton sequence would then be repeated for every stage and a fully machined cylinder block would emerge at the end of the line. This transfer line, which had a production rate approximately 100% greater than the earlier method, was considered at that time by the Ford Motor Company to be 'the greatest single advance in the production engineering

22

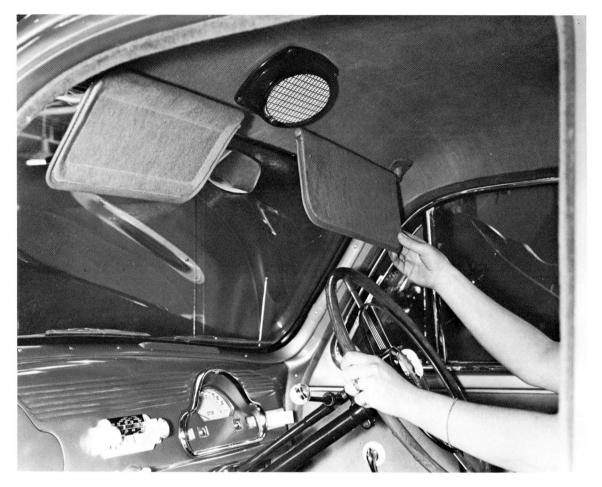

of motor vehicles since the industry commenced'. Similarly, crankshaft machining had previously been carried out in sequence on four different machines at Dagenham, but only one new machine tool was now required to complete the same four operations.

The final assembly line, too, was completely new, and once again far in advance of anything else in Britain at that time. Pit work had been eliminated, as this was felt to be particularly hard on the assembly line workers, and in order to allow the workers the fullest possible freedom of movement around the cars, the line itself had been sunk in to floor level wherever this was convenient.

Meanwhile, as the crowds at Earls Court were admiring the new cars on the Ford stand, some of the other hand-built prototypes were undergoing exhaustive 24-hours-a-day testing in Sweden, Belgium and the Swiss Alps, whilst others were taking advantage of the testing facilities of Ford France and the parent company in America. After a careful analysis and cross-checking of test reports had been completed, a production date was set, and on January 1, 1951, Ford of Britain Chairman Sir Rowland Smith drove the first Consul off the new assembly line.

Production of the four-cylinder car built up quickly over the next few weeks, and was joined on February 12 by the first Zephyr Six, although production of this version was to be in limited numbers only for some time to come, as the more economical Consul was rather more relevant in the

23

1951 Zephyr Six with whitewall tyres, and wheeltrim rings similar to those adopted later as a standard Zodiac feature.

still somewhat austere postwar world. In any case, in Britain, 1951 — 'Festival of Britain Year' — was to be a time of extreme frustration for the would-be new car buyer as, despite the fact that orders for new cars of all makes totalled more than a million at garages throughout the country, the Government were restricting the home market to an allocation of just 80,000 new cars that year. This was in order to force the manufacturers to export the bulk of their production and so earn valuable foreign currency for Britain. With this quota fixed, the Government then doubled the purchase tax on new cars to a massive $66\frac{2}{3}\%$ in the April budget, knowing full well that, with over a dozen people chasing every new car coming on to the market, even this level of taxation would not affect total sales at all. The new tax-paid prices were £662 and £759 for the Consul and Zephyr Six, which still represented quite a bargain for those who were fortunate enough to find themselves at the top of the waiting list. Many customers were placing their orders with several different garages in the faint hope that just one of these orders would bear fruit; if it did, they would then have to sign a two-year covenant on taking delivery, which prevented them from selling the car within that specified period. However, with the enforced shortage of new cars pushing used car prices up to considerably more than those listed for similar new models, there were many people quite willing to pay 'over the odds', and so in many cases much profiteering took place before a signature finally appeared on the covenant.

As soon as production was running smoothly, a Consul was made available to the motoring press, and on April 13, 1951 *The Autocar* published a full road test of this car, SHK 857. In almost every respect the Consul came in for praise from *The Autocar* test staff, who claimed: 'It is one of the outstanding cars produced since the war in the popular class

and has handling qualities that would be acceptable on a car of any price'. Of the power unit it was said that 'the engine is smooth and lively and satisfactorily quiet — full advantage has been taken of modern ideas in the design in regard to limitation of piston speed', and that 'the engine pulls very well on top gear. There is, however, everything against letting it do so beyond certain limits, in view of the fact that there is a useful middle ratio in the three-speed gearbox, engaged by a steering column lever which, because the linkage is simple, works extremely well with only finger pressure'. The performance included a genuine 75mph maximum allied to a 0-60mph time of 31.1 seconds, with the flexibility of the engine being underlined by a 20-40mph time of 13.1 seconds on top gear. Some

Despite a considerable impact, the damage to this Zephyr Six has been largely confined to the area of contact. Although some distortion of the lower part of the scuttle is evident, the windscreen pillars and the screen itself have not been affected.

Original underbonnet layout. For 1952 and later models, the coil was repositioned alongside the engine, and the starter solenoid was also removed from the bulkhead to a position on the nearside, adjacent to the battery.

criticism was levelled at the lack of a parcel shelf in the front, and also at the poor turning circle of 41ft. SHK 857 then passed into the hands of *The Motor* test staff, and their report was published in the issue of May 23. Once again, apart from the mediocre turning circle and lack of stowage space in the front compartment, it was virtually all praise. Probably as a result of more running in, the performance of SHK 857 showed a worthwhile improvement in the hands of *The Motor*, for whom it turned in a 0-60mph time of 27.2 seconds and covered the 20-40mph range in an excellent 11.1 seconds on top gear. The maximum speed was fractionally down, at a best of 74.4mph. A constant-speed fuel consumption of 36mpg at 40mph suggested that an overall 28-30mpg should be possible for the average owner. Summing up, *The Motor* stated that 'its good all round performance and quite exceptional handling qualities make it that rare vehicle — an everyman's car that is basically good by any standards'.

Whilst SHK 857 was being put through its paces in the hands of the motoring press, a fleet of 22 Consuls and 22 Zephyrs, straight from the production line, were embarking on an intensive testing programme similar to that which the prototypes had been forced to endure, in order to determine as quickly as possible whether any serious differences existed in the durability of the mass-production cars by comparison with the hand-built prototypes. This programme involved once again sending cars abroad in search of extreme climatic conditions. In Scandinavia the cars were operated in Arctic temperatures whilst, in contrast, an extract from a report submitted by the Ford Motor Company of Egypt reads: 'The cars were tested over a sand route from Alexandria to Khartoum, involving a large proportion of sandy or rocky roads, stretches of hard track and virgin terrain, heavy rain having washed away normal tracks. In some places no passenger cars had ever been before'. Allied to the tests being conducted overseas were others at proving grounds in the United Kingdom, where full use was made of facilities such as ripple-type road surfaces, *pavé* and dust tunnels. The early results were encouraging to such an extent that it was decided to continue the tests with these early production cars on an extended 'life' basis.

It was not long before the new Fords were earning foreign currency for Britain, and many of the early cars were shipped in 'knocked down' form for assembly in overseas plants. The Ford Motor Company of India were soon assembling Consuls alongside the already established Prefect, Thames trucks and Fordson Major tractors at their assembly plant in Bombay. Consuls for Malaya were assembled at the Ford plant in Singapore, whilst other Far Eastern countries were taking built-up cars from Dagenham, a batch of Consuls being included in a shipment for Japan for sale exclusively to United States service personnel and American business organizations that had been established there. In June, the first export Zephyrs, in the hands of Ford drivers, took the cross-channel ferry to Dunkirk and then motored across France, Belgium and into Germany. Joining the autobahn at Aachen, the Zephyrs headed for Cologne and a visit to the German Ford works, before turning north to their destinations in Sweden, Norway and Denmark. Soon after this, 'knocked down' Zephyrs were arriving in Bombay and Singapore. On the home market, the small number of Consuls being released were building up an excellent reputation from the start, the only regular criticism being that already referred to by *The Motor* and *The Autocar* — the lack of anywhere other than the small cubby hole in the facia to stow small items.

Meanwhile, unable to sample a Zephyr Six for themselves, many regular

Goes like a bird The smooth, exhilarating performance of the Zephyr-Six, is matched by exceptional stability on the road. The whispering power of the revolutionary O.H.V. "Over-Square" engine and the remarkable front-wheel suspension evoke a sense of effortless motion at all speeds, while the hydraulically-operated brakes and clutch ensure complete and perfect control. Truly, this is a 'Five-Star' car !

Ford MOTORING IS 'FIVE-STAR' MOTORING ★ ★ ★ ★ ★
— THE BEST AT LOWEST COST

FORD MOTOR COMPANY LIMITED · DAGENHAM

Despite the availability of some lovely photography, Ford, like most other manufacturers at the time, still favoured artists' impressions for advertising purposes like this magazine page extolling the virtues of the Zephyr Six.

The new speedometer housing can just be discerned in this scenic view of the Zephyr Six, above. A larger grille badge, and the termination of the shoulder-line chrome moulding along the rear wing top, are outward indications that this Consul, right, also features the revised dashboard layout. The model's good ground clearance is displayed here, one of the many reasons why these cars were popular abroad.

Consul facia and controls, from 1952. The knob for the starter (pull to operate) is situated centrally under the parcels shelf, and can just be seen beneath the steering wheel boss. The knob on the instrument housing is for the wipers, the toggle switch beneath is for panel lights, and the control marked 'B' is for the heater blower.

The restyled facia on the Zephyr Six. The ignition switch and starter button changed places later as, in the arrangement here, the ignition lock number could be read from outside the car. The apparently haphazard placing of the controls and switchgear was in fact a very convenient arrangement, carefully chosen so as to avoid confusion.

readers of the weekly motoring magazines were eagerly awaiting a road test report. First to oblige was *The Motor*, with a full road test published in the issue of October 3, 1951. The test staff were very favourably impressed, particularly with the car's outstanding combination of performance and roadholding, commenting that it had 'a general roadworthiness and stability which virtually take it out of the family motoring class and put it into the sports car category'. This enthusiasm was tempered somewhat by the nose-heavy weight distribution, which 'results in a decisive break-away at the rear end if corners are taken too fast'. Nevertheless they felt that 'in the general run of motoring conditions . . . the car handles in such a way as to instill very great confidence'. The maximum speed of the car tested was a best one-way of 81.1mph and 70mph was reached from rest through the gears in 29.9 seconds. This, coupled with an ability to go from 20-40mph and from 40-60mph in 8.5 and 11.8 seconds, respectively, in top gear indicated that the Zephyr Six would have no problems at all dismissing slower-moving traffic. This high performance was accompanied by a creditable overall fuel consumption of 23.7mpg. 'Finally one must say', *The Motor* concluded, 'that it represents one of the finest examples of value for money to be found today not only amongst English but also world production.'

Dagenham were quick to answer the criticism levelled at the lack of interior stowage space and, just a year after the announcement, the Consuls and Zephyrs on the Ford stand at Earls Court in the autumn of 1951 displayed a completely redesigned facia. Beneath a new dash panel of 'roll top' appearance was a full-width parcels tray, 35in wide and over 10in deep, able to accommodate objects up to 4½in high, and installed at a slight angle, sloping towards the front of the car, to prevent spillage. Also part of the redesign was a shroud encasing both the steering column and gear-change linkage, with a new binnacle instrument cluster above it. The instruments themselves were similar to the earlier type, but now had a black background and light-coloured figures, those on the Zephyr being

The optional radio in position in the restyled facia. This prototype car still retains the early throttle pedal.

'three dimensional' in appearance. A central, drawer-type ashtray was incorporated in the new dash. The control knobs were now of ivory plastic with black letters, and the Zephyr Six acquired a pushbutton starter in place of the pull-out cable which was retained in the Consul. On both cars, the original organ-type accelerator pedal operating through a hole in the toeboard was replaced by a suspended pedal, bringing it into line with those of the clutch and brake. All four doors received new trim panels with vertical flutes in the design matching those moulded into the new dash panel. In addition to these cosmetic improvements were a new door pillar striker plate incorporating a nylon block, and a reshaped petrol filler neck designed for easier filling. Cars with this revised specification could be identified externally by a new grille badge, based on the previous design but enlarged slightly and including the proud words 'A Ford Product. Made in England'. Commenting upon these changes, the Ford Motor Company explained: 'The majority of these changes refer to minor items but they do reflect the fact that our claim to a policy that is one of continuous improvement, includes every item, however small, that makes for more pleasurable and efficient motoring'.

Also exhibited at Earls Court in 1951 was a prototype Zephyr Six Convertible de Ville, and VIP visitor Princess Margaret spent a long time on the Ford stand examining this exotic looking car, although not even Her Royal Highness would have been able to purchase one as little development work had taken place and production was still a considerable time away. As a result of increases in material costs the Ford Motor Company had recently announced an increase in the prices of the entire passenger car range, and the Consul and Zephyr Six were now listed at a tax paid total of £717 and £816, respectively.

Following the Motor Show, in the motoring press in November, the Zephyr Six was certainly 'car of the month'. Raymond Mays, of prewar racing fame, had taken delivery of one of the first Zephyrs registered in Britain, and writing in *The Autocar* issue of November 9, 1951 he gave a glowing account of its performance so far. Explaining that much of his previous motoring experience had been in 'high performance vehicles of the grand luxe class', Mays went on to say of the Zephyr: 'I have never known a "cheap" car which left me at such a loss for disparagement — or so monotonously fulsome in praise. Sincerely and soberly, I regard this Ford's advent as one of the most important events in mid-century motoring'. In five months Raymond Mays had covered 11,800 miles in the Zephyr including a 2,500-mile weekend trip to Milan for the Italian Grand Prix. This trip took him over the Simplon Pass, and of this Mays said that 'the Simplon proved an eye opener; I estimate that 75 per cent of the climb was made on top gear. On that ratio we repeatedly came down as low as 20mph, then pulled away without a vestige of labouring or fuss. Always in the past when driving cars with three-speed boxes I have sooner or later found myself hankering for that fourth gear; on the Zephyr, never. If four speeds were an optional extra chargeable at £2, I wouldn't specify them'. He went on to praise its 'freedom from tilt under the stress of deliberately violent cornering tactics, rapid pick-up on top gear, roominess and superb comfort'. The only trouble Mays had experienced so far was seepage of brake fluid past a defective hydraulic seal, and he also noted that 'a just perceptible vibration' would sometimes 'creep in — although it doesn't always do so — at around 65mph'. Summing up, Mays claimed: 'The Zephyr is a truly outstanding car in almost every respect. It corners like a racing car — better than some racing cars, in fact. Where road conditions permit, you can make maximum speed and cruising speed synonymous, and it takes this sort of medicine indefinitely'.

The following week the Zephyr came in for more praise when the respected Technical Editor of *The Motor*, Laurence Pomeroy, writing in the issue of November 14 about a trip to Europe in one of the new Fords, said: 'Surely the Zephyr can be thought of as the impoverished gentleman's Aston Martin'. After this it was the turn of *The Autocar* once again with a test report of the Zephyr in the issue of November 23. This particular car was complete with the new facia panel and *The Autocar* noted that 'it now provides a parcels tray of ample proportions'. The performance of this very new Zephyr included impressive maxima in the three gears of 31mph, 56mph and 81mph, with 70mph reached in 32.1 seconds from rest. The steering and handling came in for the usual praise, with the comment: 'The steering is quite light and very positive, with good self-centering action. The slight yet definite amount of inherent understeer quickly inspires confidence and, in fact, the Zephyr steers extremely well on both fast main road bends and narrow winding roads'. Of the column-mounted gear-change it was said: 'The lever is much shorter than usual and very positive in operation; it is in some ways reminiscent of the remote control unit fitted on some sports cars'. *The Autocar* concluded: 'Judged on both performance and on value for money, the Zephyr is a very satisfactory car'.

By the end of 1951, exactly one year after the first Consul left the line, Dagenham had produced 35,667 examples of the four-cylinder car, 15,880 of which were in 'knocked down' form. The corresponding figure of 3,463 (950 'knocked down') for the Zephyr Six underlined its exclusivity so far, although a big increase was planned for 1952. The changes exhibited at Earls Court in October 1951 had only appeared on the development cars, and were not at that time ready for production, but they were to be phased in gradually during 1952. This resulted in certain cars displaying some, but not all, of the new features, and it was not until late in the year that cars exhibiting the fully updated specification were leaving the production line. In the meantime, for the benefit of owners of cars with the early flat dashboard, the Central Motor Company, of Leicester, were offering a neat accessory parcel shelf, priced at £2.

In April, Ken Wharton had driven his Consul to outright victory in the Dutch International Tulip Rally, but with long waiting lists already for this model at all Ford agencies, coupled with the planned increase in Zephyr production, there was little that Dagenham could do to capitalize on this particular success. Nevertheless, the victory added considerably to the Consul's prestige. Production continued to build up steadily throughout the year and, as the Zephyr Six was making its debut in America, the Consul was introduced in Australia, where it was to be assembled at the Ford works in Geelong, Victoria. From Geelong, the Consul would be distributed throughout Australia and Tasmania, whilst cars for New Zealand would be assembled by the Ford Motor Company of New Zealand Limited, at their plant in Lower Hutt.

The new facia panel had met with widespread approval, and so the basic design was now established for some considerable time ahead. No visible changes were planned for the 1953 model year, but a technical change was introduced in November 1952. The rear axle ratio on both models was altered, that on the Consul becoming 4.556:1 (4.625:1 previously). This raised the gearing slightly, giving a worthwhile improvement in the constant-speed fuel consumption in top gear, with a

Zephyr Six showing the repositioned badge for 1952 and later models.

figure of around 32-33mpg at 50mph. In conjunction with this change, slightly lower indirect ratios were introduced in the gearbox, actually lowering first and second gear overall, so giving improved acceleration from rest, but, on the debit side, opening up the gap between second and top. On the Zephyr, the axle ratio was now 4.444:1 (4.375:1 previously) and, as the Zephyr also received the new indirect ratios in the gearbox, its already remarkable accelerative powers were sharpened up even more. The speed at 5,000rpm in top gear was now 80.5mph, compared with 81.75mph with the earlier axle ratio, but as the engine would pull a few more revs on the slightly lower gearing the maximum speed was unchanged. At 5,000rpm on the Consul the theoretical speed would now be 76.5mph, an improvement of 2mph, although in practice the four-cylinder would not quite pull 5,000 revs on the higher gearing, so once again the actual maximum speed proved to be about the same as before.

On January 15, 1953, Dagenham's 2,000,000th vehicle was driven off the production line by Ford Chairman Sir Rowland Smith. The car, a left-hand-drive Zephyr Six, complete with whitewall tyres, was destined for the showrooms of Ford Dealers Holmes Tuttle and Company, of Los Angeles, California. An average of 400 Zephyrs a month, out of a total of 550 cars of

An early Zephyr estate car project, the 'Horsham', which did not reach production.

all models, was now being shipped to the United States from Dagenham. On the morning of January 27 the Zephyr Six was front page news; Dutchman Maurice Gatsonides had driven a standard Zephyr to outright victory in the Monte Carlo Rally. The following day, all the National dailies were carrying Zephyr adverts and, thanks to an overnight shift at a Dagenham printing works, every Zephyr leaving the line on January 28 was sporting a windscreen sticker proudly proclaiming the Monte Carlo win, whilst other batches of stickers were being rushed to dockside car parks wherever Zephyrs were awaiting shipment abroad. The winning

Zephyr was flown to London on January 30 and put on display in the Company's West End showrooms at 88 Regent Street.

During April 1953 the revised first and second gear ratios which had been introduced six months earlier were deleted in favour once again of those of the original specification. The revised *axle* ratios, however, were retained, and this new arrangement was standardized with no further modifications. So now, by comparison with the original 1951 production specification, all three gears on the Consul were raised, whilst all three on the Zephyr were very slightly lower than before, although the Zephyr was, of course, still the higher geared overall of the two cars.

In Australia the Consul had now been joined by the Zephyr Six, and the design team at Geelong, who in the past had produced variations on many Dagenham themes to suit local circumstances, were keen to produce a

One of the rare Zephyr Six utilities which Ford Australia had hoped to mass produce.

pick-up truck, or coupe utility as these are referred to in Australia, based on the Consul and Zephyr. Prototype utilities of both four- and six-cylinder models were produced, but, surprisingly, despite the enthusiasm of the Geelong team for this new version, Dagenham were not happy about building pick-ups based on a monocoque shell and eventually they vetoed the idea, so the design was shelved after only six Zephyr and five Consul utilities had been produced.

After the Monte Carlo success, many enthusiasts who had hitherto only looked upon the Zephyr as a family car were now taking another look. For the benefit of *Autosport* readers, John Bolster was busy putting a Zephyr through its paces, and his report appeared in the issue of May 8. Starting with a brief technical description of the car, he went on: 'I first took over the Zephyr in London, and I must admit that it did not endear itself to me immediately. Every time I braked at low speeds, the nose dipped considerably, and it rose sharply into the air on sudden acceleration. All this gave me the impression that, for the next few days, I was going to be stuck with a sick-making, American-style car. How wrong I was! Once out on the open road, the machine's real character asserted itself. It seemed to like cruising at almost its maximum speed, at which velocity a very level ride is provided'. Of the handling he commented: 'Perhaps the most surprising feature is the lack of serious roll on corners — the body remains more vertical during vigorous manoeuvres than is common among present day cars. The steering is light and direct, and it is "quick" enough to deal with emergencies. On dry roads, the car corners well; on wet and slippery surfaces, however, one becomes conscious that the rear wheels are relatively lightly loaded — wheelspin occurs if one accelerates violently in first or second gear, but the resulting tail slides are always easily controllable'. About the three-speed gearbox, John Bolster echoed Raymond Mays' sentiments, with the comment that 'this is one of the few three-speeders which would not be improved by a fourth ratio'. After suggesting that its light controls, good top-gear acceleration and good visibility 'makes the Zephyr an ideal woman's car', he went on: 'From my own point of view, I found that this machine invited me to drive it disgracefully hard, and I was nothing loath to oblige'. Summing up, he wrote: 'The man who buys a Zephyr gets an astonishing amount of performance and comfort for his money. It is, first and foremost, an everyday family car, but under its bonnet there is enough "zip" to make it an agreeable companion for the chap who is always in a hurry'. Checked against the stopwatch, the Zephyr had recorded a two-way average maximum of 80mph and reached 50, 60 and 70mph from rest in 12.8, 19.6 and 29.6 seconds, respectively, whilst the standing-start quarter-mile had occupied exactly 21 seconds.

Amplifying the comments by John Bolster about the wheelspin in wet conditions, it was certainly considered in some quarters that the Zephyr could be quite a handful in the wet. The vast majority of Zephyr buyers were sampling high-performance six-cylinder motoring for the first time, virtually all their previous experience having been on prewar or prewar-inspired cars, many with side-valve engines which were so lacking in throttle response that the driver was able to floor the accelerator pedal and then, quite literally, wait for signs of progress. In contrast, the Zephyr engine responded immediately to any change in the position of the pedal, and many drivers had simply never learned a progressive, light throttle technique, largely because it had not been necessary on anything they had driven before. If the Zephyr had been selling at twice the price, it is almost certain that it would never have earned this 'tail happy' reputation, as it would only have been bought by those drivers who largely were already used to powerful cars and had therefore developed the required driving technique. John Bolster's observation that 'the resulting tail slides are always easily controllable' was absolutely correct, but here was speaking a man with a vast experience of very high-performance machinery, including racing cars, to whom controlling a tail slide was, in any case, second nature. To many ordinary motorists, though, a tail slide, or 'skid' as most of them called it, was something to be feared. Writing about the same subject in the June 24, 1953 issue of *The Motor*, Technical Editor Laurence Pomeroy accurately summed up the situation with his comment that it was possible to 'promote ready wheelspin and a quick breakaway at the back. But due to the direct and positive steering such slides can be quickly ended, or accurately controlled, according to choice, and although the Zephyr can present problems to the novice, it is a safe and pleasing car for the experienced man'.

Laurence Pomeroy had commented favourably about the Zephyr on several occasions in *The Motor*, and had recently had some interesting modifications carried out on the engine of his own example. The compression ratio was raised to approximately 7.5:1 and the inlet and exhaust ports smoothed out. Double valve springs were fitted to cope with the anticipated extra rpm, and triple SU carburettors on separate induction pipes replaced the single Zenith. A large cylindrical Vokes air filter/silencer with a curved three-branch pipe leading to the carburettor intakes was mounted on the rocker cover. The exhaust arrangements consisted of two separate systems, each comprising a three-branch manifold feeding into its own silencer and tailpipe. The result of these modifications was a maximum speed of over 95mph coupled with a substantial increase in acceleration. The modifications on this particular Zephyr were very definitely on a 'one-off' basis, but elsewhere plans were in hand to market a similar conversion.

Zephyr enthusiast Raymond Mays had also been quick to realize the tuning potential of the short-stroke engine, and for some time now his Zephyr had been running in a remarkably similar state of tune to that which Laurence Pomeroy had devised. Triple SU carburettors, improved ports, double valve springs and a 7.5:1 compression ratio were all features of the Mays Zephyr. A single exhaust system was retained in this instance, although the original baffle-type silencer was replaced with one of the Servais straight-through variety. After 30,000 hard miles in this state of tune the Zephyr engine was showing no ill effects whatsoever, and Mays decided to offer this conversion for sale to the public at an inclusive price of £75.

John Bolster borrowed Raymond Mays' own Zephyr for a weekend's quick motoring, and reported enthusiastically on the experience in the *Autosport* issue of September 11, 1953. 'On taking the wheel', he wrote, 'it was at once obvious that the car had a lot more "steam" than any Zephyr I had previously driven. A full 30mph came up like a flash on bottom gear and, rather pointlessly, I was guilty of touching 60mph on second speed. On top, that "out of breath" feeling at 80mph had quite gone, and the acceleration continued in one smooth surge. To give an idea of the increase in performance I might mention that the modified car accelerated from a standstill to 80mph in the same time that the standard job took for the 0-70mph range. The maximum speed was over 90mph and at that velocity the engine was as smooth as a little dynamo. Curiously enough,

the improved high-speed behaviour of the unit made one much less conscious of the need for an overdrive. To maintain such a rate involves some pretty impressive rpm, but the short-stroke engine makes no complaint'. Summing up his impressions of the Mays Zephyr he wrote: 'After several hundred miles of exceptionally quick motoring, I came to the conclusion that Messrs Raymond Mays and Partners, of Bourne, Lincs, know just about all the answers where the Zephyr Six is concerned. It only remains to add that the success of the conversion is a fine advertisement for the basic soundness of Ford design and construction'.

With the easing of home market restrictions, more and more Consuls and Zephyrs were to be seen on the roads of Britain as Dagenham's 'Five Star Cars' firmly established themselves as the number one sellers in their particular sector of the market; and now the saloons were at last being joined by the long-awaited Convertible de Ville. Carbodies of Coventry had been building drophead coupes since the early 1920s and were first approached by Ford soon after postwar production had commenced at Dagenham, although the result was only a small number of prototype Anglia and Prefect convertibles, the projected Consul/Zephyr being a more attractive proposition in the long term. Development of the Zephyr convertible had taken much longer than had been anticipated, however, as, deprived of the steel roof, which played an important part in the strength of the saloon body, the floorpan was under too much strain and, on test, prototypes had actually suffered with cracking floors. Although it was generally accepted that convertible bodies were always appreciably less rigid than their saloon counterparts, in view of the performance available with the Zephyr it was important to reduce this difference to a minimum before production could commence, and extra bracing, in the form of a substantial X-frame, was developed by Carbodies and welded into the standard floorpan supplied by Dagenham.

The hood was in a very durable, washable, plastic fabric, and was

When in the raised position, the weatherproof hood gave a slightly lower look to the convertible models.

An early Consul convertible. The bonnet motif is non-standard and, although similar to that of the early Zephyr Six, is a Wilmot Breeden accessory in this case, which was available for £1.5s.

complete with a safety glass rear window. To and from the de Ville (half-way) position, the hood was hydraulically operated from a switch on the dashboard, and a particularly neat touch was that the rear seat tilted forward slightly as the hood was being raised or lowered, ensuring that the folds in the top did not disturb the passengers' heads. The backrest of the front bench seat was divided, with each side hinged to allow easy access to the rear compartment through the wide and rather heavy doors. All four side windows could be raised or lowered irrespective of the position of the hood, giving a remarkable overall versatility, and the only obvious shortcoming of the car was the lack of sun visors and an interior light, particularly surprising as there was ample room for both these features on the windscreen surround. At £960 the Zephyr convertible was £206 more than the saloon, but still over £300 cheaper than the nearest comparable

drophead coupe, the $2\frac{1}{4}$-litre Sunbeam Talbot 90 convertible at £1,269.

A Consul convertible, with manually-operated hood, followed quickly: at £808 it had to contend with the Austin Somerset coupe, which was very attractively priced at £705, and the rather smaller side-valve-engined Hillman Minx drophead at £723, so it was not really as well placed in its class as the virtually unrivalled Zephyr Six. Most of the early Zephyr convertibles were destined for overseas markets where, in addition to the standard range of colours, they were also available in Mandarin Red with silver grey upholstery, or Ivory with ivory. Whitewhall tyres completed the export specification.

There had not been a 'de luxe' version of the Consul or Zephyr, although a heater and leather upholstery had been listed as options right from the start. Of course owners could, and indeed often did, purchase spot lamps, wing mirrors and so on from their local garage or accessory shop. In view of the popularity of these extras, the Product Planning executives at Dagenham had decided early in 1953 that the time was ripe to add a comprehensively equipped model to the top of the Consul/Zephyr range, the specification of which would go considerably further than the typical 'de luxe' offerings of rival manufacturers. The result of this decision, the Zephyr Zodiac, was introduced to the public on October 21, 1953, the opening day of the Earls Court Motor Show, and was, in the opinion of many people, the most glamorous car yet to appear from a British manufacturer.

The new car was instantly recognizable externally in a range of beautiful dual-tone colour schemes, the division of which was highlighted by a new front wing chrome flash, incorporating the 'Five Star' motif, and a chromium-plated moulding running the length of the body. New deeper-section bumpers and overriders were introduced, as was a futuristically-styled 'aeroplane' bonnet mascot to replace the original rocket-shaped fitting. Spot, fog and reversing lamps, wing mirrors with spring-loaded stems, chromed lockable fuel-filler cap, chromed wheelrim embellishers, whitewall tyres and 9-carat gold-plated name scripts completed the exterior scene. The passenger compartment featured leather upholstery

and restyled door trims, both of which were finished in a two-tone colour scheme complementing that of the exterior paintwork. A new woollen headlining replaced the cloth lining used in the Consul and Zephyr, and a larger rubber heel pad than that of the Zephyr was incorporated in the carpet in front of the driver's seat. A cigar lighter, a vanity mirror in the passenger's sun visor and an electric clock were other standard features,

A prototype Zephyr Zodiac. The script on the bonnet front still reads Zephyr Six, though it is placed higher up on the bonnet so as not to be obscured by fog lamps; the original holes for the fixing can be seen in the lower position.

1953 Zephyr Six with non-standard interior trim, including separate front seats. This is presumably a Styling Department car, and would appear to have been involved in the Zodiac development programme.

41

Zephyr Zodiac, regarded by many Ford enthusiasts today as one of Dagenham's finest-ever cars.

and the switch in the steering column boss now operated flashing direction indicators incorporated in the front and rear side lamp units in place of the original semaphore type. For additional safety, the rear light surround also incorporated a circular reflector.

Under the bonnet was a large, heavy-duty battery, a vacuum-operated windscreen washer system and the previously optional heater and demister unit. The engine boasted a new cylinder head of 7.5:1 compression ratio, raising the power output from the standard Zephyr's 68bhp at 4,000rpm to 71bhp at 4,200rpm, and being designed to make full use of the recently-introduced premium grades of petrol, this cylinder head and its rocker cover being painted bright red. In the luggage compartment was a padded steel toolbox, placed between the spare wheel and the inner wing, and complete with two box spanners, two double-ended spanners, an adjustable spanner, a plug spanner, two screwdrivers, a tommy bar, a tyre lever and a brake adjuster, these being in addition to the grease gun, wheelbrace and jack, which were normally supplied with the Consul and Zephyr.

In addition to the three dual-tone colour schemes of Dorchester Grey upper half combined with Canterbury Green, Winchester Blue, or Bristol Fawn lower half, the Zephyr Zodiac was also available, to special order only, in single-tone black, and in this finish it came with the Dorchester Grey/Bristol Fawn interior trim combination. At a tax paid price of £851,

42

Zephyr Zodiac and Zephyr Six in traditional English settings. Apart from the wheelrim embellishers and special Zodiac insignia, the Zephyr Six had the same external brightwork as the more luxurious Zephyr Zodiac.

43

An artist's impression once again, for an advert on the cover of one of the motoring weeklies, emphasizing the elegance of the latest Zephyr Six.

A dashing turnout —

the height of elegance

ZEPHYR-6 £532

Plus P.T.

Zephyr Six interior, from October 1953 onwards. Zephyr Zodiac interior trim was similar in style, but with a two-tone finish to complement the paintwork.

the new model had no obvious rivals in its own price range and was, according to the Ford Motor Company, 'destined to take its place among the products of a select and exclusive band of British manufacturers who have set standards of quality workmanship that have become the envy of the world'. Surprisingly, a Zodiac convertible was not offered, although just one was subsequently made for Mrs Benson Ford, wife of Henry Ford's second grandson.

The new interior trim styling of the Zephyr Zodiac was now applied to the Zephyr Six, although still in single-tone PVC, with leather available at extra cost. The Zephyr Six also acquired the 'Five Star' flashes and side strips, the new bumpers and overriders, the aeroplane-style mascot and the flashing direction indicators, whilst its cloth roof lining was now of a tighter, more dust-resistant weave. The Consul received the new bumpers, but still without the overriders, which were to remain an extra-cost option on the four-cylinder car. It also received the new side strips and its own variation of the 'Five Star' wing flashes, a simple bonnet mascot and, at last, chrome inserts in the front and rear screen rubbers. Inside, the Consul now featured an improved rubber floor covering, colour keyed to the rest of the interior, and a restyled pattern on the seats and door trims, whilst under the bonnet a single windtone horn replaced the rather ineffective high-frequency unit fitted previously. Some technical changes, to improve efficiency and all-round performance rather than to increase showroom appeal, had recently been phased into production, and included improved clutch drive plates with six damper springs instead of the previous four or five springs in the Consul and Zephyr, respectively, and chromium-plated top piston rings, which would further improve the hard wearing qualities

The position of the electric clock in the Zephyr Zodiac. The interior light is manually operated.

that the Consul/Zephyr engines already displayed. Once production of the Zodiac was under way, the 7.5:1 compression ratio cylinder head was made available to buyers of the Zephyr Six as a no-cost option, retaining its red paint finish for identification.

The whole range had now been very effectively extended and updated, without having to resort to expensive retooling costs, as the body panels were exactly the same as before, and with the tax paid prices of the Consul and Zephyr Six remaining unaltered at £666 and £754, sales continued to expand.

In production, the new two-tone Zodiac bodies were first painted all over in the upper-half colour of Dorchester Grey, and this was stoved in the normal manner in a conventional convector-heated oven. The lower half colour was then sprayed on over the grey, and the body then passed into another oven with infra-red heaters adjusted exactly so as to stove the bottom half only, as restoving the top could have caused discolouration.

Consul with front wing chrome trim, a style which was not adopted for production.

Consul, as produced from October 1953, with optional overriders.

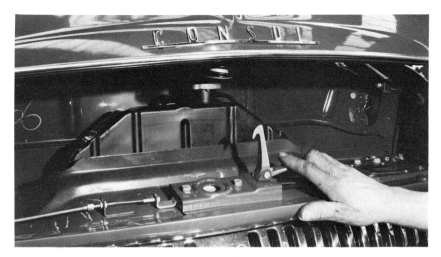

This localized infra-red oven had been designed specially for the Zodiac project by Briggs Motor Bodies in conjunction with a team of engineers from Metropolitan-Vickers Electrical Company.

In the issue of July 16, 1954, *The Autocar* published a full road test of the Zephyr Zodiac. With a price tag of £851 allied to such an impressive specification, the fittings and furnishings were beyond criticism, and even though the basic design was now four years old, the performance and handling came in for the usual praise, the test staff commenting: 'The engine is extremely flexible and pulls strongly from below 12mph in top gear up to its very creditable maximum without the slightest sign of roughness or vibration. When required, the majority of main road hills can be stormed in a very heartening fashion. . . . In addition to the excellent acceleration, it will cruise without effort at a genuine 70mph when carrying three large passengers and a full complement of luggage'. Of the gear-change *The Autocar* said: 'When it is necessary to change gear, the short, stiff, steering column-mounted lever makes the operation a pleasure', and of the ride and handling, 'the Zephyr Zodiac gives the driver and passengers an excellent ride in all circumstances. The ride in the back seat is very good and it is quite possible for two people to fall asleep in the rear compartment when the car is cruising at quite high speeds . . . the steering is positive and light . . . and the car feels as safe on wet main roads at speed as

it does on winding, badly surfaced by-roads'. The car tested reached maximum speeds in the three gears of 31, 57 and 84mph, and accelerated from rest to 30, 50 and 70mph in 5.4, 13.5 and 29.7 seconds, this performance being accompanied by an overall fuel consumption of 23.7mpg.

Many specialist tuning firms had followed the lead set by Raymond Mays and introduced conversion kits for both the Consul and Zephyr, which gave the enthusiast various stages of improved performance from which to choose. The Aquaplane Company, of Suffolk, were offering a redesigned inlet manifold with either twin (for the Consul) or triple (for the Zephyr/Zodiac) $1\frac{1}{2}$in SU carburettors, complete with air filters, priced at £28 15s and £38 15s, respectively. These twin and triple set-ups could be relied upon to produce a worthwhile increase in acceleration throughout the range, particularly so at the top end, in conjunction with a slightly higher top speed, and were also attractive because of their 'bolt-on' nature, not requiring any dismantling of the engine. For the Zephyr and Zodiac models, Sports Autos, of Bayswater, could supply two stages of tune, the first of which comprised a new inlet manifold with two additional standard Zenith carburettors, the original Zenith being utilized to complete the triple set-up whilst keeping the price down to an attractive £29 10s. Stage 2, for an extra £9, involved removing the cylinder head, polishing the combustion chambers, easing the valve ports and fitting double valve springs. Sports Autos did not quote any performance figures in their advertisements, but it would be reasonable to assume that in Stage 2 form a Zephyr would be a 90mph car with a substantial improvement in acceleration. V.W. Derrington, of Kingston-upon-Thames, offered a two-stage improvement for the Consul, Stage 1 of which consisted of a twin SU

Fixed-price routine servicing contributed to the remarkable overall economy of Consul or Zephyr ownership. On July 7, 1953 Ford had announced that new or fully reconditioned engines were available for the Consul, at £31, and the Zephyr Six, at £42, on an exchange basis.

Zephyr Six convertible, 1954 model. This particular example was a press demonstrator and was the subject of a road test published in The Motor.

arrangement and a four-branch exhaust manifold, giving a claimed 3-second improvement in the 0-50mph time and a maximum speed of 84mph for a price of £30. Another £20 would buy Stage 2, which was the addition of a reworked cylinder head and would, according to the advertisement, knock another 2 seconds off the 0-50mph time, bringing it down to 12 seconds.

Laystall Engineering experimented with both Consul and Zephyr engines, eventually standardizing a comprehensive one-stage conversion kit for both models, priced at £45 and £65, respectively, with an additional £5 fitting charge, the customer's original cylinder head being taken in exchange. The compression ratio was raised to 8.3:1, and larger valves

A 1954 Zephyr Six displays its roomy luggage compartment, although on this occasion some squashing would be necessary to close the lid! A specially shaped three-piece suitcase set for the Consul/Zephyr range was available from Auto Luggage Ltd of Barkingside, Essex, at a price of £22 19s.

were accommodated in opened-out ports and controlled by double valve springs. Twin or triple SU carburettors (Consul or Zephyr) supplied the mixture. At 4,400rpm, where the standard Consul engine was producing 47bhp, the Laystall unit was already showing 64bhp, and this continued to rise to 66.8bhp at 5,200rpm, at which revs the standard output had fallen to about 40bhp. The corresponding figures for the six-cylinder engine were: standard unit 68bhp at 4,000rpm; Laystall 87bhp, rising to 96.5 at 5,200rpm, by which time the standard unit was down to 50bhp. These figures indicated that a lot of performance was on offer, and Laystall invited John Bolster to sample both models for the benefit of *Autosport* readers. The Consul was the first available, and proved capable of a rate of acceleration through the gears that was not only an improvement over the standard model, but also over the standard Zephyr Six; from rest to 50, 60 and 70mph was covered in a remarkable 11.2, 16.8 and 23.6 seconds,respectively. A maximum speed of 84mph was recorded and the car returned an overall consumption of 23.6mpg. The normal flexibility was apparently in no way impaired, as John Bolster stated: 'The Laystall modified Consul can show a clean pair of heels to many small sports models, and yet it is in no way inferior to the standard job for shopping and business transport'. As can no doubt be imagined, the improvement with the modified Zephyr was considerable, and the figures recorded by John Bolster contrast dramatically with those for the standard Zephyr Zodiac tested by *The Autocar.*

The Autocar: Standard Zephyr Zodiac Acceleration times (seconds):	*Autosport:* Laystall Zephyr Six
0-30mph 5.4	3.2
0-50mph 13.5	8.8
0-60mph 20.4	13.0
0-70mph 29.7	18.4
0-80mph —	25.2
0-90mph —	37.4
S/S $\frac{1}{4}$-mile 21.5	19.2
Maximum speed 84mph	98mph

For those motorists who wished for something in reserve over the standard model, these conversions were certainly well worthwhile. But it would have been unreasonable, for instance, to expect to habitually use the performance of the modified Consul to the full without some extra wear and tear taking place in the long term, and in this respect the hard-driving high-mileage driver would still have been better advised to go for the standard Zephyr rather than the modified Consul. Nevertheless, these figures do show that a considerable safety margin was built in to the standard engines, and the modified Zephyr in particular was offering outstanding performance in relation to the total price.

The standard exhaust manifold did apparently cause considerable back pressure, and Servais Silencers, of Cricklewood, developed a four- or six-branch manifold for the Consul or Zephyr designed to use their 'straight through' silencer and the original Ford tailpipe. Servais advertisements quoted the following figures for the Zephyr Six with this system; recorded by *The Motor*, they are top gear acceleration times in seconds, with the figures for the standard car in brackets. 20-40mph: 7.7 (8.2); 30-50mph: 8.4 (9.4); and 40-60mph: 10.1 (11.8). Servais developed this system a stage further, and later were able to offer a complete dual system for the Zephyr/Zodiac, priced at £26 5s and featuring a pair of three-branch manifolds, dual silencer and twin tailpipes. This gave acceleration times in top gear from 20-40, 30-50, 40-60 and 50-70mph of 7.2, 7.3, 9.1 and 11.5 seconds, respectively, which represented about the best that could be achieved with exhaust system modifications only. Another firm, at first calling themselves Consul Productions, but soon changing to Consela

Productions, advertised four- and six-branch manifolds at £9 5s and £12 10s, designed for use with the original Ford silencer and tailpipe.

At Earls Court in 1954 the few changes to be seen on the Consul/ Zephyr/Zodiac range had in fact first been exhibited three weeks earlier at the Paris Show. All three cars featured a new rear light surround incorporating a reflector above the lamp unit. The rear flashing indicators were improved by a device which cancelled the appropriate stop light when either indicator was flashing. Inside, the parcel shelf had an improved covering, and the front seat adjustment range was increased slightly. The Zephyr Six acquired the larger rubber heel pad for the driver that was already a Zodiac feature, and the Zodiac's woollen headlining gave way to one of washable embossed vinyl. A clutch pedal assist spring

The rather high sill made loading somewhat more difficult than with some purpose-built estate cars.

53

Definitely not a 'van with windows', this conversion showed that an estate car could combine style and practicality.

was introduced on both the six-cylinder models in answer to recent criticism that the clutch was rather heavy to operate.

The most interesting Ford exhibit, however, was not on the Ford stand, but on that of the coachbuilders E.D. Abbott, of Farnham in Surrey. Abbotts had carried out an estate car conversion on a Zephyr saloon. The saloon rear quarter roof panels were partially cut away, and new rear side panels were welded in along the top of the wings. The roof extension was lower than the saloon roof, giving a slightly stepped effect, a deliberate feature to utilize as much as possible of the strength of the original domed roof. The extended roof section was complete with rubber-covered slats, a chromed roof rail and two strap eyes. A side-opening tailgate was employed, fitted with the original saloon rear window. By retaining the normal rear passenger doors much of the saloon's characteristic appearance had been kept, without a 'van with windows' look. Abbotts could carry out this conversion on any existing Consul/Zephyr/Zodiac saloon at an inclusive price of £145, and as the conversion met with the approval of the Ford Motor Company, arrangements could be made to have a partially completed new car converted by Abbotts, although purchase tax of £60 was then payable on the conversion.

In their issue of November 24, 1954 *The Motor* published a road test report on the Zephyr Six Convertible. The performance and handling was, of course, similar to the saloon's and were such, according to *The Motor*, as to have 'led many people to accept this model as a good substitute for a sports car'. The test staff noticed that 'at times slight shake suggests that the convertible body is a little less rigid than that of the all-steel saloon', although 'actual rattles were almost entirely absent'.

Elsewhere, another very sporting Zephyr was on test. Raymond Mays had decided to offer a genuine 100mph conversion. The weight and frontal area of the Zephyr, coupled with its relatively low overall gearing, were such that over 100bhp would be needed to reach a true 100mph, and this figure was difficult to achieve by modifying a standard cylinder head because of the restrictions imposed by the siamesed inlet ports. Mays therefore designed a new light-alloy cylinder head of 8.2:1 compression ratio, with six separate, steeply inclined inlet ports. The standard valves were retained, and the efficiency of the six-port arrangement was such that twin SU carburettors were now sufficient for the desired power output, and 106bhp at 5,000rpm was the result of these modifications. A speed of 100mph was now available, but at that rate the engine was turning over at 6,200rpm on the normal top gear ratio. Although not a Ford option, the

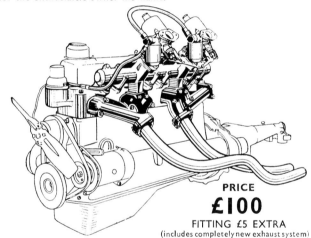

Recipe for 100mph; a Raymond Mays conversion. The earlier Mays conversion, based on the standard cast-iron cylinder head, featured triple side-draught SU carburettors, and to make room for these the battery had to be removed to a position in the boot.

An attractive way of increasing the luggage space was offered by this conversion, although situating the heavy spare wheel well outside the wheelbase would have an adverse effect on the handling qualities of the car.

Laycock de Normanville overdrive was being offered by Laycock Concessionaires G.E. Neville and Son, of Mansfield, with a fitting kit for the Consul/Zephyr range. The overdrive gave a 22.2% reduction in engine revs when engaged, which meant on the Zephyr 20.7mph/1,000rpm as against 16.1mph/1,000rpm on direct top gear. The Mays-tuned engine would pull just about 5,000 revs on the overdrive ratio, and so the true 100mph was exceeded slightly. For regular 100mph motoring Raymond Mays advised the fitting of the Laycock overdrive, although the engine conversion alone was available at £105, including a dual exhaust system and a fitting charge. The overdrive cost £72 extra, and also being offered by Mays was a set of Ferodo brake linings in racing material at £6 19s 6d, and stiffer rear shock absorbers at £6 6s.

John Bolster tested the Raymond Mays car complete with all the options, and reported his findings in *Autosport* on December 3, 1954. After describing the engine modifications, he went on: 'The car which I tried had a Laycock de Normanville device installed; this could be engaged on either second or top gear by a small switch on the gearlever, and gave the effect of a close-ratio five-speed gearbox. On the road, the first impression one gains is that the smoothness of running has been improved. This must be due to better fuel distribution, thanks to the new porting and manifold. During the tests, I changed from first to second at 30mph, second to overdrive second at 50mph, and then into direct top at 75mph. About 90mph seemed a good pace at which to switch in the overdrive on top'. Checked against the stopwatch the Mays Zephyr recorded 0-30mph in 3.5 seconds, 0-40 in 6.6, 0-50 in 9.4, 0-60 in 13.6, 0-70 in 17.8, 0-80 in 24.4 and 0-90 in 32 seconds. The standing quarter-mile had taken 19 seconds, and the maximum speed was a two-way average of 102mph. A tremendous overtaking ability was indicated by the time taken to go from 30 to 50mph in direct second gear of 5 seconds flat, and from 50 to 70mph in overdrive second in 8 seconds. The total price of the conversion, with the overdrive, hard brake linings and stiffer rear shock absorbers, would add £191 to the price of a Zephyr or Zodiac, giving a total price of £945 and £1,042, respectively, for which, in 1955, the buyer would have a truly outstanding high-performance saloon.

The cars in the Consul/Zephyr range had entered their fifth year of production well established as the leading sellers in the medium/large sector, and were continuing to represent excellent value for money at £666, £754 and £851. A worthy rival for the Consul had appeared late in 1954 in the shape of the Austin A50 Cambridge, at £678, with which

Austin were moving into the 1½-litre class; but BMC's new Morris Oxford Series 2 at £774 was too highly priced to fight for top spot amongst 1½-litre family cars. New 2.6-litre six-cylinder saloons from BMC were the Austin A90 Westminster and Morris Isis. Offering similar accommodation and rather more speed than the Zodiac, the Westminster at £834 (De Luxe) was to prove an excellent all round car, although in the event still failing to make a significant impact on Zephyr/Zodiac sales, whilst the rather ponderous Morris Isis (£801) was to be one of BMC's biggest failures. Most closely matching the big-Ford range in specification, equipment, and straight-line performance were Vauxhall's E Series Wyvern, Velox and Cresta. These had been updated with new oversquare engines of identical dimensions to the Fords, and being listed now at £702, £759 and £844 were priced competitively too, but appear not to have captured the public's imagination in the way the Fords had done, as sales of this range were on a smaller scale. Somehow, Dagenham had achieved a blend of qualities which made the Consul/Zephry/Zodiac concept seem just right to a very large number of buyers in this sector.

As well as having a wide public appeal, the Zephyr Six, with its high performance and, by now, very well proven durability, was finding increasing favour amongst the provincial police forces. Its rapid acceleration and good handling endeared it to the patrol drivers and, in one force at least, the Zephyrs had become affectionately known as the 'Fast Blacks'. A visit to the rider's car park at a league speedway track would often reveal a number of the big Fords. The professional speedway rider covered a high mileage in the course of an English league season, and a hard-working, dependable car, able if necessary to carry the speedway machine on a rack across the back, was a vital part of the rider's equipment. To see the 1954 World Champion, New Zealander Ronnie Moore, at the wheel of a Consul convertible, and England Captain Arthur Forrest with an always immaculate Zodiac, served to underline the esteem in which the big Fords were held. When the Hollywood Motor Rodeo toured England in the summer of 1955, they chose a fleet of Zodiacs to supplement the American Ford Fairlanes which they used in the United States to give their impressive display. The Zodiacs were an excellent choice, and put up some startling performances within the confines of the speedway stadiums chosen for the British tour.

A 1955 Consul convertible posing for a period press photograph.

57

The Autocar took another look at the Consul in 1955, not having put one through the full road test procedure since the original press demonstrator of 1951. The report appeared in the issue of July 22 and, four years on, *The Autocar* was still very favourably impressed, with comments such as: 'The Consul has considerable appeal, reasons for its popularity being readily apparent' and: 'Performance is impressive, the ride is comfortable, and the handling is such that the enthusiastic driver may, when he feels so disposed, throw the car into corners. . . . It is almost indifferent to rough surfaces'. Of the gearbox there was a hint of criticism: 'To use the gearbox well it is necessary to double-declutch when changing down into first, a manoeuvre unknown to many modern drivers, and one with which women usually have difficulty'. Summing up the Consul, *The Autocar* concluded: 'There is much about the Consul that is impressive, notably detail points of design that may not make themselves apparent under casual inspection. For carrying capacity, economy, performance and modest price and running cost, the Consul merits praise'. This particular car had accelerated from rest to 30, 50 and 60mph in 6.9, 17.2 and 25.9 seconds, and recorded a maximum speed of 74mph and an overall fuel consumption of 29mpg.

The success was being repeated on a worldwide basis in the various export markets. Sales of the Zephyr had received a boost in Africa in 1955 when Vic Preston drove a standard Zephyr Six to outright victory in the tough East African Safari Rally. In Australia the Consul and Zephyr had been well received from the start, and proved to be able to stand up well to the rough road conditions that existed in many areas outside the major towns. This aspect of the Zephyr's performance was reported on enthusiastically by Ian Fraser writing in the August 1955 issue of one of Australia's leading car magazines, *Cars Today*. According to Fraser: 'The Zephyr was very roadworthy in all conditions. On dirt roads the handling was nothing short of excellent. Belted along a corrugated gravel road at 80mph the car held on very well, with no tail hop at all. Driven over rough cattle tracks, the front springs refused to bottom, although one of the rear semi-elliptics went to the limit in a huge water-filled hole, which would have probably wrecked a lesser car'. He went on to criticize the Zephyr's 41ft turning circle, and thought that the driving position lacked support for persons of larger than average size, but he concluded: 'The Ford Zephyr is, without doubt, the leading car in its class. It has a couple of minor faults, but its advantages certainly outweigh these a hundred to one'.

Soon after ordering a new Zephyr Zodiac from Ford Agents Brown Brothers Motors, of Vancouver, 32-year-old Canadian Michael Schreiner learned that it would be Dagenham's millionth postwar export vehicle. Mr and Mrs Schreiner were flown to England, as the guests of the Ford Motor Company, to take delivery of their Zodiac at Dagenham. On September 5 the Zodiac was driven off the production line by The Rt Hon A. R. W. Low, Minister of State at the Board of Trade, and formally handed over to Mr Schreiner. After a tour of Dagenham in a cavalcade of Ford cars, which included a visit to the Civic Centre where the Schreiners met the Mayor, the new Zodiac was loaded on to the *MV Evanger* of the Norwegian Westfal-Larsen shipping line. The choice of the *Evanger* was an appropriate one, as, like the Schreiner's Zodiac, it too was making its maiden voyage. In the 10 years since the war had ended no other British motor manufacturer had matched Dagenham's million exports, which represented well over half of their total postwar production to that time of 1,800,000 vehicles. Just under a quarter of all Britain's export vehicles since the war had been

An interesting comparison between the Zephyr Six and the Zephyr Zodiac. The Zephyr Six shown has the optional radio. A radio exclusive to the Zodiac, featuring twin speakers, was available at £47.17s.1d.

products of the Ford Motor Company; these figures underline the tremendous contribution that Dagenham was making to Britain's postwar recovery.

The benefits to be obtained by adding an overdrive to the gearbox, particularly on the six-cylinder models, had been well demonstrated by the cars fitted with the Laycock electrically-actuated unit. Another overdrive for the Consul/Zephyr/Zodiac range was now available from Vehicle Developments, of London. Known as the Handa overdrive, this was engaged by a vacuum-operated diaphragm mechanism using manifold depression. Then, in August 1955, the Ford Motor Company themselves announced an optional overdrive for the six-cylinder models only, priced at £63. This was the semi-automatic Borg-Warner unit which incorporated a freewheeling arrangement effective below about 30mph. Above this speed the overdrive could be engaged in any gear simply by releasing the accelerator pedal momentarily: if direct drive was then needed above the 30mph cut-in speed, during an overtaking manoeuvre for example, the overdrive was disengaged by 'kicking down' the accelerator pedal past an extra switch at the fully open position, after which direct drive would be retained unless or until the pedal was lifted or the speed dropped to below the 30mph cut-out speed. In the under-30mph freewheeling range, transmission was through the ordinary gearbox ratios with normal drive on an open throttle. The combined overdrive/freewheel unit could be simply locked out of use altogether by means of a facia-mounted lever, leaving a normal three-speed transmission. The Borg-Warner unit gave a reduction of 30% in engine rpm, raising the mph/1,000rpm in top gear from the normal 16.1 to 23.0. As the six-cylinder engine was able to pull around 4,000 revs in overdrive, the Zephyrs and Zodiacs so equipped were genuine 90mph cars. Another, incidental, benefit of the Borg-Warner overdrive was that in the freewheel range, provided that the throttle was closed, clutchless gear-changes could be made, although of course the clutch still had to be used in the normal manner for stopping and restarting.

Also during 1955, the oil pump had received a modified pick-up pipe, making the pump self-priming, and the ignition system now featured an oil-filled coil. At the Earls Court Show that year there were just two visible changes: the Zephyr Six had acquired the Zodiac's vinyl roof lining, and all three models featured separate amber rear flashing indicators in place of those originally incorporated in the rear light units. Mounted in the back panel beneath the boot lid, the new indicators were a standard, off-the-shelf Tex design and as such, unfortunately, did not quite blend into the rear-end styling of the car. The only other change in the specification was the adoption of tubeless tyres.

The 'Five Star Cars' were now nearing the end of their production run as, although their sales were steadily rising — a fact reflected in the record production figure of 106,176 cars for 1955 — development work and testing of the prototypes of the projected replacement models, the Mk 2 Consul, Zephyr and Zodiac, was now well advanced. When production of the Mk 1 cars ceased on February 22, 1956, which was the day after the Mk 2 had been announced, a total of 406,792 had been produced, this figure being made up of 231, 481 Consuls, 152,677 Zephyr Sixes and 22,634 Zephyr Zodiacs.

Surprise was expressed in many quarters that the Ford Motor Company had deleted the Mk 1 models whilst still in their prime, indeed, almost certainly before they had actually reached their peak annual sales potential. But, whereas in the past Dagenham had seemed quite content to offer the best value for money in any given class, even if the cars in question were somewhat dated, they were now keen to be offering the best cars as well, and with the Consul/Zephyr range they could justifiably claim to have done just that for the last five years. To maintain this position, particularly for another five years or more, it was essential to have not just a 'facelifted' car, but a genuine development, which, whilst still following closely the firmly established and very popular basic concept, would show real advances wherever possible in the light of experience gained with the original design, so as to put the names of Consul and Zephyr once more as far ahead of the opposition as the original models had been on their spectacular Earls Court debut in 1950.

CHAPTER 3

The Three Graces

Mk 2 Consul, Zephyr and Zodiac

With the introduction of the Zephyr Zodiac in October 1953, and production of the convertible models at last under way, the development of the Mk 1 range was more or less complete. The theme was firmly established, and sales of the entire range could obviously continue to expand for some considerable time with the absolute minimum of revision to either the appearance or the technical specification. Few, if any, totally new designs had entered production so smoothly, and with so few teething troubles as had the Consul and Zephyr Six; those of the original production batch still on extended 'life' tests had by now confirmed the remarkable durability that had been indicated in the tests carried out with the prototype cars, and so the Product Planning executives and the development engineers could now start to scheme out the Mk 2 versions of the Consul, Zephyr and Zodiac.

A larger car, one which would be a generous six-seater, was decided upon. Longer by 7in in both Consul and Zephyr form, and wider by 5in, the new bodyshell shared no panels whatsoever with its predecessors, although, apart from having welded-up rear wings, it still followed the same basic concept and constructional methods of the original model, and thus inherited the great strength and rigidity that the Mk 1 cars possessed. In fact, beam stiffness and torsional rigidity were greater by about 12% as a result of carefully redesigning the inner sill area to compensate for the increased length. Deeper windows and much slimmer windscreen pillars, combined with a fully wrap-round rear screen, gave a greater field of vision than on any previous British saloon car. The hooded headlamps and mildly finned rear wings could be seen from the driving seat by anyone of average stature, and these features, coupled with a much improved steering lock giving a turning circle of around 35ft, would enable these big cars to be handled with confidence in confined spaces such as car parks and driveways.

The layout of the luggage boot, which was now of 20cu ft capacity, remained the same as before, again including a toolbox in the Zodiac. The underslung fuel tank was enlarged to $10\frac{1}{2}$ gallons capacity and had a filler cap neatly concealed from view by the rear number-plate, which was mounted on a hinged flap. The large bonnet top was now counterbalanced, and when opened revealed a truly capacious engine bay. The underbonnet layout was altered slightly, with the battery changing

The 1956 Mk 2 Zephyr. Stylist Colin Neale was responsible for this handsome line, whilst Ernie Page was the man who re-engineered the Consul, Zephyr and Zodiac into Mk 2 configuration. Seldom, if ever, had engineering, packaging and styling been in such perfect balance before.

This is the Mk 2 in Consul form. The chrome fillet on the rear screen pillar was introduced in October 1956, and has presumably been fitted retrospectively to this car which has a February 1956 registration number.

sides and now occupying a position inside the offside front wing where the heater had previously resided; that unit was now placed on the scuttle bulkhead just above the height of the engine. The hitherto awkwardly placed fuel filter bowl was now detached from the pump body and occupied a convenient position in the fuel line on the offside inner wing. The Zodiac carburettor had a large oil-bath air filter as a standard fitting, whilst the two cheaper cars retained the washable-element type. The interior arrangements were planned around 'Oscar', Dagenham's 5ft 10in, 12 stone 'average man', whose measurements and weight were based on a detailed survey of 68,000 armed forces personnel, some 80% of whom had the average measurements which resulted in Oscar. Oscar existed in several forms, ranging from a whole series of transparent templates in various positions and scale sizes, up to a full-size and weight dummy figure.

The Zodiac, now free of its 'Zephyr' forename, continued to be the top-of-the-range model, the grille and two-tone paintwork being among its distinguishing features. Circular, Zephyr-type sidelamps identify this left-hand-drive example as a pre-production car.

63

This Mk 2 Zodiac displays the vertical oblong sidelamps adopted as the production specification, a further distinguishing feature from the other models in the range.

Elegant convertibles were included in the Mk 2 range right from the start. This is the Consul; equivalent Zephyr and Zodiac drophead versions were also available.

Following the success of the E.D. Abbott estate conversions on the Mk 1 range, 'Farnham' versions of the Mk 2 cars were quickly introduced.

The Mk 2 model exhibited a sharper profile than the superseded Mk 1 range.

Although the boot was of very ample proportions, the high back panel made loading inconvenient by comparison with rival makes, a point which had been criticized on the Mk 1 models. The fact that this criticism was not attended to on the Mk 2, by deleting the back panel, is an excellent illustration of Dagenham's refusal to sacrifice overall strength for the sake of a small convenience.

As before, the Consul and Zephyr furnishings were simple in style, and the Zodiac, now without the 'Zephyr' prefix, was trimmed and equipped in a more luxurious manner. All three cars featured a combined ignition/starter switch, an arrangement making its first appearance on a British car. Apart from this, the standard equipment of the Consul and Zephyr was very much the same as previously, but the Zodiac displayed some slight changes. A more elaborate tail-end styling treatment was employed which added a further 2in to its overall length, and at the front it sported a different grille with which to distinguish it from the cheaper Zephyr when viewed head-on. The auxiliary lamps and wing mirrors were deleted from the specification, but the two-tone paint, whitewall tyres, chrome wheelrim embellishers and gold-plated badges still made it instantly recognizable as the top-of-the-range model.

Offering so much more accommodation had inevitably resulted in an

Steering wheel, instruments and controls of the Mk 2 Zephyr/ Zodiac.

1956-57 Mk 2 Zodiac interior. The dished steering wheel was making its first appearance on a British car.

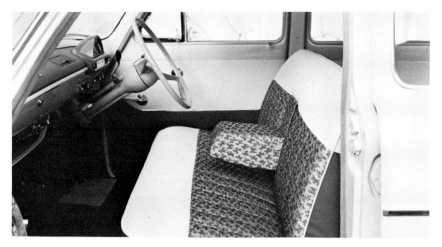

increase in weight, although experience with the Mk 1 models had shown that they were in fact carrying excess weight and that savings could have been made without loss of strength. These lessons were applied to the new cars to keep the increase to a modest ¾cwt, which was also, of course, accompanied by an increase in frontal area. In order to overcome these two factors the engineers decided to adopt greater cylinder capacities for the Mk 2 engines, rather than resort to a higher state of tune or multiple carburettors. There was plenty of 'meat' in the block, and an increase in the bore to 82.5mm still allowed ample water jacketing around each cylinder to ensure even cooling. A new, slightly longer-throw crankshaft gave an increase in stroke to 79.5mm, so the over-square characteristics were retained with only a very slight increase in piston speed, which was in any case to be more than compensated for by the adoption of higher overall gearing. As before, the crankshaft ran in either three or four main bearings

This illustration shows the fresh air ducts on the bulkhead, which were fitted when the optional heater was not specified. The four-cylinder engine fits very comfortably in the Mk 2 Consul's engine bay. This engine and gearbox was also used in the Thames 10/12cwt forward-control van introduced in 1957. Although not a Ford option, the Perkins 1.6-litre diesel could be installed in the Consul, but as the Consul engine was unusually long-lasting by four-cylinder standards, very few owners bothered with the diesel conversion.

according to the four- or six-cylinder application, and to compensate for the longer throw the bearing journal diameters were increased to 2.376in and 2.125in, respectively, for the main and big ends. Hollow webs between the big ends made this an unusually light crankshaft, and in service it proved to be just as rigid as the shorter throw Mk 1 fitting. Separate valve guides were omitted from the new cylinder head, resulting in improved valve cooling coupled with a worthwhile cost saving. The wedge shape was retained for the combustion chambers, whilst the standard compression ratio was increased to 7.8:1. A 6.9:1 head for use with 'regular' grade fuel was to be available as an option. A similar capacity cooling system to the Mk 1 was retained, but now pressurized to 7psi. The new bore and stroke dimensions gave total cylinder capacities of 1,703cc and 2,553cc for the new Consul and Zephyr/Zodiac, and the power and torque outputs showed a considerable improvement over the Mk 1 cars; net figures were 59bhp at 4,400rpm with 91lb/ft torque at 2,300rpm for the Consul and 85bhp at 4,400rpm with 133lb/ft at 2,000rpm for the Zephyr and Zodiac.

A new clutch, with an $8\frac{1}{2}$in diameter lining, was introduced for the six-cylinder models, whilst the four-cylinder cars would continue to use a clutch of the same 8in diameter as before. The gearbox ratios were to remain the same, with first gear continuing to be unsynchronized. The gearbox had proved to be particularly trouble-free in the Mk 1 range, and so the only change in specification deemed necessary here was a slight increase in the diameter of the mainshaft in order to cope with the increased power from the enlarged engines. As the larger capacity engines would be capable of pulling higher gearing, all three gears were effectively raised by the choice of new rear axle ratios of 4.11:1 and 3.90:1 for the four- and six-cylinder cars, respectively, these ratios having been carefully calculated so that once again the maximum top gear speeds would coincide approximately with a piston speed of 2,500ft/min, the road speeds now being 79.5mph for the Consul and 88mph for the Zephyr and Zodiac. The new axle ratios gave a top gear mph/1,000rpm figure of 16.9 for the Consul (15.1, Mk 1) and 18.5 for the Zephyr/Zodiac (16.1, Mk 1) and so promised rather more effortless top gear cruising in the Mk 2 models with little, if any, increase in fuel consumption. With the addition of the optional Borg-Warner overdrive, the Mk 2 Zephyr/Zodiac gearing would be remarkably long-legged, with 26.4mph/1,000rpm offering better than 25mpg economy at a 70mph cruising speed. This device was considered at one stage as an option for the new Consul, in conjunction with the lower 4.444:1 axle ratio from the Mk 1 Zephyr in order to reduce the overdrive gearing to more manageable proportions for the four-cylinder engine. However, although listed in the original Mk 2 Consul brochures, it was apparently withdrawn as a Consul option soon after the model's introduction.

The suspension and steering set-up which had been pioneered so successfully in the Mk 1 range was, of course, retained, the only alterations being those necessary to accommodate the larger and heavier body. Brake drum diameter remained the same 9in as before, but the front shoe width was increased from $1\frac{3}{4}$ to $2\frac{1}{2}$in, giving a total brake lining area of 147sq in, a larger increase than was demanded simply by the weight of the new models in order to ensure adequate stopping power from the higher speeds which could now be attained. New road wheels, of the same 13in diameter and 4 or $4\frac{1}{2}$in rim width as before and retaining the 5.90 and 6.40 section tyres, were slightly less dished than those of the Mk 1 cars. The longer and wider body had naturally allowed an increase in the track and wheelbase, the

Mk 2 Zodiac underbonnet layout. The Zephyr retained a cylin-
rical, washable air cleaner
rather than the Zodiac's oil-bath
type pictured here. From
October 1960, both six-cylinder
Mk 2s featured a pan-type air
filter with replaceable paper
element.

latter in turn allowing the engine to be mounted a little further back in
relation to the front axle line, so lessening slightly the nose-heavy bias in the
front/rear weight distribution. The difference was most marked on the
Consul, with a front/rear percentage figure of 55/45 compared with the
59/41 of both the four- and six-cylinder Mk 1 cars, the figure for the Zephyr
now being 57/43.

The new models were given the factory designation 204E (four-cylinder)
and 206E (six-cylinder) in right-hand-drive form, with 205E and 207E for
left-hand-drive cars. The first prototype to be completed, a Zodiac, took to
the road under the cover of darkness in December 1954, and by early
January had been joined by another Zodiac and a Consul. Soon after
running-in was completed, the three cars, accompanied by a standard Mk
1 Zodiac as a 'yardstick' for comparative purposes, left Dagenham for the
North Sea ferry and then motored across Holland and into Germany,
where a test headquarters had been set up in a remote mountain area.
Within a few days a prototype Zephyr had joined the first three cars in
Germany to take part in what was later described by Ford as 'one of the
most intensive proving programmes in automobile history'. Germany
offered almost ideal facilities, with many miles of badly made-up roads and
shattering *pavé*, in addition to the autobahns where full-throttle driving
could be indulged in for miles at a stretch, whilst overnight temperatures in
the mountains of around $-40°F$ were also very useful for evaluating cold
start performance. Meanwhile, other prototypes were undergoing tests at
Ford's own proving ground in Britain, whilst additional testing, principally
of the suspension, was being carried out on the uniquely rough roads of
Kenya, despite the problems being caused there at that time by the Mau
Mau terrorists.

By late 1955 much of the development work was complete, and a
production date was set for the following January. Pilot production of the
Zephyrs and Zodiacs got under way on January 26, with the first Consuls
following early in February. On Tuesday, February 21, 1956, 'The Three

Graces' — Dagenham's Mk 2 Consul, Zephyr and Zodiac — were officially announced. The Ford Motor Company hired Harringay Arena for the following weekend, to stage a lavish showing of the new cars for the benefit of Ford employees, dealers, overseas Ford officials and VIPs. In the arena, 'The Three Graces' were set in front of a background of apple blossom and cherry trees, and were surrounded by exotic flowers flown in from Egypt and the Continent.

The styling of the new cars was greeted with tremendous enthusiasm by both press and public alike, and in the opinion of many people, Dagenham's styling team, led by Colin Neale, had produced the most handsome cars ever to appear from a British manufacturer. A strong transatlantic influence was evident once again, the new cars displaying a subtle blend of features from the parent company's 1954/55 Mainline/Customline/Fairlane series, the extra length with no increase in height giving a lithe or 'graceful yet athletic' appearance as stylist Colin Neale put it. Complementary to the new appearance was a range of colours specially blended for 'The Three Graces' consisting of Carlisle Blue, Sarum Blue, Corfe Grey, Wells Fawn, Hereford Green, Warwick Green, Ivory and Black, with five two-tone combinations of these, plus Black, being available on the Zodiac.

Despite the cost of retooling and the increase in the raw materials necessary for the larger body, the new models were once again offered at prices consistent with the Ford tradition of unbeatable value for money. With the Consul listed at £781, the Zephyr at £872 and the Zodiac at £969, it was obvious from the outset that the Mk 2 models would continue to build on the remarkable sales success of their predecessors and would further enhance the excellent reputation which now came with the names Consul, Zephyr and Zodiac. Closely following the saloons into production were convertible versions of the Consul and Zephyr, the former priced at £946, with a power-operated hood as an option for an extra £75. The Zephyr convertibles were built with the power tops as standard and were priced at £1,111, although a manual top version was available to special order with the corresponding £75 reduction.

A road test report of an overdrive-equipped Zephyr appeared in *The Autocar* on April 13. In every respect the car came in for considerable praise, with comments such as: 'First impressions of the engine on the road were most favourable ... The spirited fashion in which the car tackles main road gradients and overtakes slower moving vehicles is most exhilarating for the driver ... The brakes are of Girling hydraulic type; they could not be faulted by heavy use and extreme pedal pressures. There was no unevenness or overheating, and only slight fade after exceptionally heavy use during track testing . . . The rear end is no longer skittish, nor does it attempt to break away in an over-fast corner. In the wet and with increased power, there is naturally more likelihood of the tail coming round, but not, we are satisfied, more than with any similar car'. Acceleration through the gears showed a worthwhile improvement over the Mk 1 Zephyr, with 0-30, 0-50, 0-60 and 0-70mph being recorded in 4.9, 12.3, 17.9 and 24.5 seconds, although the maximum speed of 86mph suggested that this particular Zephyr was not yet fully run-in. With the overdrive in use 32mpg was recorded on one run when the car was being driven with economy in mind, and the overall consumption figure quoted was a creditable 24.1mpg. One of *The Autocar* staff had confessed to being 'well-nigh electrified by the excellence of the new Zephyr', and the test was summed up with the comment, 'it is one of the best and most encouraging British cars in large-scale production that we have tested since the war. And there is no reason to qualify that statement'. In the hands of *The Motor*, (R/T No 9/56) a new Zodiac recorded maximum speeds in the three gears of 36, 62, and 90.5mph, and accelerated from rest to 30, 50, 60 and 70mph in 4.6, 11.3, 17.1 and 24.3 seconds, and as this particular car had already run upwards of 2,000 miles these figures were more representative of what could be expected from a fully run-in example.

A worthwhile improvement in all-round performance was also evident in the new Consul. An example reported on in the June 15, 1956 issue of *The Autocar* reached 79mph and accelerated from rest to 30, 50 and 60mph in 6.4, 15.8 and 25.0 seconds. With second gear now comfortable up to 50mph or so, the Mk 2 had a big advantage over the early Consul when overtaking in the 30-50mph bracket, with a very useful time of 8.7 seconds being recorded for this range in this gear. An overall fuel consumption of 29mpg over a distance of 540 miles suggested that the performance increase was not at the expense of economy. *The Autocar* reported: 'This new Consul is attractive in its class as it offers so much room and performance, at a price of well under £800. It combines a handsome modern appearance with technical improvements of real value, and is likely to remain for a long time in the forefront of this country's best buys'.

'The Three Graces' made their North American debut at the 1956 New York International Motor Show, and only eight minutes after the doors opened on the first day, April 28, two Ford salesmen were each claiming to have made the first sale of the show. Show Manager Gerald Martin declared a dead heat, announcing that Hans Hallendorn had made the first sale of a car for delivery in the United States, a Consul, whilst the order for a Zephyr taken by Horace Sirraco was the first from an American who wished to take delivery in Europe under a plan enabling the buyer to use his new car on a European holiday, then have it shipped to America by Ford at no extra cost. More than 50% of the Mk 2s being produced were going for export, but this flow suffered a temporary setback in July because of an industrial dispute within the rival BMC organization. Fisher and Ludlow, of Birmingham, who were a part of BMC, but also provided parts for other manufacturers, were at that time supplying Briggs Motor Bodies with certain panels for the Mk 2 range, and a strike there halted these supplies. The dies used by Fisher and Ludlow were Ford property, but attempts to retrieve them were baulked by Transport Union drivers in Birmingham refusing to handle them, even though their own Union officials tried to persuade them otherwise. To combat this situation and keep the men at Dagenham employed, Ford hastily recalled as many as possible of the 'knocked down' export cars, including those already packed and awaiting shipment at the docks.

Some of the early production six-cylinder Mk 2s had suffered from broken halfshafts, and a modification to cure this was introduced in September. A new 24-spline shaft, with the appropriate differential gears, replaced the original 16-spline shaft, an arrangement which had been inherited from the Mk 1 model and apparently could not always withstand the increased torque from the larger Mk 2 engines. The modification applied to both four- and six-cylinder cars and completely eliminated the problem.

The new models made their first Earls Court appearance in October 1956, on stand 145. Two very slight styling changes were evident; a chrome-plated fillet had been introduced on the rear screen pillars, and the flat panel across the rear of the car beneath the boot lid now featured two moulded ribs. A Zodiac convertible was being shown for the first time, and announcing this glamorous addition to the range the Ford Motor Company said: 'The distinction of the Ford range attains a new peak with the introduction of the Zodiac convertible, on which a power-operated hood is standard equipment. In this beautifully styled car is incorporated all the splendour and refinement of the Zodiac saloon plus, when required, the benefits of open car motoring. This truly superb example of convertible design has a basic price of £835 and with purchase tax costs a total of £1,253 17s'. Also being shown on the Ford stand was a Consul 'Farnham' estate car, and on their own stand, 111, the coachbuilders E. D. Abbott, of Farnham, were showing estate car versions of all three Mk 2 models. The conversion closely followed in style that of the successful Mk 1 estates and gave a very useful 36cu ft of luggage space, or 66cu ft with the rear seat squab folded flat. Stiffer rear springs and oversize tyres, 6.40 × 13 on the Consul and 6.70 × 13 on the Zephyr/Zodiac, were now included in the estate car specification. Prices were £1,028, £1,118, and £1,223 for the Consul, Zephyr and Zodiac. A new trim material, nylonweave, was announced as an optional extra on the Consul and Zephyr to replace the standard PVC, and as a no-cost optional alternative to the standard leather upholstery in the Zodiac.

Much more significant, however, was the announcement that a Borg-Warner automatic gearbox was available on the six-cylinder saloons and estates, and at a price of £187 which would make a Zephyr saloon so equipped the cheapest automatic car available outside the United States. The gearbox chosen was the Model DG; a robust unit designed to handle the torque from engines of over $3\frac{1}{2}$-litres capacity, it would be under no stress whatsoever behind the $2\frac{1}{2}$-litre Ford engine, thus promising a long trouble-free life. An automatic Zodiac was soon made available to the motoring press, and a report of the car appeared in the February 8 issue of

The Mk 2 'Farnham' estate car. The rear screen is still the Mk 1 item.

The Autocar. The car accelerated from rest to 70mph in 31.6 seconds, some 6 seconds longer than the time they had recorded with a manual Zephyr. This performance decrease could be accounted for by the power losses inherent with a torque converter in place of a clutch, and by the increase in weight — about $1\frac{1}{2}$cwt — of the automatic box. The fuel consumption, with an overall figure of 23.1mpg, was little different from that of a manual Zephyr, and was helped no doubt by the fact that on the DG gearbox the torque converter only operated on low and intermediate ratios and was locked out in top gear. In addition the automatic Zephyrs and Zodiacs were fitted with larger 6.70 section tyres in view of the extra unladen weight, and were consequently pulling slightly higher gearing. *The Autocar* summed up: 'As our experience of this latest line from Dagenham broadens, the value for money, combined with roadworthiness of a high order, becomes even more impressive. This automatic version of the Zodiac II demonstrates that a $2\frac{1}{2}$-litre engine so equipped can have a very acceptable performance and restfulness, for those who consider the normal shift to be outdated'.

The introduction of the Mk 2 in Australia quickly led to a revival of the plans for a pick-up version. The design team at Geelong produced full-size designs in 1956, based very closely on those of the ill-fated Mk 1 pick-up

Dagenham's and, some insist, Britain's most handsome convertible, the Mk 2 Zodiac.

Her Majesty the Queen's spe-
cial-bodied Zephyr estate car.

Interior of the royal estate car, which is equipped with automatic transmission and special rear seating. The enlarged window frames on the doors are of timber construction.

Tailgate details of the special estate car. After seeing considerable service over many years, KUV 1 was retired from duty and placed in the Sandringham museum.

One of the extremely rare Dagenham-built pick-up trucks, more than a prototype although never adopted for mass production.

The Australian-built Mk 2 pick-up featured a rear cab treatment quite different from the British version. This type of vehicle was always popular in Australia where it was usually referred to by the rather attractive title 'coupe utility' – often, however, shortened to 'ute'.

This interesting conversion based upon the Mk 2 coupe utility is shown whilst in service with an Australian hospital.

The Ford Australia prototype for a Mk 2 station wagon, which eventually reached production in 1959. Perhaps not quite so stylish an estate car as that of E.D. Abbott in Britain, the Australian model had the benefit of a more practical drop-down tailgate which allowed easy loading from either side.

project. One of the team, Lewis Bandt, took the drawings to the parent company in the United States early in 1957 and received authorization to tool-up for production. The prototype was tested with a 9cwt load over a 4,000-mile route in company with a Ford Mainline V8 pick-up before production commenced. Meanwhile, rather curiously in view of their original objections, Dagenham had built a Zephyr pick-up truck in November 1956, differing only slightly in detail from the Australian design, and production records show a total of 46 of these being built at Dagenham between then and August 1959; apparently these were all shipped to Australia.

Despite the Suez crisis, and the subsequent period of petrol rationing, worldwide sales of the Mk 2 range expanded rapidly during 1957, and by the middle of the year production was running ahead of the peak rate achieved by the Mk 1 models in 1955. Nevertheless, Dagenham planned several improvements designed to keep 'The Three Graces' out in front, and at Earls Court in October a Consul De Luxe was unveiled. Priced at £871, the De Luxe was a particularly useful addition to the range as, apart from the fact that the heater was still only an option, it was otherwise trimmed and equipped almost to the same standard as the Zodiac, with such items as a cigarette lighter, twin horns and windscreen washers, in addition to the leather or nylonweave upholstery, and so appealed to those buyers who appreciated the luxury trim and fittings, but had no desire for the high-performance six-cylinder engine. Externally the De Luxe model was identified by a contrasting colour applied to the roof, and chrome-plated surrounds to the rear lamps. As slight visual distinction on the Zephyr was apparent in the form of a new grille and the adoption of the Zodiac sidelights at the front, whilst the Zodiac itself remained unchanged externally. A redesigned front seat was a feature of all three cars, and both front and rear seats now also had the benefit of foam rubber padding in addition to the springing. A front seat centre armrest was also at last making its appearance, although still only as an optional extra on the Consul, and on the Zephyr and Zodiac at the expense of the one previously

Not quite right. A proposed grille design for the 1958-model Zephyr.

in the rear. Technical changes were the introduction of a Burman recirculating-ball steering box, and a new gear-change mechanism enclosed in the steering column. Completing the updated specification was a totally new range of 15 colours, including a red and a yellow, replacing the eight original shades of 1956.

For those owners wishing for a faster than standard car, the tuning specialists were offering similar conversions to those which had proved so successful on the Mk 1 models. The Alexander Engineering Company's conversion for the Zephyr consisted of a reworked cylinder head of 8.7:1 compression ratio in which the valve ports were opened out, larger inlet valves installed, double valve springs fitted and the combustion chambers polished. A new inlet manifold with triple SU carburettors supplied the mixture, and a six-branch exhaust manifold completed the conversion. The figures claimed by Alexander make an interesting comparison with those obtained by *The Autocar* for a standard Zephyr Mk 2.

Acceleration from rest (seconds):			Acceleration in top gear (seconds):		
	Standard	Alexander		Standard	Alexander
0-30mph	4.9	3.1	20-40mph	8.0	6.7
0-50mph	12.3	8.0	30-50mph	8.8	7.2
0-60mph	17.9	10.7	40-60mph	10.0	8.0
0-70mph	25.4	14.8	50-70mph	12.6	8.5
0-80mph	35.8	22.5	60-80mph	17.4	11.8
0-90mph	–	29.2			

Raymond Mays developed a Mk 2 six-port light-alloy cylinder head incorporating larger valves, stronger single valve springs, and with a compression ratio of either 8.7:1 or 9.2:1 according to choice. Complete with twin SU carburettors and a dual exhaust system, this conversion, costing £135, put the Zephyr into the 100mph-plus category, and enabled *The Autocar* to record acceleration from rest to 30, 50, 60, 70, 80 and 90mph in 3.3, 7.5, 10.0, 14.5, 19.3 and 25.5 seconds with a 9.2:1 compression ratio version. A similar Mays cylinder head for the Consul, with a single SU carburettor, boosted the four-cylinder engine's output to 90bhp.

Servais Silencers produced a complete exhaust system for the Mk 2 models, including the convertible, which, because of its additional underbody bracing, required a different system from that of the saloons. Tests carried out by Servais with a Zodiac convertible resulted in the following 'before' and 'after' figures.

Acceleration from rest (seconds):			Acceleration in top gear (seconds):		
	Standard	Servais		Standard	Servais
0-60mph	16.1	14.4	40-60mph	9.7	8.2
0-70mph	21.3	20.0	50-70mph	11.2	9.9
0-80mph	30.5	26.5	60-80mph	20.2	16.3

For the vast majority of owners, the performance of the standard models in both four- and six-cylinder form was, of course, entirely satisfactory, and converted cars only represented a very tiny percentage of the total. There was, however, a popular misconception at that time that, because the Consul was lacking a 'third' gear, its performance was handicapped. In fact, the Consul actually had a performance advantage over some similarly-priced rivals of similar power/weight ratio, but equipped with four-speed gearboxes. The Hillman Minx, for instance, had a third gear ratio which gave 10.2mph/1,000rpm, and accelerated in this ratio from 30 to 50mph in 10.6 seconds (*The Autocar*, July 1956). The Morris Oxford Series III had a third gear giving 10.0mph/1,000rpm, with which it covered the 30 to 50mph range in 9.9 seconds (*The Autocar*, October 1957). The

Almost there. The grille design chosen for 1958 on, but seen here with a badge which did not see production.

1958 Zephyr. The grille on this car displays the badge which was chosen for production.

Consul was almost exactly similarly geared in its second gear, 10.2mph/ 1,000rpm in this ratio enabling it to cover the 30 to 50mph range in 8.7 seconds (*The Autocar*, June 1956). Indeed, if we look at the second gear ratios of these two popular rivals, we find gearing of 6.2mph/1,000rpm in both cases, which is only very slightly higher than the Consul's 5.95mph/ 1,000rpm bottom gear. So these two four-speed cars had, in effect, a three-

Prototype Consul De Luxe, 1957-58 version.

speed gearbox with an additional extremely low, and largely superfluous, bottom gear. There were, of course, some excellent four-speed gearboxes around at that time, but there were also far too many of the type just illustrated, of which the extra cost in comparison with the Ford Consul/ Zephyr box was a complete waste of money. Being the smaller-engined car of the range and sharing the same six-seater body with the six-cylinder Zephyr, would sometimes lead to the Consul being saddled with an 'underpowered' tag. Yet again, a look at contemporary road test reports is all that is necessary to refute this argument. The Wolseley 1500,

Another prototype was this Zodiac Z115 high-performance saloon which was to have been powered by a rally-bred multi-carburettor engine. In the event, it did not reach production and a road accident with this car or a similar test vehicle is believed to have been a major reason for the abandonment of the project. Some years were to elapse before Ford in Britain would market a saloon with an explicitly 'performance' image in the shape of the Cortina GT.

A proposed two-door pillarless fixed-head coupe Zodiac which was definitely more than just a styling exercise but which also did not see production. This car would also have been available with the high-performance engine, although the demise of the Z115 project need not have affected the coupe. But Dagenham was already working to capacity, and an additional variation of the Mk 2 range, involving substantial bodywork changes yet having only low-volume sales potential, could not really be justified.

Below: the pillarless coupe had a very transatlantic-looking interior. Below right: the projected power unit for both the Z115 and the two-door hardtop had triple Zenith carburettors and a modified cylinder head, echoing the Alpine Rally cup-winning Zephyrs of 1956, and would have resulted in Ford of Britain's first 100mph production model.

introduced by BMC in 1957, had a 50bhp version of their 1,489cc B series engine to cope with a weight of 18cwt, and was fitted with a four-speed gearbox generally considered to have excellently chosen indirect ratios, allowing over 45mph in second and just over 70mph in third gear. During 1957, *The Autocar* tested both the new Wolseley and the Consul. The Wolseley was tested at a laden weight which gave it a power/weight ratio of 47bhp/ton, whilst the Consul had the remarkably similar figure of 46.8bhp/ton as tested. Of the Wolseley, *The Autocar* said: 'It is eminently suitable for the keen motorist who must compromise between sporting and business use'. It had accelerated from rest to 50, 60 and 70mph in 16.1, 24.4 and 43.9 seconds, and had recorded a mean maximum speed of 77.5mph with a best run of 79.2mph. The Consul, with fractionally less power/weight, and a three-speed gearbox, had gone from rest to 50, 60 and 70mph in 15.6, 25.4 and 38.9 seconds, and also recorded a mean maximum speed of 77.5mph, but with a slightly improved best speed of 80.6mph. Over the standing-start quarter-mile the Wolseley just beat the Consul with a time of 22.1 seconds against the latter's 22.7. These results show that the Consul was in fact extremely competitive, and also that within an 80mph performance range it was possible to tailor a three-speed gearbox perfectly satisfactorily to an engine of modest capacity.

Several interesting Mk 2 models came under the close scrutiny of the test staff of the various motoring magazines during 1957/58. In their issue of August 2, 1957 *The Autocar* featured a Zephyr estate car, and commented very favourably on the versatility of the Abbott conversion. Points earning praise were that the rear seat squab could be quickly detached and conveniently secured to the back of the front seat, and that the rear seat cushion and squab 'can readily be removed for use outside the car, for example, when picnicking'. When heavily laden, the Zephyr estate car had continued to handle well, *The Autocar* saying that 'we can reassure the prospective owner of a Zephyr estate car that the handling qualities are less affected by load than are those of most vehicles of this class'. A portion of the test mileage was carried out with a 6cwt burden on the rear platform in addition to two occupants, and *The Autocar* commented: 'The effect on acceleration was hard to detect; braking power was sufficient to cope with the load, even when the overdrive permitted the freewheeling below about 30mph. Steep hills were climbed without the impression that more power would be useful'. The overdrive had enabled the Zephyr estate car to record a commendable 25mpg overall for a distance of 682 miles, with a best figure of 33mpg for an 80-mile run with just two people on board.

The Motor sampled a Consul convertible (R/T No 2/58) and felt that 'it does not conceal its relationship with Detroit-built automobiles of the same name', going on to say that 'in what it does and how it does it, this medium-powered British car with an American "air" proved itself during an extended test to be a very desirable property'. Although tested in the winter months, this convertible apparently gave *The Motor* staff some enjoyable open-air motoring, as is indicated by the comment: 'As an open car, this convertible model proved very pleasant on fine winter days in the country, being immune from the buffeting around the driver's head, which can make long fast drives in some open cars very tiring'. In its closed condition, however, this particular car was apparently not entirely without draughts, and there was also criticism of the continued absence of sun visors in the Ford convertibles.

John Bolster put a Zodiac automatic through its paces, his report appearing in the June 13, 1958 edition of *Autosport*. He was particularly

1957-58 Zodiac Automatic. This particular car was tested by John Bolster for the magazine Autosport.

pleased about the driving position, having previously driven an early Mk 2 in which the pedals and seat had apparently not been in the correct relationship to each other, and he now stated: 'On taking my seat, I was at once delighted to find that the driving position has been vastly improved. Indeed, I was almost rude about this feature on the previous occasion, and it gives me very great pleasure to be able to withdraw the criticism now'. About the performance of the automatic car he continued: 'Borg-Warner gearboxes are specially tailored to give the best performance on the engine to which they are to be attached. In the case of the Ford Zodiac, a particularly felicitous marriage has been achieved, and the car is much more pleasant to drive than most automatics. The performance figures are

1958 Zodiac Automatic, with optional radio.

1958 Consul De Luxe.

just a little below those of a similar car fitted with a manual box and handled by an expert. However, the average driver would probably achieve a better all round performance with the Borg-Warner transmission. There is a Low position on the gear-lever for engine braking under difficult conditions, and a Kick-down on the accelerator to make second speed available for rapid overtaking. The engine has plenty of "punch" at all speeds, and this is a lively car . . . There is something very attractive about the easy way in which the car covers the ground, and this is a most untiring vehicle for long journeys'. Of the roadholding and handling, he wrote: 'The machine can be cornered quite fast, and remains fully controllable on wet roads. The steering feels positive, and gives the driver a sense of mastery over his mount'. John Bolster's general comments included the observations: 'The Ford Motor Company have been making cars of this type for a considerable time. The experience has been applied with considerable advantage to the latest model, and it is a thoroughly well thought out design from the point of view of all occupants'. He concluded his report with the comment: 'The man in a hurry will like this car, and so will the lady of the house who uses it for shopping. Many a family will get very fond indeed of their Zodiac automatic'. Checked against the stopwatch, this car had recorded times from standstill to 30, 50, 60 and 70mph of 5.0, 11.8, 17.4 and 28.4 seconds, respectively. The standing-start quarter-mile had occupied exactly 21 seconds and the maximum speed was 87mph.

In Australia, sales of the Zephyr coupe utility, as the pick-up truck was known, were fully justifying the faith shown in the design by the Ford engineering team at Geelong, and a test report on the 'ute' appeared in the Australian motoring magazine *Wheels* in May 1958. The design included a

stiffened rear chassis/floor and the addition of three extra leaves in the rear springs. The front end, including the passenger compartment, was standard Zephyr. The 'ute' was tested with sand bags on the rear deck, bringing it up to $33\frac{1}{4}$cwt, and at this weight it accelerated from rest to 50mph in 16.3 seconds and continued to a maximum speed of 77.2mph. The fuel consumption with this load varied between 20.3mpg 'hard driving' and 26.4mpg 'normal fast cruising'. As was usually the case with the Zephyr saloon when on test, the handling was highly praised, with the comment that 'we quickly became more confident of the Zephyr's handling qualities than we are of some cars deliberately designed for the sporting motorist!'. It was felt by the test team, however, that the normal

Consul convertible. The wing mirrors were a standard fitting on this model, and the interior rear-view mirror was mounted on the facia top to make best use of the convertible's rear window, much smaller than that of the saloon. This particular Consul was road-tested by The Motor.

saloon gearing employed in the 'ute' was rather too high for this type of vehicle, particularly for fully laden hill starts.

As the 1958 Earls Court Motor Show drew closer, large newspaper advertisements for the big Mk 2 Fords were appearing, headed 'Unchanged – Unchallenged', signifying that the Consul, Zephyr and Zodiac models on the Ford stand that year would be just the same as last. With total Mk 2 production by now running at a rate of over 2,400 per week, and at that still not always quite managing to satisfy the demand, there was certainly no need for any cosmetic changes to boost sales appeal at this stage. In fact, though, behind the scenes at Dagenham work was in hand on a 'facelift' for early the following year, designed to put the range in an unassailable position for the immediate future, and so allow time for development to begin on a replacement model.

The Mk 2 range were dominating the large-car market now, with the Consul being outstanding amongst true six-seater cars at only £818, or £871 in its more comprehensively equipped De Luxe guise. BMC's closest offering to the Consul was the Morris Oxford Series III at £884, which although somewhat smaller was also a comfortably roomy car, and very well equipped. It was of distinctly lower performance than the Ford however, and had by this time also a decidedly dated appearance by comparison. Standard were offering the Engsign, a smaller-engined (1,670cc) and more utilitarian version of their well known Vanguard, but at a price of £899 it was not at all competitive in this sector. Vauxhall were not facing the Consul head-on anymore, having replaced their large four-cylinder car, the Wyvern, with the much smaller Victor with which they were picking up more sales lower down the market. The Zephyr was a winner in every respect; its prestige regularly boosted by international rallying awards, it had continued from the start to build upon the Mk 1 Zephyr's established reputation for consistent performance and durability, and at £916 was unbeatable value by a considerable margin in the family car six-cylinder class. In fact, only Vauxhall were still offering a rival under-£1,000 six-cylinder car, this being their PA Series Velox, which for £983 gave broadly similar accommodation to the Zephyr and almost as much straight-line performance, but somehow still lacked the correct blend of qualities to lift it out of the ordinary. At £1,013, the Zodiac had to contend with the very similarly equipped Vauxhall Cresta at £1,073, and the basic Austin Westminster at £1,043. A fully equipped Westminster, the A105, was also

available, and its specification included twin carburettors for the 2.6-litre
six-cylinder engine, but at £1,235 it was not a serious threat to the Zodiac,
although a close look at either of the Westminsters would indicate that if
BMC could have reduced their prices to nearer the Zephyr/Zodiac level
without sacrificing quality, the Westminster may well have enjoyed a much
wider popularity.

On February 25, 1959, three years and four days since 'The Three
Graces' had made their debut, Dagenham announced the 'Low Line' Mk 2
models. A new panel, approximately $1\frac{1}{2}$in lower and considerably flatter,
replaced the original, slightly domed roof pressing, giving a surprisingly
sleeker appearance which was further enhanced and highlighted by
additional bright metal embellishment. All three cars acquired stainless
steel windscreen and rear window surround cappings which completely
covered the window rubbers whilst a capping of similar material was also
applied to the roof drip rail. New chrome-plated headlamp hoods replaced
the original painted fittings, and all three cars received restyled chrome
plated rear lamp covers. The Consul was given the chromed door window
surrounds and pointed rear wing tips which had always been a feature of
the two six-cylinder Mk 2s and, along with the Zephyr, it inherited the
extended rear wing side strips of the Zodiac. The Zephyr's grille badge was
now also applied to the Consul De Luxe, and the latter featured new wheel
trims in anodised aluminium, which were also replacing the chromed rings
on.the Zodiac's wheels. Exclusive to the Consul De Luxe were chrome
cappings to the ribs along the back panel.

The interior had undergone a complete redesign, and current thoughts
on safety had led to the introduction of a foam-padded facia and
instrument cowl and soft, crushable sun visors, these latter items at last also
making their appearance in the convertible. The steering wheel had always
been deeply dished on the Mk 2, and the only changes here were the
adoption of a black finish and, where applicable, a half horn ring in place of
the previous full circle. Door and seat trim patterns were new, and all

1958 Zephyr estate car. The two-tone paint division shown was applicable to estate cars only.

1958 Zodiac estate car. The off-side wing mirror was a standard estate car fitting. Zodiac estates were also available with a 'sandwich' two-tone scheme.

models now had door pull-cum-armrests front and rear, those in the front being adjustable on the Zodiac. A map pocket on the front interior trim panel under the dashboard was a new feature which was confined to the Consul De Luxe and Zodiac, whilst the control knobs on all models displayed internationally recognized symbols in place of the previous capital letters for identification. The standard PVC trim material of the Consul and Zephyr displayed a completely new grained texture, and describing this the Ford Motor Company said: 'This material represents a departure from the traditional practice of using PVC to imitate cow hide. The Company's stylists regard PVC as a first class upholstery fabric in its own right and have adopted the Cougar Grain finish which has an individual and most attractive texture'. A further optional trim material, rayonweave, was also now available.

Technical changes included the readoption of the original exposed gear-change linkage, although now shrouded in a similar fashion to that of the Mk 1 cars. A twist release handbrake was new, as was a front door safety locking mechanism, which rendered the interior door handle inoperative if the locking button on the door window sill was depressed. A final useful improvement was positive-locking quarter-lights which could not be opened from outside the car.

In all, these changes represented a worthwhile improvement in many respects, allied to a clearly updated appearance and, as they were incorporated at no extra cost, Dagenham's grip on this sector of the market was even tighter than before. Sales continued to expand steadily both at home and abroad following the introduction of the 'Low Line' models and,

A development Consul with the 'Low Line' roof panel but retaining the earlier screen surrounds and the early Mk 2 Consul cut-back fins.

Opposite and below: 'Low Line' Zephyr. The flatter roof panel gave the car an appreciably sleeker appearance and was accompanied by a very slightly deeper windscreen than on the earlier Mk 2 models.

The rear-three-quarter view of the 'Low Line' Zephyr.

The glamorous 'Low Line' Zodiac.

The 'Low Line' Consul De Luxe; Zodiac luxury allied to four-cylinder economy.

Three-quarter-rear view of the Consul 'Low-Line'.

The front and rear screen sur-rounds of the 'Low Line' cars were in a rustless chromium alloy.

apart from phasing in several new colours and deleting some of the earlier ones, no other changes occurred during the remainder of 1959. Throughout the year the Zephyr had enjoyed considerable racing and rallying success, and with the opening of the M1 motorway in November it received another publicity boost when the Police chose a fleet of seven Zephyr Farnham estate cars with which to patrol the new super highway.

In Australia, following the success of their coupe utility Consul and Zephyr models, Geelong designed a Mk 2 estate car, or station wagon, as they preferred to call it, which, unlike the Abbott conversion in Britain, was rather more of a purpose-built job to cope specifically with Australian outback conditions when necessary. Although retaining the saloon rear wings, the rear end was otherwise totally different. The rear passenger

'Low Line' Consul head and sidelight detail. Shown is the production chromed headlamp hood, which was slightly less sharp than the earlier painted hoods. Some 'Low Line' prototypes featured headlamp hoods which were chromed versions of the earlier shape.

doors had squared-up window frames and the roofline at the rear continued horizontally, van-like, to the end. Whereas the Abbott estate rear door opened sideways, the Geelong wagon featured a very neat tailgate, hinged at the bottom, which was lowered after the pillarless rear window was first wound down into it by means of a lockable handle. Inside, the front bench could be moved forward up to the steering wheel, and when in this position, with the rear seat folded flat, it gave an uninterrupted 7ft 1in long double berth sleeping area, a particularly useful feature for outback conditions. The construction of the station wagon increased the weight considerably, and a Zephyr wagon tested by the magazine *Wheels* scaled over 29cwt with just two people on board, and did remarkably well to accelerate from rest to 70mph at this weight in 26.4 seconds, although the maximum speed of 83.4mph was well down on the usual saloon figure. *Wheels* were very impressed with the Zephyr station wagon, and only offered one small criticism, this being that the inside of the tailgate was painted, and so would inevitably quickly become scratched and shabby through luggage being dragged or pushed across it during loading; they suggested that the tailgate should also be covered with the durable floor-covering material. Apparently, the Zephyr was appreciably larger, and therefore more expensive than other station wagons in Australia at that time, and *Wheels* summed it up by saying: 'The Ford Zephyr station wagon is a very nice piece of equipment for the commercial traveller, farmer,

shopkeeper, or for the ordinary family man. Rugged, practical and with a good turn of performance, the Zephyr has a slight disadvantage with that £1,430 price tag. Still, the man who wants a bigger than average wagon could hardly look past it'.

Facia and controls of the 'Low Line' Consul. The speaker for the optional radio was situated behind the grille in the panel above the radio.

A purchase tax reduction in the 1959 budget at home had brought the prices of the Consul, Zephyr and Zodiac down to an attractive £773, £865 and £957, and also helped to boost sales of all makes of car in Britain. Total production of all Mk 2 models during 1959 was a colossal 142,237, and although this peak rate was not maintained throughout 1960, the Mk 2 cars nevertheless continued to completely dominate this sector of the market. Since 1958, works rally Zephyrs had featured front disc brakes in some of the events in which modifications to the competing cars were allowed, and a *Ford News* bulletin on September 28, 1960 announced: 'There are to be no Motor Show changes from Ford this year, but today, the Company announces the introduction of power-assisted front wheel disc brakes as a production option for all versions of the Consul, Zephyr and Zodiac. The extra cost will be £29 15s including tax, making the total price of a disc-equipped Consul £803 — over £180 less than any other disc-equipped British family car. Of special interest to owners of existing Mk 2 models will be the news that Ford Dealers will soon be able to offer a disc brake conversion kit as an accessory at £32 (fitting extra). Tested and approved in the most arduous international rallies, the new Ford disc brakes are equal to all emergencies in the most severe operating conditions'.

At Earls Court in 1960, the centrepiece of the Ford stand was a dual turntable projecting the 'two-car family' theme, featuring a Zodiac and an Anglia, both of which were in a special white finish, with white hide upholstery edged in black and embossed with gold stars, whilst every single

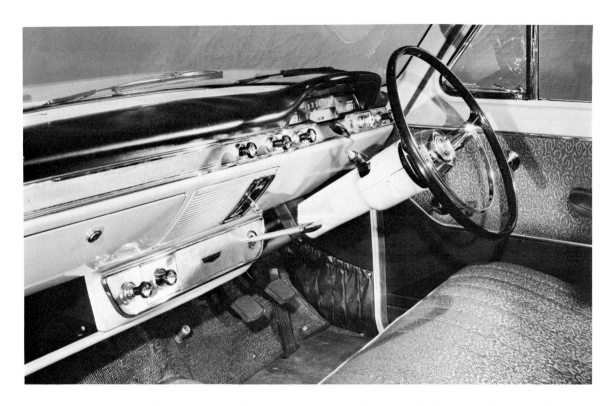

'Low Line' facia and controls, Zodiac and Consul De Luxe. The handbrake was of the twist-release type on these cars, and the instruments included a temperature gauge in place of the previous ammeter.

Ease of entry and exit was always an excellent feature of Dagenham's big-car range.

interior and exterior bright metal part, right down to the tyre valve caps, was finished in 22-carat gold plate. The 542 separate parts in the Zodiac and 306 in the Anglia had been given the 'golden touch' by the Harris Plating Works, of London, and a full quarter-pound of the precious metal had been used. Backing up this glittering display were 10 production Fords, ranging from the 100E Popular to the Zodiac, and no less than five of these cars were awarded medals in the Motor Show Coachwork Competition that year which was organized by the Institute of British Carriage and Automobile Manufacturers. Gold medals were awarded to

The amazing amount of equipment which was swallowed up by the Motorway Patrol Zephyr estates.

the Zodiac, the Consul De Luxe and the Anglia De Luxe. A silver medal went to the basic Consul, and a bronze to the Zephyr, whilst on the Carbodies stand the Zodiac convertible was awarded the silver medal in the Convertible Coachwork category.

Away from the glamour of Earls Court was another Zephyr which certainly deserved a medal. This car was owned by the Goodyear Tyre Company and had spent all its life testing tyres. An account of its amazing record appeared in the *Ford Times,* the report saying: 'As an outstanding example of what performances Goodyear test cars have achieved, a 1958 Ford Zephyr recently completed the astonishing mileage of 417,554 miles in 20 months, using only two engines. The original engine gave 158,000 miles and the replacement engine — still running completely satisfactorily — had totalled 259,554 miles when the car was taken out of the test fleet. As a matter of record, the gearbox was repaired at 217,435 miles; new engine mountings were fitted at 231,871 miles; the back axle had a major overhaul, and new wheel bearings were fitted at 263,792 miles, and the universal joints were replaced at 310,966 miles. This 1958 Ford Zephyr completed the last five months of its test life, running three shifts per 24-hour day on the M1 motorway, at a constant speed of 70mph for one month, followed by four months at a constant 50mph. The car ran on the M1 carrying an all-up weight of 34cwt, a definite overload. Indeed, throughout its running life in the Goodyear test fleet, the Zephyr had never carried less than a 34cwt all-up load, and for the first 12 months of its life on the A5 test route was regularly carrying 38cwt all-up'.

A late technical change was introduced in January 1961. A new gearbox mainshaft, on which the speedometer driving gear was held in position by a nut instead of a circlip, replaced the earlier arrangement, in which it had not been entirely unknown for the circlip in question to break, allowing movement in the gearbox and consequent selection problems. Improved circlips introduced earlier had apparently not been entirely effective in curing the problem, which did not seem to afflict Consuls, but could

The Ford Zephyr estate car.

sometimes occur on high-mileage Zephyrs and Zodiacs where the gearbox was handling the extra torque of the six-cylinder engines.

The Motor put a Zephyr convertible through their road test procedure in the spring for what appears to have been the last road test report on one of the Mk 2 models. Writing in the issue of May 10, 1961, the magazine's staff pointed out that the Mk 2 Zephyr had recently 'quietly celebrated its fifth birthday' and as a result had now 'graduated to the select company of cars which, because they have pleased the customers, sell readily year after year without requiring more than very minor detail improvements'. As far as the performance was concerned, *The Motor* felt that 'for a $2\frac{1}{2}$-litre car to be timed at 90mph is no longer remarkable', but that 'the fine surge of top gear acceleration anywhere in the speed range still makes the Zephyr a brisk moving car on give-and-take roads'. There was praise, too, for the disc brakes with the comment that this option 'may be regarded as adding the finishing touch to a sensibly priced modern version of a high-powered touring car'.

The Motor expressed the belief that the majority of buyers were specifying the disc brake option, and this was indeed the case, to such an extent that in June 1961 this feature was absorbed into the standard specification along with the adoption of sealed-beam headlamps. The Mk 2 models in this final form could be recognized by the deletion of the name script from the upper rear wing and, on the Consul only, by the addition of '375' to its name. The Mk 2 Consul was given the full title Consul 375 at this late stage in its career in order to distinguish it from a recently introduced medium-sized Dagenham product, the full title of which was Consul Classic 315, or, in certain export markets, simply Consul 315. Dagenham had already decided to delete the Consul name from their large car range with the introduction of the appreciably more sophisticated Mk 3 version which was scheduled for the following year. The Consul replacement would be named Zephyr 4 (four-cylinder) with a Zephyr 6 and Zodiac completing the line-up. The Mk 3 range was intended to be considerably more 'up market' than the Mk 1 and Mk 2 models had been, and it was felt at Dagenham that the well respected Consul name would be more appropriate now on a new medium-sized car. Hence the Consul Classic, and the temporary 315/375 identification tags. As the Consul Classic was not in any respect a derivative of the Consul/Zephyr range, and therefore

The space required in which to lower the hood and sidescreens reduces the width of the rear seat on the convertible. The adjustable armrest/doorpull, exclusive to the 'Low Line' Zodiac, can be seen in this view.

Sunshine Express: the 'Low Line' Zodiac convertible. The interior mirror was positioned as on the saloons now, and met with criticism as it was rather too high in relation to the raised hood's small rear window. These glamorous cars were to be the last of the big Ford convertibles, their relatively low sales volume being quoted as the main reason for their discontinuation with the coming of the Mk 3 Zephyr/Zodiac range.

was not a 'real' Consul, apart from this mention it has no other part at all in the Consul/Zephyr/Zodiac story.

Production of the Mk 2 models was now running at a little more than 1,600 per week, a considerable reduction from the production rates of 1958-60, although very few sales were in fact being lost to rival makes. Many established customers, whilst certainly not in any way 'in the know', had nevertheless correctly reasoned that with the Mk 2 model now well into its sixth year of production, Dagenham must surely be at an advanced

101

The 'Low Line' Zodiac. Big, bold and beautiful, one of Dagenham's all-time greats.

stage of development with the projected replacement car, and many who had reached this conclusion were now quite prepared to wait and see just what the new model would be. Overseas, too, the sales had taken a downward turn and, through no fault of its own, the Zephyr had now lost its Australian market. A market survey there some time previously had convinced the Ford Motor Company of Australia that a 100% locally built six-cylinder car would soon be needed to satisfy the growing demand, and that the Zephyr would fit the bill. Unfortunately, however, Ford Australia were unable to reach the necessary agreement with Dagenham which would have enabled the Zephyr to be manufactured in Australia. The stumbling block, apparently, was the price Dagenham needed for the Mk 2 Zephyr dies which, of course, they would have had to supply, and so, as the parent Company in the United States were by now producing a Zephyr-sized 'compact' car, the 2.3-litre six-cylinder Falcon, Ford Australia made a successful approach to Dearborn which resulted in the Falcon, rather than the Zephyr, going into production 'down under'.

As production of the Mk 2 models drew to a close, some rather late, but interesting, publicity came their way when the BBC launched a new television programme entitled 'Z Cars'. This featured the escapades of two Police patrol crews who answered to the call signs 'Z-Victor 1' and 'Z-Victor 2'. The two cars were 'Low Line' Mk 2 Zephyrs, and they featured prominently in the early series of this popular programme. These gleaming 'white' Zephyrs were, in reality, painted yellow, as this colour is apparently 'whiter than white' in black-and-white television transmission.

In April 1962, production of 'The Three Graces' came to an end. In just over six years slightly more than 650,000 saloons and convertibles had been produced, with the latter accounting for an exclusive 2% of this total, in addition to which there had been some 30,000 estates, Australian station wagons and coupe utilities. Added to this impressive total, of course, were the preceding 406,000 'Five Star Cars', making a grand total of more than a million Consuls, Zephyrs and Zodiacs in an 11-year period, which remains a production record for this class of car in Britain. Between them they had introduced the comfort and performance characteristics of 'big car' motoring to more people than any other British car before them, and at a new low level of overall economy of operation for this type, which some would insist has never been equalled elsewhere.

CHAPTER 4

The third generation

Mk 3 Zephyr, Zodiac and Executive

With Mk 2 sales climbing steadily throughout 1958, and the improved 'Low Line' versions on the way, the all-new 105E Anglia set for a September 1959 launch, and the development of the new mid-range model (Consul Classic) nicely in hand, the company were able to turn their attention to the eventual replacement for the big cars.

The mechanical aspect of a Mk 3 Consul/Zephyr/Zodiac series would present no serious problems, but, having as it did to follow Colin Neale's supremely handsome Mk 2 range, the new model was to be the cause of much concern during its development in respect of its outward appearance. Neale had left some time earlier to work in America, after which, according to styling team member Charles Thompson, the styling department floundered somewhat, with their schemes for a new generation of large cars being rejected, before Neale, accompanied by American stylist Elwood Engel, returned to Dagenham for a short period in order to assist with the Mk 3 design. However, that move failed, as Engel's and even Neale's ideas were considered by the management at Dagenham to be a bit too transatlantic for British and European tastes. Outside help was now considered, and the Italian styling house of Frua were commissioned to produce a prototype.

Frua quickly came up with a striking design which rather cleverly retained a hint of the established Zephyr/Zodiac characteristics at the front, thus maintaining the continuity of style which could just be detected between the Mk 1 and Mk 2 sixes. Little information about the Frua prototype seems to have survived, but from studying a rare photograph and a Charles Thompson drawing dated August 1959, it appears that it was built around the existing Mk 2 six-cylinder car's track, wheelbase, overall length and width, but with slightly reduced overall height. It would seem to have been a suitable enough design, but in the event it failed to gain the approval of Dearborn, as the parent company felt that the big British Fords should if at all possible maintain the world-wide corporate image. The Mk 1 and Mk 2 models had of course conformed to this ideal, reflecting the lovely Dearborn 'FortyNiner' and subsequently the big Mainline/Fairlane cars, whereas the Frua proposal, quite understandably, did not echo the forthcoming American Galaxie and Falcon models scheduled for 1960. Indeed, the concern in America was such that one of Dearborn's stylists, Canadian-born Roy Brown, was sent to Dagenham to

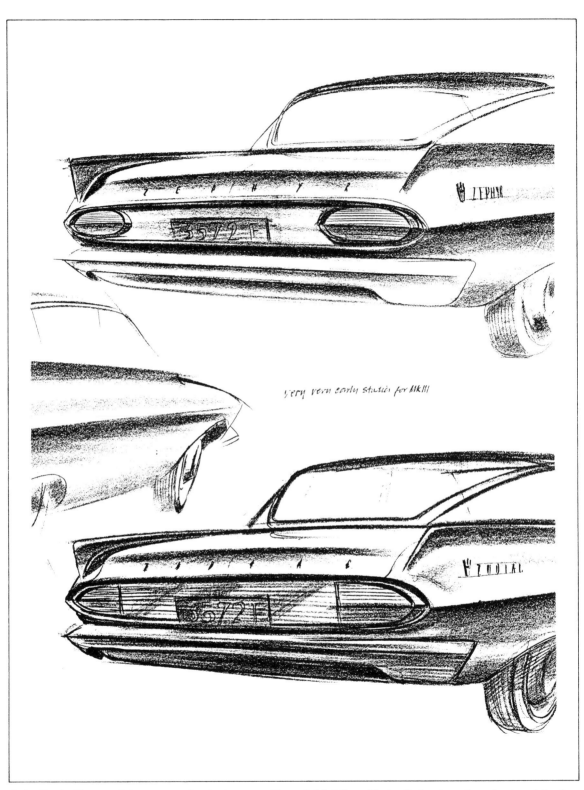

Stylist Charles Thompson's first tentative ideas for the outward form of a Mk 3 Consul Zephyr Zodiac range, these drawings dating from 1957.

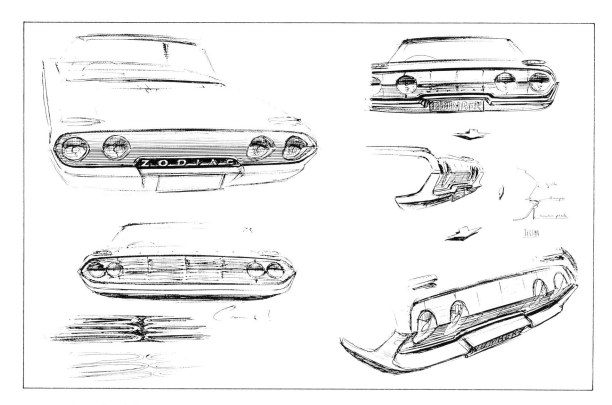

assume the role of chief stylist there, with the Mk 3 Zephyr/Zodiac range as a priority. In the event, Brown evidently saw much that he liked in the rear-end treatment displayed by the Frua design, and was to blend quite successfully a lowered and rather more full-width version of the Frua rear half with a completely new front, also retaining the curved side-window treatment of the Italian design.

Prototypes of Brown's design with a Galaxie-type rear roof line and broad rear quarter panels were produced for the Consul, Zephyr and Zodiac replacements. But the Frua glazed and triangulated rear quarter panels were eventually decided upon for the top-of-the-range Zodiac, giving further distinction than previously between it and the lower-priced models. Very sleek in profile, with an illusion of greater length and width due to being some 3in lower than the 'Low Line' Mk 2, the new body was based upon the same wheelbase (8ft 11in) as the Mk 2 six-cylinder cars, and had a common bonnet length now for both four- and six-cylinder versions. Front and rear track measurements were also the same as on the existing Mk 2 range, as indeed was the overall width at 5ft 9in.

Certainly very stylish, the bodywork did however take less account than should have been the case of passenger accommodation, for although the adoption of the Frua curved side windows resulted in greater hip and shoulder width than on the Mk 2, the situation was less satisfactory in other respects. The rather more streamlined rake of the windscreen necessitated resiting the front seat slightly rearwards, this in turn requiring the centre pillar, or B-post, also to be moved back. As the rear seat was remaining a similar distance ahead of the rear axle line as on the Mk 2 series, the overall effect was a noticeable reduction in rear compartment knee-room and somewhat restricted access through the considerably narrower rear doors. And it was not only the passenger accommodation which suffered, as the

When Ford commissioned a design for the Mk 3 from the Italian styling house of Frua the result was this full size model, retaining a quite deliberate front-end likeness to the Mk 2 six-cylinder cars.

low build of this model also resulted in a change in the running gear: the MacPherson strut front suspension had to be inclined more sharply inwards to conform with the low bonnet line, necessitating changes to the internal arrangements of the struts themselves. So, whereas within their overall dimensions both the Mk 1 and Mk 2 cars had displayed total harmony of styling, passenger accommodation and engineering, this was not quite the case with the Mk 3, in which styling had very definitely been allowed to overrule.

Once satisfied with the overall shape, Roy Brown left the finer details of his creation to other members of the styling department, and it fell to Charles Thompson to scheme out the three different grille designs which would distinguish the new Consul (as it was still being called at that time), Zephyr and Zodiac. At this stage, there was apparently still some disquiet amongst the management at Dagenham about this new design, as Thompson recalls how he was asked to include if at all possible some visual hint that this latest Zodiac in particular was a genuine descendant of the much admired Mk 2. This was achieved by incorporating a similar vertically-slatted upper portion to the new Zodiac's grille, linking it directly to the Mk 2 Zodiac in this respect, whilst at the rear introducing a series of horizontal bright metal mouldings giving a broadly similar effect to the preceding Zodiac's fluted, silver-painted back panel. Now with four headlamps whilst the cheaper cars retained two, its own exclusive bumper bars and the glazed rear-quarter treatment already referred to, the Zodiac did indeed appear further removed from the Zephyr than had previously been the case. Reflecting changing fashions however was the adoption of single-tone paintwork only and black-sidewall tyres for the new Zodiac, in pursuit of a rather more restrained elegance than hitherto.

Of even greater structural rigidity than the outgoing model, the Mk 3 bodyshell featured slight constructional differences and also introduced the use of galvanized steel for the more vulnerable of the underbody areas. Noticeable at the front were the redesigned inner wings of more box-like shape than before, without the previous turret-shaped accommodation for the MacPherson struts. These new, much broader inner wings obviated

106

the need for the diagonal bracing pieces across to the scuttle which had characterized the underbonnet scene on the earlier models. The counter-balancing arrangements for the very large and heavy bonnet top were situated on the rear of each inner wing's horizontal upper surface. The four doors differed considerably, being of an altogether more modern design with their slender window frames removing the previous rather heavy carriage-door look. Swivelling front quarter windows were again provided, but pivoted to move in a different plane and so keep out rain when slightly open whilst also reducing the wind noise generated. Slight additional overall length by way of longer rear overhang provided an even larger luggage compartment than before, the fuel tank's upper surface now forming part of the boot floor itself. Increased in capacity to a more useful 12 gallons, the centrally mounted tank, bolted to the car rather than being strapped underneath as previously, continued to enjoy the excellent protection of the chassis-type side members and the unyielding, well mounted rear bumper bar.

As it was not until a late stage in the development programme that the decision was finally taken to drop the Consul name altogether for the larger-car range, three distinct trim levels broadly in line with before were applied. Surprisingly, although in overall terms it was moving relatively more upmarket than the cheaper versions, the new Zodiac did not now feature leather upholstery as standard equipment. Instead came a new, very soft but nevertheless extremely durable grade of PVC, named 'Cirrus' by its manufacturer, which was to prove an excellent choice. A foam-padded leading edge and sides to the seat cushions, and similar treatment along the outer edges of the squabs, resulted in slightly larger and

Alternative front-end treatments proposed for the Frua model. Those on the left, by Charles Thompson, have a hooded-headlamp affinity with the Mk 2 but with a more modern grille design. Going a stage further, some consideration was given to grafting an Elwood Engle-style nose onto the Frua body, right.

Two sketches by Charles Thompson for possible Mk 3 rear ends, utilizing much of the Frua design including the glasshouse.

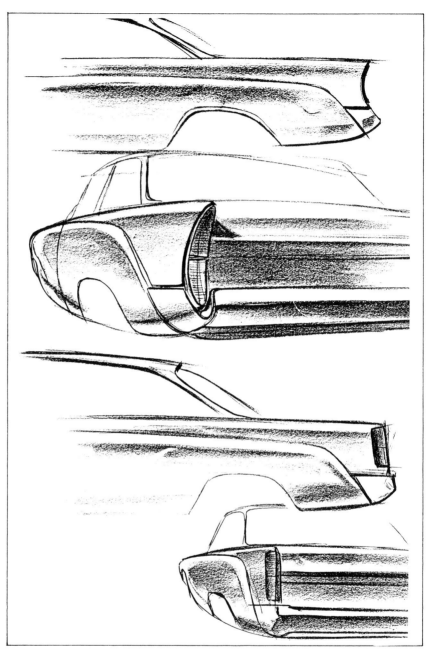

decidedly plushier seating in the Zodiac than in the other two cars, whose seats were in a less expensive vinyl and without the padded rolls. The Zodiac had a folding centre armrest in both compartments, but this equipment was only to be found in the front on the Zephyr 6, whilst being entirely absent in the case of the four-cylinder car. An excellent new feature to be found in all three cars were interior door handles neatly situated beneath and almost within the combined armrest/doorpulls on all four doors. Easy to use when needed, by simply squeezing upwards into the armrest, these handles were virtually impossible to operate inadvertently, a very worthwhile new safety feature. Zero-torque locks, which allowed

108

In the event, a Galaxie-style roof and rear window line was wished upon Dagenham by the parent company who sent stylist Roy Brown over from America. The Zodiac trim on this prototype indicates that the top-of-the-range car was originally to have shared an identical shell with the Zephyrs . . .

the doors to be closed with only gentle pressure, were making their first appearance on a Ford. A parking light arrangement in which the nearside front and rear sidelamps could be switched off was another new feature, with its switch wired in such a way that the engine's starter motor could not be operated when the nearside lights were out. Also new was a headlamp flashing facility, with a button on the end of the direction indicator stalk. Perhaps most welcome to the majority of buyers, particularly of the four-cylinder on which the previous vacuum-operated wipers had been the cause of some frustration, were the new electric windscreen wipers which came complete with two-speed control.

Whilst all these innovations were standard throughout the range, it remained something of a disappointment that the two cheaper editions of the Mk 3 series were still without the benefit of a heater or even a windscreen washer amongst their standard equipment.

The anxieties which surrounded the development of the Mk 3's outward appearance did not of course apply to the mechanical elements. No fundamental changes at all were necessary, and at the beginning of the programme even the four-speed gear box which eventually emerged had

. . . but when it appeared, the Mk 3 Zodiac did in fact have the roof and rear window arrangement of the Frua design as a measure of exclusivity. This photograph shows a full size glassfibre mock-up of the Zodiac in final form, complete with all panel lines and details accurately represented.

In the metal: two views of the production Mk 3 Zodiac which made its public debut two weeks before the Zephyrs. With its squared-up rear door windows, the Zodiac required a rear door wider at its trailing edge than that of the Zephyr, because during manufacture the window had to be inserted into the door end-on and then rotated into position, a move not possible with the original door shape.

been under consideration only as an optional extra. However, as investigations along these lines progressed it was found that very few Mk 2 owners were critical in any way at all of their cars' three gear ratios, and that precious few of them would be prepared to pay extra for an additional gear. So if the four-speed option were to go ahead the company would be producing two entirely different gearboxes of which the poorer selling would have involved considerable new investment. It might appear, then, that simply retaining the existing three-speeder on its own would have been the best bet, but in fact it was not quite so simple a decision as that. Whilst well satisfied with three ratios, many owners of the Mk 2 were by this time becoming quite critical of the continued lack of synchromesh on first gear, and resolving this criticism alone would involve the company in substantial investment. That, and the fact that a four-speed gearbox would give greater scope for increased top-end acceleration and maximum speed

Rear view of the production Zodiac: the bumper looks altogether more elegant than the heavy style shown on the earlier prototype. Being mounted rather close to the body, however, the Mk 3 bumpers offered less protection to the paintwork than had those of the preceding models.

A truly massive boot was a feature of the Mk 3 range. The spare wheel cover included a tool pocket, but only came as standard equipment on the Zodiac, not the Zephyrs.

Under the Zodiac's bonnet. The heater unit was now on the passenger side of the bulkhead but the heater hose connections remained accessible from the engine compartment. This pre-production car has the black-painted rocker cover and air cleaner as on the Zephyrs, whereas production Zodiacs had these items finished in pale yellow.

on the one hand, with rather more relaxed and economical cruising on the other, resulted in the decision to develop a new four-speed gearbox, with synchromesh throughout, and to abandon the old three-speeder entirely. The synchromesh was again of the excellent baulk-ring type and gear selection was still by means of a steering column mounted lever.

Of the same 8 and 8½in diameters as before, but lighter to operate now, the clutches again included an over-centre assist spring in the withdrawal mechanism, of which the arm now pivoted on a knife edge. Although there would of course again be differing axle ratios for the four- and six-cylinder cars, two sets of first and second gear ratios were now also provided, the lower geared of these being for the four-cylinder car. The third-gear ratio would be the same for whichever engine.

The provision of three indirect gears allowed the use of higher axle ratios, with the former six-cylinder model's 3.9:1 final drive now to be found on the new four-cylinder car, and a new crownwheel and pinion set of 3.545:1 being introduced for the latest sixes. These gave mph/1,000rpm figures of 18.5 and 20.3 in conjunction with 6.40 x 13 tyres which were now standardized throughout.

Supplementing the manual gearbox if required was the Borg-Warner overdrive, which differed slightly from that used previously in that the ratio was only 0.77 rather than 0.70, this 23% reduction being calculated to maintain the 26.4mph/1,000rpm for overdrive-top of the previous cars

Entry into the front of the car and general roominess were good, although the lower roof line necessitated a driving position a little lower and not quite so alert as on the earlier models.

With the driver's seat set well back the rear seat kneeroom was less than satisfactory in the early Mk 3s. The door release catches are almost completely hidden beneath the armrest/doorpulls.

Less ornate than the Zodiac, the two Zephyrs were easily identified by their broad rear quarter panel. A simple front grille, beneath which a small figure '4' appeared in an oval emblem, was to be seen on the Zephyr 4, while a divided, full-width grille signified the six-cylinder version. Model designation of the Zephyr 4 was 211E, that of both the Zephyr 6 and the Zodiac was 213E.

despite the new higher axle ratios. As the Mk 3s were to get higher-power engines, the overdrive was now considered valid on the four-cylinder car, but with a lower axle ratio, down in this case to 4.11:1.

The optional fully automatic transmission was also by Borg-Warner, the new and much lighter Model 35 three-speed gearbox which featured torque conversion throughout rather than just on the low and intermediate ratios as before. The larger of two torque converters available with the Model 35 was used on the Mk 3 application. An advantage of this gearbox was the lock-up facility which gave some manual override in the selection and retention of the low and intermediate gears. With this arrangement and the torque conversion on top gear, this option too was at last considered suitable for the four-cylinder car. For either engine, four- or six-cylinder, the automatic gearbox would be mated to the high 3.545:1 axle which, on the four, would help in returning similar fuel consumption to the manual car, albeit with a further reduction in acceleration.

Reference has already been made to the more powerful engines; in fact they were very substantially as before. The 1,703cc and 2,553cc capacities

of the existing units were considered by Dagenham to be at their (perfectly safe) limit, and further capacity increase was therefore ruled out. In the quest for greater power, attention was now focussed on increased compression ratios and improved breathing. Much work of this nature had of course already been carried out on Mk 2 engines, both by outside tuning concerns and by the company's own Competition Department, and with this experience upon which to draw it would not be difficult to endow the Mk 3 models with usefully greater performance. These were however to remain first and foremost touring cars, in which tractability and total lack of temperament were important considerations, and so no attempts were being made to match the more spectacular results achieved by some specialized Mk 2s. A modest increase in compression ratio, to 8.3:1, accompanied by improved porting, larger valves and stronger valve springs were the principal differences to be found in the new cylinder heads, whilst larger Zenith carburettors on improved inlet manifolds also played a part in providing greater power and torque outputs. With the retention of the simple Mk 2-type exhaust manifold, the four- and six-cylinder units now produced 68bhp at 4,800rpm and 98bhp at 4,750rpm respectively, the corresponding torque figures being 93lb/ft at 3,000rpm, and 134lb/ft at 2,000rpm. In conjunction with the revised gearing these outputs were sufficient to provide both better acceleration through the

The only feature distinguishing between the Zephyrs when viewed broadside were the bright metal door window surrounds, as seen here, on the Zephyr 6 only. The shallower curve of the Zephyr's rear door trailing edge is also evident in this view.

Zephyr rear view shows that the two cheaper cars had smaller rear lamps with less wrap-round than on the Zodiac. Whitewall tyres were optional extras which suited the Mk 3 very well.

There were echoes of the 'Low Line' Mk 2 in the new Zephyr facia, this example being a Zephyr 4. On the new six-cylinder car an imitation wood veneer replaced the corrugated bright metal panels, and a horn ring was added to the steering wheel.

Zephyr 4 underbonnet layout. All Mk 3s had blown glassfibre insulation on the passenger side of the bulkhead, extremely effective in reducing the mechanical noise entering the car. In the right foreground is the vacuum reservoir tank which provided some servo assistance for the brakes in the event of a dead engine.

gears and maximum speeds some 5 or 6mph greater, but at the expense of top-gear acceleration in the low and middle ranges. With the Zodiac set to move more upmarket, a greater performance than the less expensive six-cylinder Zephyr was deemed necessary, including a 100mph maximum speed. This was achieved by a further change to the larger Zenith 42 WIA-2 carburettor and the provision of a dual exhaust system. The latter was arranged so that the two pipes running the length of the car curved inboard to run alongside the propellor shaft in the transmission tunnel before sweeping over the axle. Here each pipe met with its own silencer, these being mounted transversely end-to-end immediately behind the axle; a short tail-pipe from each silencer completed the system. Thus equipped, the Zodiac's power unit developed 109bhp at 4,800rpm, and 137lb/ft torque at 2,400rpm. In view of the increased outputs at higher rpm than before, the slightly cooler-running Champion N5 spark plugs (N8 previously) were adopted for all three engines.

Slightly strengthened pistons, still of the autothermic type, were fitted, whilst white-metal now gave way to lead-bronze for the big-end bearing

shells, with this material also being used for the main bearings on the Zodiac engine. Larger connecting-rod bolts completed these internal changes, incorporated in order to maintain the same reliability and longevity of the previous units despite the higher power outputs. A redesigned crankcase breather tube was introduced to obviate the slight oil loss sometimes experienced on the earlier models during sustained high-rpm operation. The cooling system was now pressurized to 13psi, and featured what appears to be the first application in Britain of the American wax thermostat which was claimed to open more smoothly than the conventional bellows type. Completely new, the heater and demisting unit achieved its temperature variations by air blending rather than the usual water metering methods, and could be set to give warmth in the lower part of the car but with cool air at face level. Very large demister vents were provided for the windscreen, and the booster fan motor was quiet enough to warrant a warning light fitted alongside its facia-mounted switch.

Although following closely the established layout, the running gear included several refinements in the interests of improved riding comfort

An early Zephyr 4 in pleasant outdoor surroundings. The Zephyr 4 was to prove a popular car with taxi and private hire operators, and also with the Ministry of Defence who purchased many for armed forces staff and other duties, their sage green or airforce blue liveries suiting them rather well.

The Mk 3 estate cars were surely the sleekest of their type to date. Although still Abbott conversions, they were completely free from the 'add-on' look, the removal of the saloon rear quarter panels enabling the design to appear totally integrated.

But sleek lines were not achieved at the expense of a capacious interior, the tailgate opening up to reveal a roomy and convenient load area.

and road noise suppression. The pronounced inward inclination of the MacPherson strut has already been mentioned, and in view of the reduced effective strut height which resulted, the internal working parts were now situated lower down in the casing in order to maintain the same generous up and down wheel movement as before. Although chosen for body height reasons in this case, there are advantages in this strut inclination in respect of riding qualities in that during cornering the strut is subjected to rather less bending forces, and therefore operates more smoothly. From the handling viewpoint however there was a slight disadvantage in evidence on the Mk 3, resulting in a greater degree of understeer, to an extent which could not be so readily counteracted when desired by skilled use of the throttle as had been the case with the earlier models. Slightly softer coil springs than before completed the front suspension. A variable-ratio worm in the recirculating-ball steering box gave approximately the same ratio as before around the straight-ahead position, so maintaining good initial response, but was of appreciably lower ratio towards the extremes of lock in order to ease the effort during parking manoeuvres with these slightly heavier cars.

At the rear were completely new leaf springs. Of only five leaves each (against six on the Mk 2) and slightly softer than before, these included full length butyl rubber inserts between the upper four leaves. A 2in-diameter rubber bush was used at the forward attachment point beneath the passenger compartment, with ample rubber insulation also to be found at the point where the spring was fixed to the rear axle casing by the usual U-bolts and plate attachment. Girling lever-arm dampers were to be seen once again here. In addition to reducing quite considerably the road noise entering the car, the refinements introduced into the suspension system at both front and rear were to result in overall ride qualities which were very close indeed to the best which can reasonably be expected from a conventionally-suspended car.

The braking system utilized the Mk 2 discs, calipers, and pads at the front, and was linked to the same vacuum servo unit as before. At the rear, the drum brakes were of the same 9in x 1¾in dimensions as the Mk 2 cars on the new four-cylinder model only; on the sixes the 9in diameter drums were increased in width to house brake shoes 2¼in wide. This change introduced on the two more expensive Mk 3s was in order to increase the brake lining life to similarly high mileages as were normally being attained by the front disc pads with this system on the Mk 2 models. Roadwheels of 13in diameter again completed the running gear, this time equipped with 6.40 x 13 tyres on all three cars, with those of the Zodiac now being of the high-speed type which were of nylon cord construction rather than the usual rayon. The recommended tyre pressures were 22psi to 28psi all round depending upon load for both the Zephyr 4 and 6, and 24psi to 30psi for the Zodiac, with the further advice 'For extensive high-speed driving, increase pressures slightly' now appearing in the owners' handbooks for each model, in recognition of the implications of the then relatively new but expanding motorway network.

Although the car was a development of an existing and well-proven theme, Mk 3 prototype testing was undertaken on a world-wide basis to such an extent that considerably more than a million miles were accumulated between mid-1960 and the April 1962 launch. From the mechanical reliability viewpoint, this testing on top of an excellent pedigree, plus the valuable additional experience gained and lessons learned by successfully campaigning the Mk 2 Zephyrs in the East African

A six-branch manifold and complete dual exhaust system was soon available for the Mk 3 from Servais; it differed completely from the Zodiac's standard twin exhaust layout.

NEW
"LIVE-DRIVE"
HIGH EFFICIENCY EXHAUST SYSTEM FOR
Zephyr 6 - Zodiac Mk III

These photographs show the Servais Exhaust System for the latest six-cylinder Ford cars. The manifold, intermediate pipes, Servais straight-through silencers and all clips and hanging brackets are sold under Part No. HEM 128. The price is 25 guineas.

MOTOR SHOW STAND NO. 352 *BY* **SERVAIS**

SERVAIS SILENCERS LTD · Ashford Works · Ashford Road · London N.W.2 · *Tel:* GLAdstone 0023 · and at Northampton *Tel:* Northampton 179

Safari Rally, made the Mk 3 range probably the most fully-sorted new car released by a British manufacturer up to that time.

Prior to the model's public release, the official preview for the motoring press was staged at the Silverstone racing circuit where the new Zephyrs and Zodiacs could be sampled well away from the popular gaze. On hand in order to demonstrate the latest Zodiac's performance to the full was former BRSCC Saloon Car Championship winner Jeff Uren who, in addition to enjoying an unofficial dice with one of the scribes present who also possessed an outstanding driving skill, put in many laps of the circuit in a consistent 2min 18sec, which equated to an average speed of just under 77mph.

In keeping with its rather more exclusive image than before, the new Zodiac was the first to be revealed, on April 13, 1962. Thanks to a purchase tax reduction in the spring budget only two days before, it arrived at the very attractive price of £1,071 rather than the £1,135 it was expected to be. At its manufacturer's basic price of £778 (before tax) the Mk 3 Zodiac was £68 more expensive than the outgoing Mk 2 – a 9½% increase – which reflected the inclusion of the four-speed all-synchromesh gearbox, twin exhaust system, high-speed tyres etc, and also the fact that the car was 1cwt or so heavier now. £110 extra was required for the automatic transmission, £58 for the overdrive, and a rather hefty £33 for the optional crushed-hide seating.

Road test reports appeared the following week, *The Motor* being first in their issue of April 18, and commenting at the beginning: 'With the new Zodiac Mk III, a 100mph saloon with sports-car acceleration, the largest and most expensive British Ford moves into a new performance category . . . . The new car looks bigger and more imposing than its predecessor and yet, in fact, its size is largely an optical illusion . . . . In external appearance the separate influences of current American, British and Continental fashions are blended harmoniously rather than strikingly.' It was then noted that, 'No other large saloon available on the British market can offer speed and acceleration of the same order at a price as low as £1,070. A

The Peco improved-perform-
ance exhaust system retained
the Zodiac's transverse silencer
arrangement, albeit with a new
replacement box, and featured a
handed pair of the popular Peco
booster units to give a four-
tailpipe effect.

genuine two-way 100mph was achieved by our very new test car which
had done less than 1,500 miles when the figures were taken.' When
accelerating through the gears the Zodiac had reached 50, 60, 70, 80, and
90mph, in 9.2, 13.4, 18.2, 24.2, and 37.9 seconds. The standing-start
quarter-mile had taken 19.2 seconds, and impressive maximum speeds of
39, 56, and 84mph had been attained in the three lower gears. The new
gearbox received the anticipated praise with such comments as '.. . Fords
have elected to fit synchromesh on all the forward gears, a particularly wise
decision for a box which has well-chosen and fairly close ratios and lower
gears which are intended for use rather than emergency . . . . One can only
criticise the Zodiac column gearchange on the grounds of rather a long
travel which puts third gear at arm's stretch.' When dealing with the
Zodiac's handling qualities, *The Motor* noted, 'On wet roads or dry a
noticeable understeer characteristic persists right up to the well-balanced
breakaway point; the back wheels can be made to slide first if a lot of power
is used but the handling is only slightly throttle sensitive . . . .' It was pointed
out that axle tramp could be induced by full throttle acceleration in second
gear when cornering, but nevertheless, '. . . the handling was characterized
by lack of vice and by first-class controllability which imparted considerable
confidence when hurrying over fast main roads.' There was criticism
regarding the allocation of space within the car, with *The Motor's* opinion
being that a slightly longer passenger compartment at the expense of some
of the very ample luggage boot space would have been a better
compromise. These thoughts could be detected in the final summary: 'We
see this new Ford as a car which will appeal particularly to the long-distance
business motorist by virture of the outstanding performance and
impressive appearance at such a low price. It may have less attraction for
the buyer who seeks maximum passenger space inside a car of compact
overall dimensions.'

Another Zodiac was being tested at the same time by *Autocar*, whose
report appeared in the issue of April 20. This car proved to have an almost
identical performance, reaching 60mph from rest in 13.5 seconds. A mean

John Mitchell's Stage 3 Zephyr 6 conversion offered a substantial performance boost at a reasonable cost, and adding Wooler's excellent floor gearchange conversion as well would result in a very sporting Zephyr whilst leaving a few shillings change out of £100.

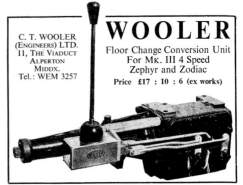
maximum speed of 100.3mph was attained, with a best one-way speed of 103.5mph. On the latest edition of Dagenham's excellent in-line six-cylinder engine, they said, 'Usually extra power is extracted from a given engine with some sacrifice of smoothness and quiet running. Of the new Zodiac the reverse is true, and a deal of thought and application given to sound insulation has, in fact, appreciably reduced the mechanical noise reaching the passengers. The unit remains refined and notably unobtrusive at high engine revolutions, and the car can maintain 80-90mph on a motorway with most agreeable ease.' Other comments suggested that in all respects this car had behaved almost exactly as the one tested by *The Motor*, and there was agreement regarding the relative lack of rear knee-room which was, claimed *Autocar*, '. . . its one considerable shortcoming.' Both these Zodiacs had returned overall fuel consumption figures of only a little over 19mpg, but in each case this was considered quite reasonable by the testers as the cars had been driven extremely hard throughout much of the test routine.

Sleek, plushy, powerful and with the magic of that three-figure maximum speed, the Mk 3 Zodiac had arrived on the scene with an impact which somehow took the shine off the debut of the lower-priced Zephyrs which followed two weeks later, although a close look at these would reveal at least the same overall value for money as the more glamorous top-of-the-range car. The tax-paid list prices of £847 and £929 for the Zephyr 4 and Zephyr 6 included a manufacturer's increase of just £37 and £30 respectively, with the apparent £7 discrepancy here in fact taking into account that the four-cylinder model this time shared the longer bodywork of the six. To these Zephyr prices of course a further £20 12s 6d had to be added if the optional heater was required, plus an additional £8 13s 3d for the necessary, but not then mandatory, windscreen washing equipment.

Both the manual and automatic transmission versions of the Zephyr 4 came under the scrutiny of *Autocar* in their issue of April 27, in which it was seen that the performance with a manual gearbox was appreciably quicker in almost every respect by comparison with the Mk 2 Consul. A maximum speed of 84mph was recorded, and the car accelerated from rest to 60 and

For 1964 the Zephyr 4 grille was set lower in the front panel. Sometime earlier, the four-cylinder car had acquired the rustless bright metal cappings to the door windows which had at first been confined to the Zephyr 6.

70mph in 19.6 and 32.1 seconds. Also, it was noted, '. . . the Zephyr 4 will cruise without fuss at over 70mph and, with its high 3.9:1 top gear ratio, it is particularly restful when cruising at about 60mph. This same high top gear does bring the need for an earlier downchange, both in slow traffic and for overtaking, but this is the natural outcome of the pleasant new four-speed box and sensibly-selected ratios.' Indeed, just as had been found with the Zodiac, although flexibility was still very good, there was a slight decrease in the acceleration when pulling hard from low and medium speeds in the higher top gear. But of course the new third gear could be employed very profitably to considerably greater speeds than the maximum attainable in the second gear of the old three-speeder. With the automatic transmission, the Zephyr 4 proved to be appreciably slower than the manual gearbox version, eventually running completely out of breath at only 77mph, although its ability to reach 60mph from rest in 23.3 seconds was nevertheless rather better than could be achieved with the

Studio portraits of the 1964 Zephyr 6. These later Zephyrs, both the 4 and the 6, also had the vertical bright strip on the centre pillar which had originally been a Zodiac-only feature.

superseded Consul. Pick up on the move from medium speeds was very poor, with a distinctly leisurely 50-70mph time of 34.8 seconds serving to underline *Autocar*'s comment, 'Overtaking usually needs careful timing and plenty of space.' The automatic's overall fuel consumption for the entire test however was a creditable 23.1mpg which was closer than one might have expected to the manual car's 23.8mpg overall. Of the detail changes in the suspension, *Autocar* said, 'The outcome is somewhat less firm springing and a softer ride. Roll is restrained, although when a full load is carried the back of the car will take on appreciable bank when cornering fast; this in turn has some effect on the cornering characteristics.' With their less nose-heavy weight distribution these four-cylinder Zephyrs exhibited nearer neutral cornering qualities, with an initial roll-oversteer sometimes being evident when heavily laden. Of the roadholding in general it was said, 'Adhesion in dry weather is very good indeed and it is difficult, with the power available, to make the back of the car move across unless the road surface is unusually rough. In wet conditions the adhesion is also good and definitely an improvement on that of the previous model.' And when it came to summarize these cars, *Autocar* thought that, 'With the introduction of their new Zephyr 4s Ford have again made substantial improvements over the models replaced; they offer greater refinement and several new features which owners will appreciate. Equally important, the price has been held at a very competitive level.'

Having been in production for some time before their public appearance, in fact from December 1961 in the new Zodiac's case, the Mk 3s were widely available from the start, were quickly seen in quite substantial numbers at home and abroad, and in general were soon earning considerable praise. It was not only *The Motor* and *Autocar*, however, who criticized the rear compartment knee-room, as this shortcoming had been noted in almost every journal, and there were many of them, who had sampled these new Fords. There was no doubt that a mistake had been made in this respect, but rectifying this was not easy. Had the wheelbase been lengthened at the design stage, this problem would not have occurred; but this option was no longer available, as a significant increase in this measurement now would involve considerable changes to the bodyshell including the rear-end outer panelwork. There was however a compromise solution. As the Mk 3 had retained the Mk 2 track measurements, but was of greater width across its rear flanks, it was possible to widen the rear track sufficiently to allow the rear seat to be repositioned slightly rearwards with its squab just between the (wider apart) wheelarches, but with the cushion still comfortably ahead of the axle line so as not to impair riding comfort. This did involve changes to the rear floorpan and wheelarch pressings, and of course necessitated a pair of longer halfshafts and a new axle casing. But this quite costly modification, which was introduced into production in time for an eve of Motor Show announcement in the October of 1962, was very worthwhile as it provided almost 2in additional knee-room. Whilst not a generous increase this did improve the situation considerably, going a long way towards ridding the Mk 3 of the one really glaring fault in an otherwise extremely good all-round car.

Also announced for the Earls Court show was that the Zephyr 4 interior was being upgraded by adopting the Zephyr 6's mock-wood facia, horn ring and door trims, these being accompanied by a modest price increase of £7. The two Zephyrs therefore had become even closer together, the four-cylinder model now having almost totally lost its 'Consul' image. Indeed, there were those within the company who had wanted the Zephyr 4 to adopt the six-cylinder model's grille, and so just leave discreet badging to identify the 4 or 6; but fortunately this move was blocked by others who quite rightly felt that buyers of the larger-engined and more expensive car should retain some visual distinction of their choice. This edging upmarket of the Zephyr 4 of course coincided with the release of the company's new Consul Cortina, a smaller and much cheaper but nevertheless roomy car which, as it was going into production alongside the medium-sized Consul Classic model which had appeared the year before, would double the choice in that sector, and so lessen the need to retain a really inexpensive version in the big-car range.

A new upholstery option being introduced for the Zodiac only was a washable nylon velour, whilst a technical change to be found on each of the Mk 3s was a new brake servo unit which had in fact been incorporated into the production specification during the preceding month. This change came about because Girling went into production with their own design of vacuum servo unit, the Supervac, having previously manufactured the Bendix-designed Mastervac under licence. Designed to regulate the amount of servo assistance according to pedal load, the Supervac was claimed to give more positive feel to the driver when operating the brakes.

The anticipated estate car variants also arrived at the Motor Show, with a dark blue Zodiac representing this line of development on the Ford stand, whilst a pair of Zodiacs and one each of the Zephyrs could be examined on the stand of E.D. Abbott who were once again being entrusted with the conversion of these particular big Fords. Arguably the sleekest looking estate cars yet produced, with not a hint of the added-on look which had been evident on the preceding models, these latest Farnhams were more

practical too thanks to the adoption of a lift-up tailgate in place of the previous side-hinged rear door. Now of glassfibre construction, the tailgate utilized the rear window of the Zephyr saloon. Being counterbalanced for easy operation, its lower edge was raised to 5ft 9in from the ground when open, so permitting easy loading without much stooping for tall persons. With the rear seat squab folded forward there was a 5ft 10in-long loading area, this measurement being a useful 6in greater than on the Mk 2, although the maximum capacity of 61cu ft was a little smaller than before as a result of the Mk 3's lower build. A stainless steel bar running the width of the upper edge of the squab served as a handle when raising or lowering the squab, and acted as a safety barrier when the squab was down by retaining any objects which might slide forward. An extra leaf in the rear springs plus an increase in tyre size to 6.70 x 13 were in accordance with the additional carrying capacity. At £1,172, £1,245 and £1,387, these estate cars were again substantially more expensive than the corresponding saloons, due of course to their being partially coach-built.

Not actually at the Motor Show, but available for inspection over the same period in London SW1, at the Carlton Tower Hotel, was an example of a super-luxury Zodiac conversion being offered by Hooper Motor Services Limited. Completely new seating was installed, with a choice in the front of either Reutter reclining bucket seats, each with a folding armrest, or a bench seat with a separately adjustable split squab arrangement and a pull-down centre armrest. Connolly's best quality hide was used as the trim material, and there was new deep pile carpeting throughout with a covering of this on the lower portions of the door panels. Each door incorporated a small compartment complete with a sliding cover, whilst in the rear centre armrest was situated a vanity box. Above each rear door pillar was to be found an adjustable reading lamp, and facing the rear seat occupants were a pair of pull-out picnic tables set into the back of the front seat squabs. Grab handles on the centre pillars were provided to assist the passengers when leaving the rear compartment. Although the usual Zodiac instruments and switchgear were retained in the Hooper conversion, these were now situated in an entirely redesigned facia board finished in real wood veneer; a lockable glove box was set into

Restyled overriders with rubber inserts were a small recognition feature on the Zodiac from October 1963.

this on the passenger's side. Lining up with the facia were veneered door window sill fillets which continued across the centre pillar and right to the rear of the passenger compartment. A similar polished wood finish was also to be seen on the picnic tables.

Externally could be seen a pair of reversing lamps set into the rear panel at each side of the number plate, but far more likely to identify the Hooper Zodiac was the glass-like paint finish achieved by applying no less than 14 coats of cellulose, in any colour specified by the purchaser. All of this added £575 to the price of a Zodiac so treated, giving a total of £1,645, and in addition there were a number of optional extras available from Hooper, amongst which was a glass partition to separate the front and rear passenger compartments.

Not available to the public at any price, but nevertheless being shown on its own plinth on the Ford stand at Earls Court was a black Zephyr 6 specially fitted out for police work. In addition to appropriate instrumentation and the obvious external police equipment, these Z cars featured the 109bhp Zodiac engine and nylon high-speed tyres on special heavy-duty rims. Either a 3.9 or the regular six-cylinder model's 3.545:1 axle could be specified on these Zephyrs, which were also of interest in that

The Zephyr estate cars were based on the Zodiac shell, partly to avoid duplication of parts for this low-production model. The Zodiac rear doors and larger tail lamp clusters are evident in these views of a Zephyr 4 estate car.

because of the additional amount of electrical equipment necessary, the usual dynamo was replaced by an alternator in what appears to be the first application of such an item on a production car in Britain.

Purchase tax reductions in the November of 1962 saw the Mk 3 range down to £773, £837 and £971 for the Zephyr 4, Zephyr 6 and Zodiac saloons, with the corresponding estate cars now listed at £1,051, £1,115 and £1,249. Automatic transmission now added only £96 to these totals, and it was complete with this equipment that a Zephyr 6 was at last submitted to a major magazine early in 1963 for the purpose of a road-test report, which duly appeared in a special 'Ford' issue of *The Motor* dated March 27. Interestingly, this Zephyr 6 proved to have almost identical acceleration to that of the automatic Mk 2 model, reaching 50, 60, and 70mph from rest in 12.4, 17.5, and 28.6 seconds, whilst taking 21.2 seconds to cover the standing-start quarter-mile. A mean maximum speed of 87.4mph and a best one-way speed of 91mph were a little better than the automatic Mk 2, but an overall fuel consumption of just 16.1mpg was decidedly poorer as were the constant-speed mpg figures in top gear. This was no doubt due to the fact that there was now torque conversion on top gear, and it appeared in this installation to be more than nullifying any advantages there may have been with this lightweight Model 35 gearbox over the former heavier Model DG with its direct-drive top gear.

NEV 1C was a late model Zodiac estate with raised roof built for the Royal Household and delivered to the Royal Mews in April 1966. The colour scheme, like that of the earlier royal Zephyr Mk 2 estate, was dark green.

Commenting on the acceleration figures obtained, *The Motor* report said, ' . . . not outstanding figures, these, for a 2.6-litre car, but it should be remembered that dependable long-distance transport on give and take roads is the prior motive behind this car, rather than high performance, which is catered for more by the Zodiac Mk 3. ' Referring to the fuel consumption, it was felt that this, '. . . must be partially regarded as one penalty of automatic transmission, which tends to be more wasteful at lower speeds than manual control.' Much favourable emphasis was placed upon the effortless nature of this car, and the ease of driving which it provided; there was qualified praise for the steering and the cornering

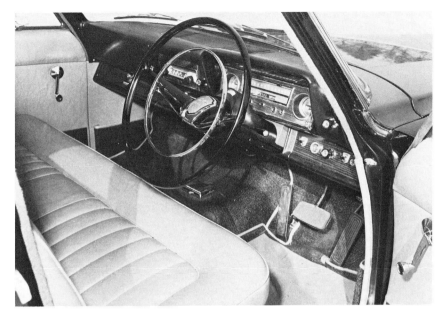

Apart from plainer door trims, the interior appointments of NEV 1C were largely as on the standard Zodiac. A dog grille originally installed across the back of the rear seats had to be replaced by a wider one when some of the smaller royal canines found they could squeeze past the sides. After service at Sandringham, Windsor Castle and Buckingham Palace, this car was sold back to the Ford Motor Company.

characteristics of which the latter, it seemed, were perhaps better than one might expect from a big six-seater saloon. In summing up, *The Motor* said, 'Withal, this is a sound, rugged and willing performer, ideal for the big-mileage man who demands comfort and dependability without having to break the £1,000 barrier to obtain it.'

As was to be expected, there had been little of a mechanical nature that had needed change during the first year of production, although modifications, twice, to the selector forks and linkages of the new four-speed gearbox had been made to improve the gearchange as some difficulty in shifting between reverse and first gears had been experienced on a number of early production cars. A small but very important change was the introduction during April 1963 of armoured front flexible brake hoses to eliminate a potentially dangerous situation discovered on some Mk 3s where this hose had been chafing on the suspension strut. The original flexible hose was in fact the Mk 1 item which had continued in use on the Mk 2 models. On the Mk 3, due to a change in the layout of the hydraulic pipework, the flexible hose now had a different run which took it around rather than away from the suspension, and in some cases it was apparently flexing the wrong way whenever steering lock was applied and so momentarily coming into contact with the strut. The armour on the replacement hoses consisted simply of a flexible metal coil around their full length.

Some 80,000 Mk 3s had been built during their first year, and production was now running steadily at just over 1,600 cars per week, which was almost exactly the figure the preceding models had maintained during their last year in production. The breakdown this time, however, was quite different, with the four-cylinder model having lost some of its market and now only accounting for about a third of this total, whilst the two six-cylinder cars were actually building up on the respective Mk 2's final-year figures. In some cases this simply represented a shift from four to six cylinders by existing Ford buyers, this move seeming logical to them now that both models were of identical body size. Many others, though,

The individual reclining seats, centre console and oddments tray fitted to the Executive model are seen here. Production versions also had a radio and front seat lap-and-diagonal safety belts as standard equipment.

who had placed some value on the previous Consul's rather more compact dimensions, were looking elsewhere within the Ford line-up, to the Classic and Cortina, to satisfy their needs; this of course had been actively encouraged by Ford who initially badged these new models as the Consul Classic and the Consul Cortina. Even so, it seems likely that Ford did lose a not insignificant number of former Consul buyers to other makers at this period.

Excellent value though it was as a big family four, at £773, the Zephyr 4 was indeed now a very large car: offering excellent accommodation within a rather smaller package, and also at least the performance of the Mk 2 Consul, were BMC's 1.6-litre Austin A60 Cambridge, and Morris Oxford Series VI which, at £756 and £766 in their De Luxe guises, came more fully equipped than the Zephyr 4 and were selling on a much larger scale.

Leaving Dagenham at a rate of more than a 1,000 cars per week, the Zephyr 6 and Zodiac were maintaining Ford's position as the leading producers in the six-cylinder field. Moving the Zodiac upmarket had actually increased its share of the sales in Britain where it was now outselling the Zephyr 6, whilst conversely the Zephyr 6 was the top export car in the range, its overseas sales throughout 1963 being some 50% greater than at home. These figures for the six-cylinder Fords were all the more creditable now that the traditional opposition in this sector from Vauxhall had been strengthened considerably by the introduction of their new PB series Velox and Cresta late in 1962. These 2.6-litre, six-seater models had been recognized instantly as much better than the outgoing PA Vauxhalls, and, whilst not quite able to equal the Mk 3 Zodiac's performance, they could most certainly match the speed and acceleration of the Zephyr 6; with prices of £840 and £943 in their Velox and Cresta configurations they also represented excellent value, and were pushing Ford hard in the sales race. BMC's contender was still the Austin Westminster, which by this time had acquired larger, Farina-styled bodywork and a 2.9-litre version of the BMC C-series six-cylinder engine. Another 100mph car, the Westminster included overdrive as standard in its very comprehensive specification, but at £1,052 it was proving to be just that bit too expensive to seriously threaten the Ford and Vauxhall sixes.

Two more of the Ford six-cylinder models came under close scrutiny during the early summer of 1963 when *Autocar* tested an example of the Zephyr 6 estate car whilst John Bolster of *Autosport* sampled a Zodiac saloon. Of the estate car, in their edition of May 24 *Autocar* said: 'Seafaring folk might well describe this estate car as a spanking big craft with a nice turn of speed. It is big, by our standards, but one soon forgets this as the ease of handling and the unusual smoothness and quietness become apparent . . . . This 2,553cc six-cylinder Ford engine gives the impression of being a glutton for work, if not for fuel, and is particularly smooth and quiet throughout its range. It started readily, hot or cold, except when the carburettor fuel level produced jet starvation on a 1-in-3 test hill . . . On all four gears the synchromesh operation was beyond reproach. The steering column gearchange mechanism was quite good, but there was just that trace of whippiness in the lever and the slight lag in response that make many drivers prefer a floor change for its directness. Like the engine, the transmission had no vibration periods . . . . The clutch itself proved well up to all demands made on it, including several attempts to start on a 1-in-3 gradient. This proved just too much for the Zephyr, although it gets away happily on 1-in-4.' By comparison with the Mk 2 estate car tested previously by *Autocar*, this latest Zephyr was appreciably faster all-out with

133

Z car; Mk 3 police cars were used by forces all over the country and proved popular with police drivers and mechanics alike.

Inside the police Zephyrs, the standard speedometer was replaced by a highly accurate, specially calibrated and tested instrument which was centrally mounted on the facia so it could easily be read by the non-driving observer.

a mean maximum speed of 91mph (83mph previously). There was a useful improvement in acceleration through the gears too with 0-60 and 0-70mph times of 16.1 and 22.8 seconds comparing very favourably with the previously recorded Mk 2 figures of 18.7 and 27.3 seconds. The new third gear had of course played a major part in the improved 0-70mph time, but the higher overall gearing and a small increase in weight had combined to take the edge off the top gear acceleration, with the latest car proving inferior to the Mk 2 in this respect throughout the 20-70mph range. In respect of its riding and handling characteristics, *Autocar* had much praise for the Zephyr 6, commenting that, 'Most estate cars behave quite differently between running light and fully loaded. Not so the Zephyr, which very nearly ignores such minor irritations as a 6cwt load of concrete blocks in the back . . . . In normal trim its ride qualities are impressive, and it sails along on good and indifferent road surfaces without exhibiting any vices. Little road noise is transmitted to the interior and even on quite sharp corners the amount of heeling over is small. Perhaps because of Ford experience in the East African Safari, the suspension shows up particularly well on a simulated "washboard", or corrugated surface.' This Zephyr had shown up less well, though, on Continental *pave* roads, which had left it '. . . bouncing around quite a lot' – but overall this was an impressive test report.

Equally enthusiastic was John Bolster's report in the *Autosport* issue of July 5, this time on the Zodiac saloon. A feature of this Mk 3 which immediately impressed Bolster very much was the gearchange: 'As one takes one's seat and drives away, the first impression is that the gearchange is absolute bliss . . . and though the lever is on the steering column, it is as smooth and sensitive in action as the best central change.' The Zodiac's cornering capabilities also earned praise, bringing the comments, 'Corners may be taken in a spirited fashion, the handling inviting such rapid manoeuvres . . . . The big Ford is by no means clumsy and handles like a smaller machine than it is, while the degree of roll is not excessive for a saloon. The Zodiac is a fast car, with a cruising speed close to its maximum, while the accurate steering and dependable roadholding make it easy and enjoyable to exploit these qualities.' The Zodiac's ride, however, did not particularly impress in this instance, as John Bolster continued, 'Personally – and I emphasize that this is my personal opinion – I was disappointed with the ride. I am aware that to obtain both roadholding and comfort at the same time is difficult with a rigid rear axle and I am glad that Fords have chosen to underline the former quality. Nevertheless, it should be possible

No doubt enjoying himself immensely, a police driver demonstrates both his skill and the controllability of the Zephyr with some opposite-lock cornering on the skid pan.

to achieve a better compromise for a car that is, in all other respects, ideal for fast Continental journeys.' Having accelerated from rest to 30, 60, and 80mph in 3.9 , 12.8, and 24.0 seconds, covered the standing quarter-mile in 18.5 seconds, and recorded a two-way average top speed of 103.7mph, the *Autosport* Zodiac appears to be the quickest of the Mk 3s tested, and its performance makes an interesting comparison with that of the Raymond Mays-modified Mk 1 Zephyr tested by John Bolster nine years previously (see Chapter 2). Those 1954 figures, considered quite spectacular then, and only achieved with an expensive engine conversion, were now being matched or bettered by the standard product, and still for less than £1,000.

Even with this sort of performance available 'off the peg', there were still a number of people searching for and willing to pay quite substantially for further increases in speed and acceleration. Again out to satisfy these demands were several specialist outfits, including the Raymond Mays concern with new six-port cylinder heads designed specifically for the Mk 3 models. Larger valves were a feature of these, and in order to maintain valve and piston clearance the compression ratio provided by the Mays head was a modest 8.5:1. Taking into account the Mk 3 car's lower bonnet line led to the adoption of a sidedraught arrangement for the carburation. Either twin or triple H6 SU carburettors were offered with this conversion, providing 130bhp and 140bhp respectively, and coincidentally being priced at £130 and £140. A similar conversion for the Zephyr 4 offered a claimed 90bhp with a single H6 SU, or 100bhp with a twin SU set-up; but with prices of £85 and £105 representing considerably more than the price difference between the standard 68bhp four-cylinder car and the 98bhp Zephyr 6, it seems unlikely that many four-cylinder conversions would be sold. The same can be said of the four-cylinder items in the range of bolt-on equipment from the Aquaplane Co Ltd, whose modifications for making the big Fords go faster once again consisted of twin SU carburettors and inlet manifold complete at £34 18s 0d for the Zephyr 4, and a corresponding triple carburettor arrangement for the six-cylinder engines at £41 15s 0d. Fabricated four- and six-branch exhaust manifolds complete with 'high efficiency' silencers and tail pipes were also offered by Aquaplane at £18 18s 0d and £24 3s 0d. Overall, any equipment of this

nature would be best applied to the Zephyr 6: the standard Zodiac had of course already the benefit of an extra 11bhp thanks to its larger carburettor and dual exhaust system, and the addition of a triple SU arrangement would only result in a further 6bhp or so. If identical equipment were replacing the lesser carburettor on the standard Zephyr 6, a gain in the region of 10bhp could be expected. If performance were the only criterion, then going all the way by adding the Raymond Mays 140bhp conversion to the Zephyr 6 would result in a decidedly quicker car, albeit a less luxurious one, than the standard Zodiac for only approximately the same total financial outlay.

As had been the case with the Mk 2 models, the estate version of the Mk 3 Zephyr was ideal for motorway patrol duties, and was able to carry equipment to deal with almost any emergency.

The big Fords on show at Earls Court in the October of 1963 displayed a number of cosmetic changes, the two Zephyrs in particular now having a more expensive look about their interiors which had undergone a subtle but effective redesign. The vinyl used for the trim was without the almost metallic sheen seen on the previous Mk 3 Zephyrs; a new pattern was applied to the seats, and there were restyled door trims of rather less flamboyant design. The burr-finish facia panels were replaced by a straight-grain American walnut finish, this style also replacing the burr on the Zodiac's facia in which was a redesigned central ashtray. The lower sections of the Zodiac's door trims now acquired a carpeted finish, this necessitating the deletion of the stowage bins built into the front doors. Instead, elasticated pockets were provided on the front side trim panels ahead of the doors. New interior door handles had been introduced throughout the range, of chromed metal now rather than the earlier plastic fittings, and protruding below the armrests slightly for easier operation.

A floor gearchange became an optional extra now, with the lever aimed towards the driver's side and cranked backwards to come easily to hand. This could be specified with the normal front bench seating, but seemed much more appropriate if ordered together with the optional individual front seats, although, unlike in some export markets where there was indeed to be a Zephyr 6 Sport model with the individual seats and floor change as standard, the combination does not appear to have been advertised as a package deal in Britain. A refinement now incorporated into the steering gear was a damper in place of the idler arm; this served to eliminate any residual steering wheel shake which might be apparent if a particular tyre and rim assembly was difficult to balance completely.

Externally, the changes to be seen were few, on the Zephyrs being confined simply to lowering the front grille slightly on the four-cylinder car and repositioning its name just above, whilst the latest Zodiacs could be identified by their redesigned overriders which now each included a rubber insert, and additionally at the rear by the provision at last of a pair of reversing lamps set into the bumper just inboard of the overriders.

The Motor were quick to sample a Zodiac with the new optional floor change, their report appearing in the January 1, 1964 issue: 'The new floor gearchange for the four-speed all-synchromesh gearbox is smooth and light. It is bent through a right angle, bringing the substantial knob close to the driver's left knee, and moves through an unusual plane at a shallow angle to the horizontal. Movements are short against powerful (but not heavy) synchromesh and they can be made quickly . . . . To guard against inadvertent engagement of reverse, there is a neat sliding ring around the lever, below the knob, which is pulled back naturally when selecting reverse.' This was one of *The Motor*'s newly introduced 'Extended Road Test' reports in which the cars were looked at in greater depth, and an analysis of the model's running costs was given. Fuel consumption figures were taken under specific sets of circumstances, those recorded for the Zodiac being 19mpg for a cold start journey of 5.3 miles (with choke for ½ mile) at a 24.4mph average speed; 13.8mpg over a 27.9-mile stretch of motorway at an average speed of 88mph; and 22.1mpg under gentle driving on main roads. Ford's own Zodiac Service Voucher maximum labour charges were quoted, £4 10s for the 5,000-mile service, plus an extra £1 charge every 15,000 miles to cover additional checks to be carried out on the running gear at these intervals.

In respect of their servicing requirements the Mk 3s had always differed from the earlier cars in that the greasing of the suspension, steering, and propeller-shaft joints was only required at 5,000-mile intervals rather than the previously recommended attention every 1,000 miles, so bringing this aspect of the car's lubrication into line with the 5,000-mile engine oil change periods. Improved ball-joint gaiters and the advent of grease containing molybdenum disulphide had made this servicing change possible, whilst further developments in this respect eventually resulted in the adoption of sealed-for-life joints on the Mk 3 range in January 1964. Also in the same month came a redesigned clutch mechanism which was without the former assist spring, as this fitment had sometimes impeded the pedal's return action. Other detail development continued. A slight change on the engines was an improved rubber for the valve stem oil seals, as the earlier ones, which in fact were still the Mk 1 items, could eventually become brittle with age and mileage, leading to some oil burning due to seepage down the valve guides. In June 1964 an offside front coil spring longer by ¾in than its opposite number was introduced to eliminate the excess front offside tyre wear which could occur under driver-only running.

The changes announced for the 1964 Motor Show were aimed at further comfort and refinement. A no-cost option on the Zephyrs was Knit-weave PVC upholstery, whilst Curzon cloth seating could now be ordered at extra cost. More deeply padded seat cushions were introduced, whilst deeper underfelts and redesigned silencers would result in even quieter running than before. The heater and windscreen washers at last became standard equipment on the Zephyrs, albeit with an adjustment in the price. On the Zodiac, too, attention to further improvements in the application of sound-deadening materials was to result in a quieter car for the occupants.

A new range of colours, apparently coinciding with the adoption of acrylic paintwork on the Mk 3s, identified the latest cars; included amongst these were Malabu Gold and Alcuda Blue, both of which were metallic colours and available only at extra cost.

The basic prices had risen slightly, and the Mk 3 range entered 1965 at £805, £877 and £1,017 for the Zephyr 4, Zephyr 6 and Zodiac saloons, with their respective estate car variants now being £1,083, £1,156 and £1,294. Those occupying the top positions in Ford Motor Company management did of course use Zodiacs, and it was the existence of some of these cars which had been personalized with non-standard fittings, notably a central division/armrest between the individual front seats, which prompted the product planners to call for an additional top-of-the-range model which appeared at the end of January, 1965. This was the Executive Zodiac, on which all the normally catalogued Zodiac extras were supplied as standard, these being: automatic transmission; individual front seats; crushed hide seat coverings; radio (front and rear speakers); front seat belts; fog lamp and long-range driving lamp; wing mirrors; and a locking fuel tank cap. Additional new features included a dipping rear-view mirror; heavier sound-deadening material; fully carpeted boot and spare wheel cover; engine compartment lamp; and a 30-amp generator. The normal Zodiac's twin exhaust system had always emitted a rather sporting note, which was not considered appropriate for executive transport, and so the twin downpipes from the manifold were now arranged to feed the gases into a single large-bore system. Extreme quietness was the result of this change, which was also adopted for the standard Zodiac at this time as was the improved sound-damping. For the Executive Zodiac just four colours were standardized, these being the Malabu Gold and Alcuda Blue metallics, along with Sable (dark brown) and Midnight Blue. Any of the other Mk 3 colours could however be supplied to special order without any price differential. All of this was available for £1,303, or to special order with manual gearbox and overdrive at £1,257.

The Executive was seen by Ford as a possible means of moving considerably further upmarket, with instructions going out to Ford dealerships to aim this car at the professional classes who would perhaps normally be prepared to spend in the £2,000 region; but as no breakdown of production figures distinguishing between the Executive and the standard Zodiac appears to have survived, it is impossible to say just what impact this car had at any level. Based solely on price, the Executive had only one obvious rival, in the shape of BMC's Wolseley 6/110 Mk 2 which was £1,276 in its automatic transmission form but without radio and seat belts. Adding those two items would take the big Wolseley past £1,300, so making the two cars closely comparable in both price and equipment level. This of course was the top BMC C-series 3-litre model which (thankfully) had not been given BMC's so-called 'advanced-engineering' treatment, and therefore remained a sensibly straightforward and good-looking car with a 'quality' air about it. In its automatic form this Wolseley was a fraction quicker than the Executive Zodiac, but no more thirsty. As was usually the case with other manufacturer's big cars it was not nearly so agile as the Ford, although this perhaps mattered only a little at this level of executive transport. In all, it seems likely that the Executive Zodiac would appeal mostly to existing Ford buyers who had more to spend than was required for the standard Zodiac model. Within a few weeks of its introduction the price of the Executive Zodiac had risen slightly, to £1,315, as a result of a manufacturer's increase in basic price which also applied to the Zephyrs and the Zodiac, these now being listed at £818, £890 and £1,029.

For many weeks each year throughout the Mk 3's production run, the Zephyr 6 received prime-time television coverage as the star of BBC Television's police drama series 'Z Cars' which, as mentioned in the previous chapter, had at first featured the Mk 2 Zephyr. The choice of the Zephyr for the original series had been quite correct, as the adventures related in the programme were taking place in and around a fictitious north-western town, an area where in reality some 80% of police patrol cars were indeed Ford Zephyrs. Authenticity, therefore, had demanded the use of the Zephyr, but nevertheless, fully aware of the advertising value of this programme to Ford, the BBC did attempt to redress the balance somewhat by using other makes of car, in rotation, in the minor roles. This may however have backfired, as it tended to mean that at all times the good guys were driving Zephyrs whilst they apprehended the baddies who were driving other makes – a sort of 'Zephyrs Rule OK' situation, and all great stuff for Ford. In real life, the Mk 3 Zephyr 6 had of course soon been seen in action throughout the country alongside the police Mk 2s, so much so that during 1965 production of the special police edition of the car passed the 1,000 mark. Even with the availablity of a purpose-built Zephyr from the factory, many forces still opted for further differences in specification depending upon the locality to be patrolled. For M6 Motorway work the Cheshire Constabulary had some of their Mk 3s fitted with Raymond Mays cylinder heads and triple HD6 SU carburettors, whilst a small number of their Zephyrs for patrolling the Stockport town centre and adjacent hilly areas were equipped with a special low-ratio axle, known amongst the drivers as the 'town diff'. This limited the maximum speed to around 75mph, but gave shattering acceleration in the streets and an outstandingly rapid hill-climbing ability.

On September 1, 1965, Ford readjusted their prices throughout, from basic Anglia to Executive Zodiac, in a surprise move doing away with the extra delivery charge which the company had always levied in line with all other British manufacturers, but which was never shown in the price lists. Being based broadly on actual costs incurred in delivering a vehicle from the factory to the dealer, these charges naturally varied quite considerably in different parts of the country and had resulted in some people paying much more than others for the same new car. Now, with these costs averaged out and consolidated in a new list price, Ford buyers anywhere on the British mainland all paid the same price, and knew exactly what that price would be. This did mean of course a further increase in list prices, with the Mk 3 range now being £836, £909 and £1,048 for the Zephyr 4, Zephyr 6 and Zodiac, and the estate cars at £1,114, £1,187 and £1,326. The Executive Zodiac was now £1,335. With no other manufacturers following suit, these all-in prices could perhaps have made the Mk 3s look a little expensive to some people at first glance, although in reality the range was as good value as ever.

It was somewhat ironic that this welcome change in pricing policy regarding delivery charges coincided with a delivery drivers' strike, which resulted in the stock-piling of some new Ford cars and a consequent spell of short-time working. Also, a change of government the year before had resulted in a change in economic policy, with a credit squeeze bringing about a reduction in the number of buyers and lower production throughout the motor industry in Britain by comparison with the previous year. A reduction in the number of large cars accounted for much of the cutback, and of the Mk 3 Fords it was the Zephyr 4 which suffered least in these suddenly more stringent times in which the Zephyr 6 and Zodiac were hit rather harder. Nevertheless, in their reduced market the two Ford sixes alone were still accounting for more than 50% of the over-2½-litre sales in Britain as they continued to be regarded by the majority as the best of the big-car buys.

The changes to the Mk 3s during 1965 were small. The chrome strip running along the sills and its continuation on the front wings were deleted in the middle of the year, whilst in September separate amber flashing indicators were introduced at the front although still housed in the same nacelles as the previously combined white indicator/sidelamp unit. The cloth upholstery option was deleted at this time, after which the Mk 3 range continued in production for a further three months or so only. In January 1966 the model was terminated after 291,940 examples, as the company began a build-up of the all-new Mk 4 cars in readiness for their scheduled April 1966 launch.

As these forthcoming replacements were based upon a completely new train of thought in which no account had been taken of the original Consul/Zephyr concept, the production demise of the Mk 3 Zephyr/Zodiac series signalled the end of what can now be seen to have been the outstanding era in big-Ford design. Over the preceding 15 years this line had achieved everything that its designers could possible have been hoping for in the late 1940s as they schemed out the Mk 1 cars. Revolutionary though they were upon their appearance in 1950, they were also built on the soundest of engineering principles in all aspects of their design. That they were considerably over-engineered for home and many other market requirements is beyond any doubt, but as this had never been reflected in the prices asked it was simply a real bonus in durability to be enjoyed by many through whose ownership these big Fords passed.

CHAPTER 5

Starting afresh

Mk 4 Zephyr, Zodiac and Executive

On February 10, 1961, with the forthcoming Mk 3 Zephyr/Zodiac models still more than a year away from their introduction, the Product Planning Committee at Dagenham first discussed the development of a Mk 4 range. The reasons for this early consideration of a fourth generation of large cars were several: the Mk 3 could be seen in some respects as the ultimate development of the original theme; a range of completely new large-capacity V-configuration engines suitable for both future car and commercial vehicle applications was already being mooted; and due to political changes abroad there were indications that the company would lose many of its African markets, with their extremely rough road conditions for which the preceding generations of postwar Fords had been designed. The large-car range for the late 1960s therefore, it was thought, would need to be planned around somewhat different criteria than before. After due consideration over the ensuing weeks, the Product Committee reached its decision on May 5; work was to begin on the Mk 4 project – code named 'Panda'.

Thanks wholly to the compact nature of the V engines, Panda would be able to offer appreciably more passenger and luggage space within the same overall dimensions as the forthcoming Mk 3, and early package studies were to approximately these outside dimensions. In one respect, however, the V engine installation was problematical in that as it only required a short bonnet it upset the established British and European notions of large-car proportions. At least one full-size clay mock-up was built around the short V engine theme, and its relatively snub-nosed, long-tailed proportions did indeed look all wrong. It was eventually when stylist Ron Bradshaw suggested locating the spare wheel at an angle in the front of the engine compartment ahead of the engine that the Mk 4 really began to take shape. This idea was attractive also in that it left a completely uncluttered luggage boot, although this point and the subsequent claims that the front-mounted spare wheel was a safety feature, whilst valid enough, were definitely afterthoughts. Styling considerations alone had brought about this layout in the first place. Early package drawings around this arrangement still suggested the Mk 3 model's overall length, and were apparently approved by the Product Committee in mid-1962; but although the layout endured, the overall dimensions did not.

Mindful that the Mk 2 sixes though very popular had nevertheless not made significant inroads into those rather more exclusive markets where cars like the Humber Super Snipe, the Rover 3-litre and the big Wolseley were favoured by higher ranking large-company executives, there were one or two at Dagenham who felt that a larger car than the established Zodiac was needed if Ford were to score in this sector. This thinking, and the appointment at Dagenham late in 1962 of a new Director of Engineering, American Harley Copp, was to have a considerable influence on the Mk 4. Copp felt that the Zephyr/Zodiac line should be the European Ford equivalent of the parent company's upmarket Lincoln models, which were promoted across America as 'The fine car from Ford'. A bigger car, therefore, the Mk 4 was now to be, and it is interesting to note that the track and wheelbase measurements of 4ft 9in and 9ft 7in and the overall width of 5ft 11½in adopted were as on the mid-range American Ford Fairlane of 1962.

Although viewed with disappointment, and in fact with foreboding, in some quarters at Dagenham, this enlargement was naturally welcomed in the styling studios, where it offered considerable scope. Indeed, Charles

An early clay mock-up for a Mk 4 car, taking into account the shortness of the V engine and showing alternative front corner treatments at each side.

Much better proportions were achieved once it had been decided to locate the spare wheel ahead of the engine. Again alternative bumper, wing and side treatments can be seen, the design now showing definite Lincoln influence at the front whilst retaining a Mk 3 Zodiac window theme.

Thompson, by this time one of the two senior stylists at Dagenham, recalls how they were told to make the car look as big as possible within the dimensions chosen. Both Thompson and Ron Bradshaw produced mock-ups, with one of Charles Thompson's designs eventually getting the management's approval.

Whilst of course being a completely new structure, from both the general constructional viewpoint and in a number of specific details, this large bodyshell had much in common with the Mk 3, its floorpan and

144

Detail proposals for the front end schemed out by Charles Thompson at the time. Clearly visible is the low air intake resulting from the spare wheel position.

145

September 1963: a glassfibre-bodied Mk 4 comes under the scrutiny of some of Ford's top brass. Product Planners Maurice Sury (left) and Terry (later Sir Terence) Beckett are seen exiting the car, whilst Director of Engineering Harley Copp looks into the driving compartment. This car's styling was almost wholly by Charles Thompson and was approved for production largely as seen here.

underbody bracing layout being a scale-up virtually of the preceding car in most respects. Being built around a longer wheelbase presented a slight problem at the front in that the suspension struts were now further ahead of the scuttle into which their loads were transmitted. Box-like inner wings of even greater robustness than those of the Mk 3 type were therefore necessary, and at least one Mk 4 prototype ran with the addition of a diagonal bracing arrangement from the suspension top mounts to the bulkhead in a manner which echoed the Mk 1 and Mk 2 cars, although this former level of over-engineering was avoided in the production Mk 4s. In fact, now having as it did to include a spare wheel carrier, the extreme front cross-structure of the latest cars was of greater strength in itself, and proved sufficient to tie the longer front end together. Also of dimensions close to those of the American Fairlane, the passenger compartment offered far greater fore-and-aft room than any of the previous Consul/Zephyr series. It was a particular improvement over the Mk 3 in this, and in respect of rear entry and exit too. A slightly taller build than the Mk 3 gave another inch or so of headroom, and in maximum internal width also there was an improvement, with no less than $4\frac{1}{2}$in greater shoulder room which was a remarkable achievement as the car's external overall width had increased by $2\frac{1}{2}$in only. With a 6in front seat adjustment, and the introduction of a new steering column adjustable for height by $1\frac{1}{4}$in, this was indeed a well-planned passenger compartment in which very few occupants would ever have difficulty in finding a very comfortable travelling position.

At the rear, Charles Thompson's gently sloping 'bow back' style hid a luggage compartment much larger than its outside appearance suggested, with a very conveniently shaped 20cu ft capacity, although strength considerations again resulted in a high back panel with its associated difficulties for some loading operations. Residing in the same position as before, and with its upper surface forming part of the boot floor as in the Mk 3 cars, the fuel tank was now of 15 gallons capacity. Being based

Cold-climate trials being carried out with very thinly disguised Mk 4 prototypes. A false, lengthened rear end to conceal the car's true proportions can be detected in the second picture.

closely on the Mk 3's build, but longer by 5½in, this Mk 4 body had lost a little in torsional rigidity by comparison. But the Mk 3 body was the strongest of the whole series in this respect, and that the latest bodyshell still matched the rigidity of the earlier Mk 2 cars says all that is necessary regarding the Mk 4's strength.

At the front of the car were to be found the established MacPherson strut suspension and recirculating-ball steering gear, but with further refinements incorporated plus slight changes dictated by this larger and heavier vehicle. Again inclined inwards, the MacPherson struts were now embraced by coil springs angled further inwards than the struts themselves. In this arrangement the springs exerted an opposite pressure to the bending force exerted on the inclined strut when running in the straight-ahead position, so reducing the internal friction. Additionally, there were now PTFE-impregnated bearings which eliminated the initial resistance to movement within the strut usually referred to as 'stiction'. Compliance, a slight fore-and-aft movement to reduce the initial impact shock of striking a ridge or whatever in the roadway, was also built into the MacPherson strut system for the first time, and was achieved quite simply by locating the anti-roll bar, and the track-control arms at their suspension ends, in compressible bushes. Whilst most satisfactory results on the road could be confidently expected from all of this, the same could not be said of the

Mk 4's steering. Taking into account an increase in overall weight, of which some 58% would still be carried by the front wheels on the six-cylinder cars, the steering gear was now of the extremely low ratio of 20.6:1 which equated to almost five turns of the steering wheel from lock to lock. Making matters worse in this respect was the introduction of a flexible coupling in the steering column made necessary by the decision to offer a steering wheel adjustable for height. Vagueness on the open road and a lot of wheel-twirling when manoeuvring were the only possible outcomes here, although there was a redeeming feature in a turning circle of 36ft which was excellent for a 15½ft-long car.

The company had been evaluating independent rear suspension systems for some years prior to the Mk 4 programme, and had found them unsuitable in general terms because they either did not work well, or if they did were far too expensive to incorporate in the specification of the traditionally low-priced Ford. Moving the large-car range further upmarket however would perhaps bring them into a sector where the cost of such sophistication could just be borne, and if so the new cars would have a definite plus point here by comparison with the other British executive heavyweights such as the big Rover, Super Snipe, etc. Even so, that the pros and cons of independent rear-end arrangements were quite evenly matched can be seen by the fact that it was not until January 1963 that the decision was finally taken to introduce such a system on the Mk 4. Inexpensive swing-axle systems in which the driveshaft is pivoted only at its inboard end were never under serious consideration, for although these arrangements do normally result in slightly improved riding under most circumstances, the handling qualities displayed at not much above average touring speeds often vary between poor and, in extreme cases,

A prototype car undergoing some rough-road durability testing at a research facility.

dangerously unpredictable. The more elaborate semi-trailing wishbone layout with driveshafts pivoted at both ends is really the only way to achieve good results, but with this system there are conflicting arcs of movement which have to be compensated for. Variable-length sliding-spline driveshafts are the usual method adopted here, but they are not actually an ideal solution as they can lock up under driving torque, are subject to wear, and are expensive to produce. These factors resulted in Ford's devising a layout in which a swinging-link inboard attachment for the semi-trailing wishbone provided the necessary compensation, and so allowed the use of simple fixed-length driveshafts. In the interests of keeping unsprung weight to a minimum, the wishbones were of cast aluminium, and for absolute safety were each to undergo an X-ray flaw-detection process in production. Coil springs and telescopic shock absorbers completed this independent rear suspension, which on its own was to add in the region of £75 to the tax-paid total price of a Mk 4 car.

Testing this new suspension mounted directly to the car's underside resulted in too much road noise being transmitted, and so a simple subframe arrangement to which the suspension arms could be attached was devised. This was achieved by introducing a pair of crossmembers, to

149

one of which was bolted the rear of the differential casing, and to the other the pinion casing which protruded well forward of the differential assembly. Rubber-bushed mounting points, one each at both ends of the two crossmembers, provided for a well-insulated four-point attachment.

An all-disc braking system was decided upon for the Mk 4, in part because of the uniform front/rear fade characteristics; the idea was also made more attractive now due to the development by Girling of a swinging caliper single-piston rear brake assembly which combined an effective integral handbrake mechanism for the first time with a disc brake. Viewed from above, and with unworn wedge-shaped-section brake pads, the caliper was mounted at an angle to the disc, on a vertical swivel pin. The single hydraulic arrangement was inboard, and when under pressure and operating the inboard pad caused the caliper to want to rotate around the swivel pin, thus forcing the outboard pad onto the disc face without the need for a separate hydraulic cylinder and piston. In normal use the wedge-shaped pads would eventually wear down to a uniform thickness until, when they were worn out, the caliper would be in line with the disc having gradually moved round on its swivel pin as pad wear progressed. The hydraulic cylinder also contacted one end of a rocking lever, the other end of which was operated by a cam at the end of a normal mechanical handbrake linkage which when pulled exerted pressure on the inboard pad with precisely the same swivel effect again being brought into play. Cheaper than a conventional twin-cylinder caliper, because of its simplified hydraulics and interconnected handbrake, the Girling swinging caliper was making its debut on the new big Fords. The whole system was linked to

In sharp contrast to the earlier snowy scenes, hot-climate testing was carried out in Spain – apparently to the total indifference of the local transport also seen here.

Girling's SuperVac 50 servo unit, and the braking effort was split 65% front and 35% rear.

Roadwheels of 13in diameter and 4½in section were retained, but this time equipped with 6.70 x 13 tyres for the rather heavier six-cylinder Mk 4 whilst the four-cylinder car retained the previous 6.40 x 13 covers.

No less interesting than the braking and suspension systems were the all-new power units, which were the result of a separate line of development and had come about solely because of the desirability, on production economy grounds, to have common large-capacity engines throughout the large-car, large-van/light-truck range in the future. The previous 1,703cc Consul/Zephyr 4 in-line unit had been used in the Thames 10/12/15cwt forward-control van introduced in 1957, but this was something of a compromise installation, and as in any case this engine could not be increased in cubic capacity, something new would be needed

151

for the eventual Thames van/pick-up replacements with which greater payloads would be sought.

Following the large-bore oversquare principle, a new four-cylinder in-line unit of the 2-litre capacity reckoned to be necessary in the future would have taken up considerable space lengthwise, to the detriment of cargo carrying capacity, and so the extreme shortness of a V4 cylinder arrangement seemed the most attractive proposition for a new generation of Thames vans and their derivatives. Just as with an in-line engine, it would be easy to add another pair of cylinders and so continue to provide a powerful six-cylinder engine for a top-of-the-range car, and with quite considerable space-saving benefits in this application also which could be translated into extra passenger space. Amongst other benefits of the V engine are that even large bores can still be surrounded by ample water jacketing in a nevertheless compact engine overall; a water-heated inlet manifold is easily provided in the centre of the V, and as the carburettor sits centrally the more efficient crossflow combustion chamber design is a natural outcome.

However, for a variety of reasons V-configuration engines, and in particular V4 and V6 units, are appreciably more difficult and therefore more expensive to produce than corresponding in-line units. One of these reasons is the inevitable duplication of some assembly operations, such as fitting two cylinder heads, two exhaust manifolds etc, and of course the need to provide pairs of items such as these, albeit slightly smaller individually. Also, as a simple V4 unit is inherently extremely rough-running irrespective of the V angle chosen, an additional balance shaft not required by an in-line four has to be provided. This shaft, which is gear-driven directly from the crankshaft and therefore rotates in the opposite direction, has strategically placed weights which go some way towards countering the fore-and-aft rocking motion which is an unwelcome characteristic of the V4 layout. A balance weight built into the crankshaft pulley and another incorporated in the flywheel are also necessary, but even then secondary out-of-balance forces still remain, and as these are of greater magnitude than those remaining in the in-line four-cylinder engine, the V4 at its best is a less smooth unit.

Fortunately, although also requiring the crankshaft pulley and flywheel weights, the V6 layout does not demand the additional balance shaft, although matters are still somewhat complicated here. Unlike on an in-line six-cylinder where all that is necessary for both near-perfect balance and equally spaced firing impulses is a relatively simple three plane counter-balanced crankshaft, or on 90-degree V8-cylinder engines where provision of a four-plane crankshaft also achieves perfect balance (although still with irregular firing in this instance), to achieve an acceptable standard of smoothness with a V6 unit a narrow angle (60-degree) block and an extremely complicated six-plane crankshaft are necessary. This arrangement does give equal firing impulses whilst also cancelling the primary out-of-balance forces, but still leaves one secondary out-of-balance force which cannot be corrected. Therefore, even in its most appropriate configuration, a V6 does not operate quite so smoothly as do six cylinders when arranged in line.

Both the casting and machining of V-shaped engine blocks are considerably more complicated operations than are required with in-line

An independent rear suspension assembly being made ready for testing under load on a rolling-road rig.

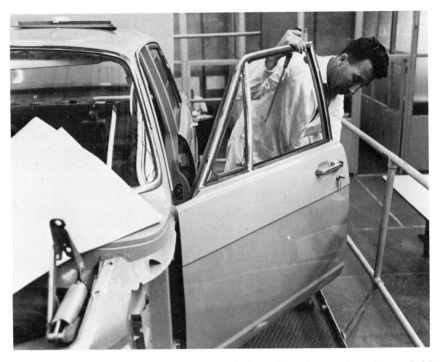

cylinder blocks, and by comparison with the relatively simple right-angle V block which suffices for an eight-cylinder engine, the required narrow angle of the V6 presents further manufacturing problems. The same comments apply to the necessary six-plane crankshaft of the V6, of which the usual counterweights now have the added responsibility of combating the out-of-balance forces introduced by the angled cylinders.

Overall, therefore, the arguments against introducing V-configuration engines would seem to be decisive, and certainly from the foregoing it is easy to see why no manufacturers in Britain were producing either V4 or V6-engined cars. However, Ford's foundry techniques were almost legendary, and their production-engineering expertise was unrivalled in Britain. Also, as the company were transferring tractor production to Basildon, there would be ample space for expanding engine-building

facilities at Dagenham so enabling the more complex transfer machinery required for V engine production to be installed without seriously upsetting existing engine lines. And so, as Ford were extremely keen to be the undisputed leaders in the delivery-van markets, the space-saving arguments in favour of the compact V4 engine won the day.

Both the four- and six-cylinder blocks did of course feature the 60-degree angle, and there was a common bore size of 93.7mm, with bore centres so widely spaced as to suggest excellent cooling properties. As with the in-line engines, these new blocks were of the deep-skirt type, giving great rigidity, but more advanced casting methods ensuring greater accuracy and consistency in wall thickness now resulted in slightly thinner walls throughout and a saving of something in the region of 20lbs in weight by comparison with the old straight-six. In order to satisfy a wide market, several cubic capacities were needed from this basic engine line, and so two different stroke measurements were chosen in order to achieve four engine sizes, with the longer of these strokes, at 72.4mm, providing a 1,996cc four and a 2,994cc six-cylinder unit. With the alternative 60.3mm stroke the swept volumes became 1,663cc and 2,495cc, the smaller of these two capacities being outside the Zephyr story as the four-cylinder Mk 4 would be powered exclusively by the 1,996cc engine. (The 1,663cc engine powered the economy version of the new van, which appeared as the Transit late in 1965, whilst the 2-litre V4 was also to be found in the bigger payload variants of this model, and both V4 engines were used in the company's middleweight Corsair passenger car range. These applications plus the Zephyr/Zodiac cars did indeed amount to far greater utilization than had been possible with the original Consul/Zephyr engines.) This of course necessitated two crankshafts each being provided for four- or six-cylinder use, but there was still considerable bottom-end interchangeability of moving parts between all the engines. Unlike in an in-line engine where it is possible to fit a main bearing between each cylinder, the practice which was now being adopted by Dagenham for its 1.6-litre 'Kent' in-line power unit, the maximum number of main bearings possible on a V engine of course is limited to one between each pair of side-by-side cylinders, and so three main bearings for the V4, and four for the V6 were provided in the new 'Essex' engines. All the crankshafts featured a 2.5in main bearing journal diameter, and a big end journal diameter only very slightly less at 2.37in; the bearing shells throughout were either copper-lead or aluminium-tin. Although two different crank throws were involved, the same length connecting rods were used in all the engines, the shorter-stroked units therefore having pistons which were taller above the piston pin than those in the longer-stroked engines, so maintaining the same top-dead-centre height.

Recesses in the piston crowns formed the combustion chambers, these being very accurately machined to give precisely the same compression ratio in each cylinder. Common combustion chambers in conjunction with two cylinder capacities resulted in compression ratios of 8.9:1 with the 72mm stroke and 9.1:1 on the shorter-stroked engines. With this bowl-in-piston arrangement a perfectly flat-faced cylinder head can be used, in which the valves are installed vertically to the head and can be of the largest diameters that the cylinder bores permit; the new Ford cylinder heads also featured very generous water passages. Replacing Ford's usual steel shim cylinder head gasket were new ones of a synthetic rubber/asbestos composition, reinforced with steel wire.

Eliminating a timing chain, the camshaft was mounted centrally in the V and operated directly from the crankshaft by means of a large gear-wheel which was of compressed fibre construction for silent running. Hollow tappets (cam followers) and tubular pushrods operating individually stud-mounted rocker arms completed a lightweight valvegear set up which resulted in reduced inertia loads.

A single Zenith carburettor, complete with automatic choke, supplied the mixture on the V4 engines and the 2½-litre V6, whilst a twin-choke Weber instrument, again with automatically controlled rich mixture for starting, was exclusive to the 3-litre six-cylinder unit. With the carburettors residing in a hot location directly above the V engine, a new feature in the fuel system was a return pipe from the carburettor to the tank, so providing continuous fuel circulation even with a closed throttle and avoiding any possibility of vapour lock occurring in the pipes. The respective net power outputs for the 2, 2½, and 3-litre engines were 88bhp at 4,750rpm, 112bhp at 4,750rpm, and 136bhp at 4,750rpm, with the corresponding net torque outputs being 116lb/ft at 2,750rpm, 137lb/ft at 3,000rpm, and 181.5lb/ft at 3,000rpm. These figures suggested substantially greater performance for both the four-cylinder Zephyr and the new Zodiac, which was to be the 3-litre car, but less so for the Zephyr V6 which although gaining a little in bhp did not have the advantage of the larger cylinder capacity now enjoyed by the other two cars. The cooling system capacities were 15.3 pints and 19.5 pints for the V4 and V6 units respectively, and were again pressurized to 13psi. Owing to the front mounting of the spare wheel obliquely ahead of the engine, a very wide low-mounted radiator was installed, drawing its cooling air through a grille beneath the bumper.

A lavish launch party for the motoring press was held in Tunisia, where it seems that in addition to Zephyrs and Zodiacs a somewhat older form of transport also came under scrutiny.

Overall, it can be seen that a considerable amount of thought had gone into the design and application of these V power units, with the result that many of the inherent drawbacks, including those of manufacture, had been successfully overcome. (In more recent years several other manufacturers have adopted V6 power for space-saving reasons, but usually in the much easier-to-build but irregular-firing and off-balance 90-degree form.) Nevertheless, the Ford V4 engine remained a relatively rough-running unit, more than adequate no doubt for the Transit van, but not really quite good enough for so large and impressive-looking a family car as the Mk 4 Zephyr. By comparison, the V6 fared much better altogether, although still of course lacking perfect balance and so unable to endow the Mk 4 Zodiac with that special touch of 'class' inherent only in the straight-six-cylinder layout.

Sensibly still actuated hydraulically, at a time when cable operation was gaining favour elsewhere, the clutch was now of the latest diaphragm-spring type with a pedal load reduced to 30lbs or so. A new manual gearbox was required to handle the torque of the 3-litre engine, so what can be regarded broadly speaking as an uprated version of the Mk3 gearbox was provided for the new six-cylinder cars. With the same ratios as before, this gearbox suited the $2\frac{1}{2}$-litre car well, but the indirect gears were rather too low for the immensely torquey 3-litre V6. Tailored more accurately to the engine's requirements were the indirect ratios for the four-cylinder Zephyr, which was equipped with a very low bottom gear, and second and third gears slightly below those of the sixes. Linkages were provided in all cases for both a floor or column-mounted gearchange mechanism. A Laycock overdrive could be specified at extra cost on the Zephyr V6 and Zodiac only, and gave an 18% reduction in engine revolutions when engaged. With its simple in or out stalk operation and power-sustained changes this was much easier to operate than the previous Borg-Warner device.

The previously optional automatic gearbox from Borg-Warner had gone too, to be replaced by Ford's own American C4 automatic transmission. A conventional torque converter and three-speed epicyclic gearbox, the C4 was equipped for both D1 and D2 drive-range operation. With D1 selected the car would start from rest in low gear and progress through the intermediate ratio and then into top gear, whilst if D2 was in operation the low gear was blocked, thus giving more economical, albeit more leisurely intermediate-gear starts; this was useful in heavy traffic stop-start low-speed crawling conditions as it eliminated hunting between low and intermediate ratios. A kick-down facility was provided as usual for instantaneous downward changes on the move, and there was a low-gear hold position on the selector with which to retain the lowest ratio for situations like very steep hill descents.

With independent rear suspension the final-drive/differential assembly is of course at a fixed height, in this case as already mentioned forming part of a subframe arrangement. The fixed height therefore applies also to the propeller shaft, so in turn allowing a shallower transmission tunnel in the passenger compartment floor. A long gearbox tailshaft was provided as in the previous cars which, in conjunction with an unusually long pinion shaft from the final-drive, resulted in a relatively short single-piece propeller shaft on the Mk 4 despite the new car's considerably lengthened wheelbase, thus obviating the sort of vibrations which can occur with an over-long shaft. The final-drive ratios for the six-cylinder cars were chosen with acceleration in mind, a 3.7:1 ratio for the Zodiac being rather lower than on

Zephyr V6, in a studio pose revealing what Ford referred to as 'the elegant thrusting look'. Ford's model designations for the Mk 4 cars were 3010E (Zephyr), 3008E (Zephyr V6) and 3012E (Zodiac).

the Mk 3 (3.545:1) and in fact over-compensating slightly for the larger tyres now fitted to give just 20mph/1,000rpm; a 3.9:1 ratio for the Zephyr V6 gave 19.1mph/1,000rpm. Chosen in the interests of economical open-road cruising with the four-cylinder Zephyr was the 3.7:1 axle, which with this car's 6.40 x 13 tyres resulted in 19.4mph/1,000rpm.

The electrical systems were now negative-earth, and all models were equipped with a pre-engaged starter motor. Exclusive to the Zodiac was an alternator rather than the usual dynamo still to be found on the latest Zephyrs.

Apart from the fact that there was once again a four-cylinder car in the range, the original Consul image had gone completely, with the four- and six-cylinder Zephyrs appearing identical externally apart from a small V6 script on the bonnet front, boot lid and nearside wing of the 2½-litre car in addition to the 'Zephyr' lettering front and rear common to both. No reference to the power unit ever appeared on the four-cylinder model which was to be promoted now simply as 'Zephyr'. Inside the Zephyrs were bench front seats and a steering-column gearchange as standard, the one difference here being a front centre armrest as standard equipment on the V6 whilst available only at extra cost on the four. Rear centre armrests were optional in both cases, as was a front seating package comprising individual fixed-back bucket seats, a centre console and a floor gearchange all-in at an extra charge. All the seating was covered in vinyl, with a cloth option for export only. Both cars were fitted with loop-pile carpets throughout. Electric windscreen washers, cigar lighter and the heater were standard, as was the excellent 'aeroflow' fresh-air ventilation system first seen on the Ford Cortina, which in its Mk 4 application completely changed the air inside the car every 25 seconds.

Distinguishing the Zodiac externally were four 7in headlamps, full width rear reflectors, bumper overriders and full wheelcovers. Inside were a pair of reclining front seats, centre console and floor gearchange as standard, but with a bench seat and column gearchange as a no-cost option. The seating was once again in Cirrus PVC, with hide or cloth available at extra cost. Deep, cut-pile carpeting covered the floor and was repeated on the lower part of the doortrims. Additional instrumentation consisted of a

tachometer, ammeter and oil pressure gauge, whilst there was also an electric clock.

In all, therefore, these big Mk 4 Fords were technically advanced and in some respects innovative cars, and were very fully equipped by the standards of the day. Their development programme, however, would prove unfortunately to have been flawed in two important respects in that strict limitations on the development time, and on component costs, had been imposed. The development of the previous generations of big Fords and the company's small Anglias and Prefects had always been seen through most thoroughly by the development engineers, and it was generally not until they were reasonably satisfied that all would be well with a new car, that production and release dates were finally brought into sharp focus. With the Mk 4, in July 1963, at a time when the car still only existed on paper and in the form of a few as yet unapproved clay models, the project was subjected to a master 'Product Timing Plan' which set out start and finish dates for each of the principal activities involved in bringing a new model into being. At the same time a 'Red Book' was compiled for the Mk 4 which gave the planned cost of every component and was to become, according to the company, 'the financial bible of everyone concerned with the design and manufacture of the car'.

These methods, referred to today by some ex-Ford personnel as 'discipline', had first been tried, and worked very well it must be said, with the company's new Cortina which product planner Terry Beckett (later Sir Terence Beckett) and engineer Fred Hart had seen through from the first simple idea for a new car to a production model in an astonishing 21 months. But the Cortina was an utterly conventional Ford, able to draw on the experience of a decade at Dagenham of building the best and most modern conventional cars in Britain. It was also a relatively downmarket car, where the tightest cost-control techniques can indeed count very much towards success. The projected Mk 4 Zephyr/Zodiac range could not have been in sharper contrast: mechanically, it was breaking new ground for Ford in several very important respects, and in Zodiac form it was supposed to be taking Ford into the prestige market. These factors would seem to have been quite sufficient to justify a proving programme largely

Zodiac Mk 4. 'The Mark of Distinction' was the slogan adopted for advertising purposes, one previously associated with the Lincoln name. Apart from their 'Five Star' centre insignia the Zodiac's ornate wheel covers were of identical design to those of the 1962 Ford Galaxie.

The simple rear-end styling was relieved on the Zodiac by the full-width red reflector strip. The filler cap was again neatly concealed, but the 'bow-back' styling resulted in very poor driver vision when reversing.

free of any constraints, but in the event both the Product Timing Plan and the Red Book prevailed. Also not helping matters throughout the development period was an unfortunate situation which had arisen at Dagenham following the arrival of Harley Copp. There had been American personnel holding the Director of Engineering post at Ford of Britain before, and harmonious relations had always been maintained between them and Dagenham's engineering staff. Copp, however, had arrived with an 'America knows best' attitude and appears to have failed to appreciate or even recognize that the Dagenham team had been very successful so far in postwar Britain, with a string of well-planned big-selling and very profitable cars to their credit. He was himself apparently wholly committed to the principles of these overriding product plans, and his constant antagonism toward's Dagenham's established proven ways of going about the engineering and building of big cars served only to hamper the Mk 4 project and eventually to destroy almost totally the enthusiasm of the engineers involved – and as a consequence of this friction the Mk 4 suffered further.

In addition to some early testing of an independent rear suspension set-up in a Mk 3 Zephyr 6, from October 1963 onwards there were nine phase 1 prototypes which were actually Ford Fairlanes running with modified underbodies to take the proposed Mk 4 mechanical elements. These were followed by 11 Mk 4 prototypes with the correct body from the beginning of 1965. Overall, according to the company's figures, the prototypes covered approximately 300,000 miles of test running, which included 100,000 miles or so overseas across Europe and in Scandinavia.

Additional testing was conducted over the winter of 1965/66 with pre-production cars assembled by teams of production operatives from mass-produced Mk 4 parts. These tests, which took place on the roads of Essex and East Anglia, always overnight under the cover of darkness, were principally to iron out any production problems before putting the Mk 4 into mass production for public consumption, and were not really concerned with design development. Three production Mk 4s were

The V4 engine looks almost lost in the Mk 4 engine bay. This would appear to be a pre-production car, as there is a mounting plate on the bulkhead and bolt holes near the suspension strut tops to take the bracing piece depicted earlier on a prototype. Possibly this was fitted to some export cars but recent research has failed to confirm this.

completed at the end of December 1965 and by launch day, April 20, 1966, there were already some 8,000 in dealers' showrooms worldwide. Not only cars are required for a new model launch, as sales brochures, leaflets and so on are also vital if everyone's curiosity is to be satisfied, and for the Mk 4 a staggering 450 tons of sales literature had been distributed throughout the dealer network during the previous month.

The schedules had been kept, but some of the Mk 4 programme so far would prove to have been inadequate; a number of detail defects began to show up as the production models were building up mileage in normal service. Also, the car was to display a definite shortcoming in one respect of its road behaviour, and overall there was need for considerable further development before all would be well.

At prices of £933, £1,005, and £1,220, which were again all-in (heater, delivery etc. included) the Mk 4s were between 10% and 16% more expensive than the outgoing models (£836, £909, & £1,048) but taking into account the new specification were perhaps even better sheer value for money than ever before at face value. Certainly, the company were confident enough to predict 80,000 sales worldwide in the first year, with 100,000 annually being the target spoken of thereafter. However, this was not to be. The tremendous public interest shown in these cars at their launch did not translate into tremendous sales. The largest group of potential buyers of a new Mk 4 were of course already driving around in

Zodiac underbonnet layout, with the spare wheel removed. Fears that the spare tyre might suffer deterioration through being 'cooked' in the engine compartment were to prove unfounded.

Zephyrs and Zodiacs, mostly Mk 3s by this time, although still a good number in late Mk 2s, and many of these simply took one look at the Mk 4 and said 'too big'. That it was in fact shorter than the also new Vauxhall Cresta PC series, the Austin Westminster, and the Rover 3-litre was irrelevant; it was slightly wider than all of these, but more important was that it was larger all round than the Mk 3 Ford, and that car was considered quite large enough by more owners than not. Indeed, most who had been driving big Fords for many years considered the older, Mk 2 versions to have been the best all-round package in both their four- and six-cylinder forms, and by comparison the Mk 4 seemed huge.

On the road, of course, with its 3-litre engine the Mk 4 Zodiac would quite comfortably out-accelerate any previous Zodiac, as *Motor* magazine found out when putting a new model through its paces (R/T 16/66). Going from rest to 30mph, 50, 60, 70, 80 and 90mph in 3.5, 7.5, 11.0, 14.2, 20.1 and 28.1 seconds, this car had also covered the standing-start quarter-mile in 17.9 seconds, figures which prompted *Motor* to liken it to the Triumph TR4 sportscar in this respect. Perhaps even more impressive were the top gear/third gear acceleration figures quoted for the usual 20mph increments, 20-40mph in 8.0 seconds/4.8 seconds, 30-50mph 7.1/4.5, 40-60mph 7.0/5.4, and 50-70mph 7.7/6.5 seconds. With a mean lap speed of the test circuit of 102.5mph and a best one-way maximum only 1mph above this, the top speed was little different from the old Mk 3, but that this much livelier, larger-engined and heavier car had returned 18.4mpg overall, and whilst cruising at the legal 70mph maximum speed would manage 21.5mpg, was a pleasant surprise indeed for those contemplating a purchase and spoke well of the efficiency of this Weber-carburettered engine.

By comparison with this, the performance of the Zephyr V6 with only 2½ litres was inevitably something of a disappointment. When tested by *Autocar*, whose report appeared in the issue of April 22, 1966, the 2½-litre car recorded 0-30mph, 50, 60, 70, 80 and 90mph times of 4.6 seconds, 10.6, 14.6, 20.4, 28.7, and 49.1 seconds, whilst requiring 19.6

Zodiac boot. The short tail hid a very large and uniformly shaped luggage compartment.

163

A front bench seat and column gearchange were standard Zephyr equipment, the alternative individual front seats and floor change being extra-cost options. The 'eyeball' vents for the Aeroflow system can be seen on the facia. Protruding below the facia, next to the ignition key, is the handle for the steering column height adjustment.

seconds to cover the standing quarter-mile. Accelerating from 20-40mph, 30-50mph, 40-60mph, and 50-70mph in top gear had required 9.6 seconds, 9.7, 10.7, and 12.0 seconds, whilst covering the same speed ranges in third gear produced figures of 6.1, 6.8, 7.8, and 11.6 seconds. A mean lap speed of 96mph had been achieved, with a surprisingly high 102mph along the most favourable quarter-mile straight. Whilst the Zephyr V6's overall fuel consumption, at 19.4mpg, was 1mpg better than the Zodiac tested, its figure of 20.1mpg for the 70mph cruise was worse by almost 1½mpg, which suggested that the 3-litre car might well prove to be just as economical as the smaller-engined six-cylinder model under most conditions. Of the 3-litre V6 engine itself *Motor* said: 'It always remains smooth, although not as silky as the best straight sixes, but the engine note becames rather looser and harsher as the speed rises over 4,000rpm.' In *Autocar* it was noted of the 2½-litre unit that, 'In terms of smoothness there are no noticeable vibration periods, yet the sweetness of a straight six has been lost somehow, particularly at the top end of the rev range.' Both the Mk 4s tested were equipped with the floor-mounted gearchange, which received praise in both cases but more particularly from *Autocar* whose test staff thought, 'The gearchange is well up to the high standards set by smaller Fords, and in many ways it works and feels just like that of a GT Cortina.'

The Mk 4's behaviour in respect of its independent rear suspension was of course of great interest to many, and it was evident not only from these early road test reports but also from the experiences of a number of owners of the production Mk 4s coming into service that the results on the road were unfortunately not so good as had been hoped for. On the credit side, the ride was extremely level, and although a little on the hard side with the car lightly loaded, became really good indeed with all seats occupied; directional stability was also excellent. With the very important proviso that the rear seats were fully occupied, the cornering capabilities were quite high for this class of car and perhaps even better than the Mk 3 under similar (fully laden) conditions. However, the picture changed considerably for the worse if the front seats only were occupied. In this condition, if the car were cornered at all vigorously, as often as not the

In the Zodiac, a very comprehensive set of instruments faced the driver. The instrument panel, like that of the Zephyrs, was a one-piece phenolic resin moulding, the integral instrument bezels and panel surround having a rather cheap-looking imitation chrome effect which unfortunately did not last well.

165

outside rear wheel would fail to adopt the intended negative camber in the
cornering attitude and instead tuck under on full positive camber. This was
in part due to the static rear wheel camber angles chosen, of which more
later, and also because the weight transfer in the turns imposed down
forces on the outside rear corner which prevented the suspension's
swinging link at that side from moving in the designed manner. The result
would usually be a change from the stable, understeering attitude in which
the car had entered the turn to a sudden and quite pronounced roll-
oversteer, possibly very quickly followed by rear-end breakaway. In
extreme cases, the jacking effect as the outside rear wheel tucked under
was sufficient to raise the inside rear wheel several inches clear of the road,
the car therefore behaving in the very manner of the cheap swing-axle
designs which it had been hoped to avoid. As recovering from this situation
was hampered somewhat by the low-geared steering, even the skilled
quick-thinking driver could find the Mk 4 something of a handful at this
point.

Taking into account that the great majority of cars are driven most of the
time with their rear seats unoccupied, Ford had chosen rear suspension
geometry in which the wheels had very slight positive camber (wheel
leaning outwards at the top) in the static unladen condition, took up a
vertical attitude under normal straight-ahead running with only the front
seats occupied, and only adopted a negative camber attitude with the car
laden at the rear. This geometry would give overall tyre life and wear
characteristics almost as good as those with a conventional beam axle
(where of course the wheels remain upright irrespective of load), much
better than with a swing-axle layout or even a semi-trailing type similar to
the Mk 4 but with the more usually seen unladen negative camber.

166

Consequently it was really only in the well-laden condition that the Mk 4 would enter a turn with its rear wheels already obliged to take up their ideal cornering attitude; hence the car's normally very good behaviour in this laden condition and its unpredictability otherwise. Even though the swinging link mounting was rendered less effective under load than had been anticipated, a change to a slight static negative camber geometry would have overcome much of the early criticism of the Mk 4's handling, at the cost of a small increase in rear tyre wear. But Dagenham were not convinced at this stage that they had got it wrong as there was another problem serving to confuse the issue which does not appear to have been of Ford's making. Many Mk 4 users, including police forces, were complaining of a serious lack of wet road adhesion which affected all four wheels, under even quite gentle driving. This, it was reasoned, simply had to be down to the tyres, and if they were indeed so bad in some cases then it followed that they were no doubt responsible for exaggerating the rear-end breakaway characteristics. Investigations revealed that of the three makes of tyre supplied as original equipment, Firestone, India, and Goodyear, it was the latter which were causing the complaints of poor grip. The Goodyear G8 had been in production since the early 1960s, and was a very popular tyre, but apparently at about the time of the Mk 4's introduction Goodyear changed the specification to a different rubber mix which was proving inferior to the original. Whether the Ford company were informed of this change officially by Goodyear is not clear, but certainly the senior engineers in charge of the Mk 4 were not aware of it. However, identification of these tyres as the cause of the adhesion problem quickly brought about an improved 'Two Star' Goodyear G8, which was immediately fitted to new Mk 4s in production and from October 1966 offered free of charge on an exchange basis to owners whose earlier cars were still running on the inferior tyres.

Quite a few owners however had by this time sorted the situation out for themselves, by scrapping their original tyres and fitting radial-ply ones instead, the Pirelli Cinturato and the Michelin X being popular choices.

Problems with lack of adhesion were encountered by many early Mk 4 users, and Ford experimented with several different tyre fitments, including the Michelin X radial-ply covers seen here. Of the then-conventional cross-ply types evaluated, the Uniroyal Rain Tyre was found to give excellent results on the Mk 4, though it was never adopted as initial equipment.

Actor Stratford Johns, who played Barlow, one of British television's best-known policemen, with the Mk 4 version of the 'Z car'.

Individual front seats were fitted in the police Mk 4 Zephyrs, and the central console housed the radio and switches for the auxiliary equipment.

As in earlier versions, the specially calibrated police speedometer occupied a central location on the facia.

E.D. Abbott were again responsible for the estate car derivations, which this time came with vinyl-covered roofs and featured extensive use of rustless bright metal window trim.

Ford, too, had in fact experimented with the X tyre, successfully it seems, but apparently there were political reasons within the industry preventing a Ford/Michelin tie-up at that time. Interestingly, though, at least one batch of early Mk 4 police cars which had been returned to Dagenham for the rectification of a number of faults, and with accompanying claims of poor adhesion, when subsequently returned to the force arrived with 14in rims of greater offset than standard and fitted with 7.50 x 14 Michelin X covers.

Although the better quality cross-ply tyres were now considered adequate, the radial-ply type seemed to suit the Mk 4's suspension characteristics much better, and so these became listed as optional extra-cost equipment late in 1966, in the 185 x 14 size. The one inch increase in rim size was necessary as, with their lower profiles than cross-plies, the appropriate 13in radials would have lowered the gearing quite considerably; even with the 185 x 14s the mph/1,000rpm came down from 20.0mph to 19.7mph. Either Goodyear G800, Firestone F100, or Pirelli's Cinturato could be specified, and in view of the radial-ply tyre's almost neutral steering characteristics the recommended pressures were changed from the 24psi all round with cross-plies to an understeer-inducing 24psi front/28psi rear.

The availability of a police specification Mk 4 Zephyr from the start did result in a number of examples of this brand-new car immediately going into hard and very intensive use, which proved beneficial from the development angle as mileage build-up was of course much quicker than with privately-owned cars. The batch of cars already referred to belonged to the Cheshire police, and had been returned to Ford for rewiring after one car had suffered a total electrical system burn-out, whilst on others the switches were found to be welding themselves together. The front struts were proving to be a weak point, barely lasting between the 6,000 mile service intervals, and one of the force's mechanics was being employed full-time simply reconditioning MacPherson struts. Gearchange problems required a modification to the gearlever nut at the back of the single rail; there were modifications to the swinging caliper, and the brake discs themselves were proving shortlived under the severity of police use; tappet adjustment was required every 1,000 miles or so; a permanent stock of windscreen wiper arms was needed, as these kept lifting off altogether and

Interior details of what were claimed to be the roomiest estate cars in production in Britain at the time.

being lost; and the window winding mechanism was prone to failure due to rapid wear on the splined drive.

However, that not all Mk 4s were giving serious trouble indicated that basically this design was very sound, but that assembly was not always nearly so good as it should have been (although in fairness this was largely due to unfamiliarity and a very complex car) and that quality control of individual components was uncharacteristically very poor. In respect of the latter, it seems that the 'financial bible' had left little or no safety margins, as apart from its robust bodyshell, the Mk 4 somehow seemed to lack that comforting degree of over-engineering which had characterized so many earlier Fords. In all, therefore, it had been an unhappy debut for this technically advanced and in many ways very impressive car. But the

170

reliability problems were being tackled, and would eventually be largely overcome; and on the bright side there was the debut of Zephyr and Zodiac estate cars and a lavish Executive saloon at the Earls Court Motor Show in October 1966.

These latest Farnham models from E.D. Abbott had of necessity retained the saloon's broad rear quarter panels as these accommodated the extraction arrangements for the car's built-in aeroflow ventilation system, and so the latest estate cars looked rather more of a conversion job and less rakish than had the Mk 3 Farnhams. At £1,379, £1,453 and £1,672 the big Ford estate cars were the most expensive of this type of car being built in Britain, the Zephyrs being undercut by the Humber Hawk estate car at £1,342 whilst the Zodiac was beaten on price by the estate car version of the Humber Super Snipe which was listed at £1,618 and Vauxhall's Cresta at £1,507. However, the Humber large-car range as a whole was soon to disappear without a replacement model, and as BMC were not offering estate car versions of their big sixes, the Ford Mk 4 models only had the Cresta estate car to contend with in this sector in future.

Prices of the three original Mk 4 saloons had been raised slightly by Ford to £949, £1,023 and £1,241, and coming in above these now was the Executive at £1,567. Carrying the all-in theme a stage further than with the corresponding Mk 3 model, the new Executive saloon featured power steering and an opening sunroof in its remarkably comprehensive standard specification. Retaining some feel, the Hydrosteer power steering was fitted in conjunction with a higher ratio steering box of 18.4:1 , and these arrangements, which were also to be available at extra cost on the Zephyr V6 and Zodiac, would generally be judged much better than the standard set up. Of the steel panel sliding type, with hand winding

The luxurious Executive as it first appeared in October 1966. The 'Lincoln Star' on the grille was making its first appearance.

mechanism, the sunroof was of Wilmot Breedon design, and had been tested by Ford under both tropical and polar conditions as well as in a dust tunnel before being adopted for the Executive. No-cost options on this top-of-the-range car were cloth upholstery in place of the standard hide, metallic paint, and the manual gearbox plus overdrive rather than the standard automatic transmission; whilst at extra cost were white-banded sidewall cross-ply tyres or the 185 x 14 radial-ply equipment, the latter costing an extra £18 8s 9d. Cars offering broadly similar roominess and other amenities to the Executive, although without independent rear suspension, were the Vauxhall Viscount at £1,483, the Rover 3-litre automatic at £1,933, and BMC's Westminster-based but Rolls-Royce-engined Vanden Plas 4-litre R for which £2,030 was being asked.

Autocar tested the Executive early in 1967, publishing their report in the issue of May 4. At a laden weight of 31½cwt this car accelerated from rest to 60mph in 13.1 seconds and to 90mph in 39 seconds, these figures being some 2 seconds and 10 seconds inferior to the rather lighter (29.6cwt laden) manual transmission Zodiac tested by *Motor* the previous year. However, the Executive remained a genuine 100mph car, and the fuel consumption of 17.2mpg overall was quite a reasonable figure for a 3-litre automatic car when subjected to one of these inevitably hard-driven test routines. Although commenting about the independent rear suspension, '. . . one cannot help but wonder if a well-located live axle would not have been cheaper and equally effective,' the report nevertheless continued, 'The ride comfort is good, with irregularities being absorbed well by the suspension; on the test car there was some slight harshness caused by the Goodyear G800 radial-ply tyres, which are extra. This could easily be forgiven for the vastly improved grip they gave under all conditions, although on greasy town roads wheelspin going away from traffic lights

The sumptuous Executive interior, this view of a car without doors emphasizing the spaciousness of the Mk 4 passenger compartment.

was provoked too easily.' The Executive's directional stability was such that it ran 'straight as an arrow' on rough and badly surfaced Continental roads, over which it apparently fared much better than a Mk 3 Executive which *Autocar* had taken on the Continent some time earlier.

Apart from on some export cars and those for the police which had featured stiffer heavy-duty road springs from the start, new road springs softer by 20% than the original standard equipment had been introduced into the domestic model specification right across the range in December 1966. This change was in answer to criticism from some that the ride qualities were a little harsh for this class of car; whilst redesigned rear bump-stops introduced at the same time were to reduce roll stiffness and so lessen that tendency towards sudden oversteer which had also resulted in complaints. Whether the Executive tested by *Autocar*, which was a 1966-registered car, included these modifications is not clear, but whatever, it seems likely that only very few buyers would have got the benefit of these changes rightaway as many of the 50,000 Mk 4s built during 1966 were languishing in compounds and dealers' showrooms well into 1967. This situation inevitably resulted in drastic cutbacks in Mk 4 production as the year progressed. There was certainly more to this than just antipathy towards the Mk 4 range however, as big-car sales generally were falling rapidly, in part due no doubt to the ever expanding variety of well-appointed medium-sized models such as the Triumph 2000/2500 series, the Rover 2000, and Ford's own Corsair range which included a comprehensively equipped 2-litre executive model.

In a determined effort to boost Mk 4 sales, Ford reorganized and expanded the Zephyr/Zodiac range in time for the October 1967 Motor Show, with a series of revisions which included some price cutting, the introduction of De Luxe versions of the Zephyrs; and a most beneficial change to the rear suspension throughout the range. The standard model Zephyr and Zephyr V6 were now reduced in price to £906 and £980 without any reduction in their equipment level, but with the deletion of the individual front seat and floor gearchange extra-cost option. At £961 and £1,035 the new De Luxe Zephyrs featured the fixed-back individual front seats and floor gearchange as standard (with no bench seat, column change option) and were trimmed in a superior grade of vinyl to that of the cheaper cars. The 185 x 14 radial-ply tyres were standardized on these De Luxe Zephyrs, which could also be identified by their own grille design making its appearance at the front. Both the former radial-ply tyres and power steering options were now included in the Zodiac as standard

A year or so later, and the Executive now has a bonnet motif and 14in wheels with radial-ply tyres.

equipment, accompanied by a slight price rise in this instance of £41 to a tax-paid total of £1,282, whereas on the Executive the price remained at £1,567 despite the adoption here too of the 185 x 14 tyres and rims.

This move towards radial tyres with their generally heavier steering characteristics resulted in a change of steering ratio on the manual steering Zephyrs to an extremely low-geared 23.5:1 which meant more than six turns of the steering wheel were required between the extremes of lock. At the rear came the revised suspension geometry which the car should really have had from the start, as it at last gave a slight negative camber to the rear wheels in the static unladen condition: on the road it would now require a violent change of direction, or attempts at extremely fast cornering, to 'catch out' the outside rear wheel and find it tucking under.

It must have been particularly disappointing to Ford, therefore, after having submitted a Zephyr De Luxe to *Autocar* for a road test report, to see the car pictured in the magazine (August 15, 1968) being cornered very hard with the outside rear wheel tucked under and its opposite number some inches above the ground. However, this had occurred, '. . . at the limit on a closed track,' and overall the report was not really critical of the rear suspension which, it was thought, '. . . provides a comfortable ride, in a swooping, soft sort of way.' As the car under scrutiny was a four-cylinder model, there at last appeared a set of performance figures for the lowest-powered Mk 4, which were quite impressive for what was after all a rather heavy 2-litre car. From rest to 60, 70 and 80mph was accomplished in 17.7, 26.9 and 44.7 seconds, with the Zephyr V4 continuning to a mean maximum speed of 95mph, and a best only 1mph short of the magic three figures. Acceleration in the high top gear was inevitably rather leisurely with 30-50, 40-60 and 50-70mph requiring 12.6, 14.3 and 18.4 seconds in this ratio, but third gear offered a considerable improvement over top in this respect right up to 70mph, the corresponding figures here being 8.3, 9.8 and 15.2 seconds. An overall fuel consumption for the 1,238-mile test distance of only 21.1mpg suggested that this Zephyr had been driven hard for much of the time; in contrast the constant-speed mpg figures in top gear were excellent, with 32mpg being recorded at 60mph and a most creditable 21.5mpg when the V4-engined car was cruising at as high a speed as 80mph.

Revamping the Mk 4 range had paid off, with production increasing late in 1967 from a one-month low of 948 cars in July to above the 2,000 per month rate for November and December, this level in fact being maintained on average throughout 1968.

Although in general terms it was by this time a reasonably reliable model, and certainly of good build quality, the Mk 4 was not yet fully sorted. As mileages had built up there had proved to be a number of design weaknesses in the V engines, which despite some attention had not been fully eradicated. Excessive tappet noise was due on the one hand to the rocker arms quickly going out of adjustment and on the other to rapid wear on the bottom of the pushrods. These were hollow tubes of which the end was simply turned over to form the bottom end, and this would quite soon

The Zephyr De Luxe interior, showing the revised Aeroflow outlets with adjustable flap valves which were introduced throughout the range in October 1967. The padded steering wheel seen here denotes a post-October 1968 car.

Six-cylinder Mk 4 cars with an overall length stretched to exactly 18ft to increase passenger carrying capacity were produced by Coleman Milne of Bolton, Lancashire. Early versions were called Diplomat but this title gave way to Dorchester for the Zephyr V6 conversion and Grosvenor for the extended Zodiac. 1969 prices were £2,788 and £3,460, excellent value to large companies, embassies, funeral directors and the like, and several hundred examples were sold through distributors Stormont Engineering of Tunbridge Wells. The only mechanical change was a longer prop shaft, specially balanced by Hardy Spicer, so the Ford warranty still applied to the running gear, whilst Coleman Milne and Stormont operated a bodywork guarantee.

wear away completely, so making accurate valve adjustment very difficult. A redesigned locknut, improved oil feed and, later, redesigned rocker arms would eventually cure these problems completely.

More disturbing was too high an incidence of failed cylinder head gaskets, and similar failures of the gasket for the water-heated inlet manifold. As either of these failures could result in water mixing with the lubricating oil there were numerous cases of confused diagnosis, and therefore many cylinder heads being needlessly removed. The complex inlet manifold gasket was a tricky one to fit correctly and great care was needed if trouble was to be avoided. The head gasket problem was baffling, as so short and stiff an engine should have been absolutely trouble-free in this respect. Changes in the gasket specification and later slight changes in the block and head castings to further increase the stiffness largely overcame this problem. But, according to some mechanics, it was not a fault in the engine, rather a result of incomplete attention being given to it at the free-of-charge 600-mile service following

A conversion of a quite different sort transformed this Zodiac into a high-speed stretcher carrier for ambulance duties.

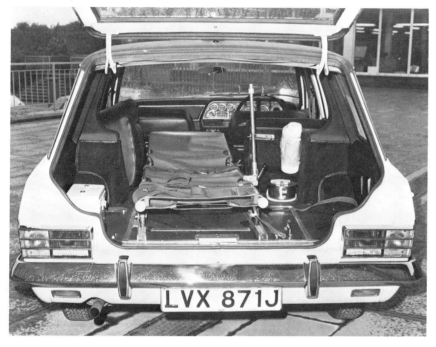

An ingenious tilting and swivelling rear seat section allowed space to accommodate a stretcher.

running-in. With this compact unit installed at the back of the large engine compartment the rearmost cylinder head bolts were rather inaccessible to anyone and extremely difficult to reach for someone of small stature, and it is reckoned that on many Mk 4s these bolts were never tightened down as instructed at that first important service. Bearing this out is the fact that Mk 4s with a blown gasket were very often found to have cylinder head bolts little more than finger tight, and they also tended either to suffer from this problem at relatively low mileages or not at all.

The engine overheating often caused by these gasket problems is also thought by some to have been a contributory factor towards another too-frequent failing on this engine, that of a stripped timing gear. A boil-up certainly could 'cook' the fibre timing wheel, rendering it too brittle to withstand much further use before the teeth would strip. Such a failure was of course usually disastrous, as with the flat cylinder head design any valves remaining open were contacted by the pistons as they reached the top of

177

their stroke. Equally disastrous was the loss of oil pump drive which occurred when the corners of the hexagonal driveshaft became rounded off by wear. The onset of serious wear in the shaft could sometimes be detected by a tendency to slow pressure build-up after starting the engine, but there were occasions when total failure was quite sudden – and expensive. Although remaining of basically similar design, modified oil pumps and driveshafts were introduced late in 1968.

From November 1967 the automatic transmission option had been changed to the Borg-Warner Model 35 gearbox, but on the 3-litre cars there was a reversion to the Ford C4 for a period from late in 1968. This appears to have had something to do with police requirements; at that time several forces were taking delivery of specially converted four-wheel-drive Zephyrs from Harry Ferguson Research Ltd, whose development work on the project had begun with a C4-equipped car. These 4WD cars were not a part of Ford's own Mk 4 programme but were nonetheless extremely interesting and important – see Chapter 8.

Ford continued with detail improvements throughout the Mk 4 range: in October 1968 came a safety-type padded steering wheel, and for some export markets the availability of dual-line brakes. An improvement to the engine's cooling system early in 1969 was the deletion of the remote header tank; this had shown a tendency to develop cracks at its mounting point, although water loss from here was usually only slow seepage. The revised system had the filler cap directly on the thermostat housing, with a tube to a plastic bottle which accommodated any overflow due to expansion and from which the radiator would automatically be replenished as the system cooled.

By this time purchase tax increases had raised car prices in Britain, with the cheapest four-cylinder Zephyr now listed at £975, whilst £1,714 would now be required to purchase a Ford Executive. The most expensive Mk 4 however was not as might be expected the Executive saloon, but the Zodiac estate car, at £1,862, an example of which complete with the optional overdrive, which added a further £58 to the price, was tested by *Motor* during the summer of 1969 (R/T No. 42/69). Commenting that this estate car was almost £460 more expensive than a Zodiac saloon, *Motor* continued, 'For this you get an extremely comfortable hold-all with none of the draughts, squeaks and rattles which go with some of the less expensive car/van compromises and one which retains all the cosiness and amenities of a luxury saloon . . . . As the price suggests it is an estate car in the grand manner and one likely to remain sufficiently uncommon to carry prestige appeal in addition to its considerable practical value.' In respect of this car's handling and braking, it was noted, 'Power steering is standard on the Zodiac and generally well liked by our drivers. Requiring $4\frac{1}{2}$ turns from lock to lock, it still feels too low geared and calls for excessive winding in confined spaces; it does offer some resistance to wheel movement, which goes a long way to correct the sensation of insecurity engendered by the extreme lightness of some systems . . . the driver tends to be discouraged from fast cornering by the suspension softness and sheer size though, thanks to the larger wheels, radial tyres and the revised rear suspension camber settings, cornering power is now quite high and the car can be hustled round twisty roads briskly . . . the once alarming tendency for the tail to slide when a bump or wave raised it and changed the camber angles has been reduced and was seldom noticed . . . . The brakes are extremely good – powerful, light and progressive. Barely 70lb pressure was necessary for a straight-line stop of better than 1g.' Loaded to

Late Zodiacs were distinguished externally by their new wheel-arch trim and a waistline rubbing strip . . .

. . . whilst inside, the Zodiac had now acquired the walnut veneer instrument panel previously reserved for the Executive.

31½cwt, this Zodiac reached 60mph and 90mph from rest in 12.7 and 34.1 seconds, and when accelerated hard in top gear covered each of the 20mph increments from 20-40mph through to 50-70mph in either 8.7 or 8.8 seconds, so amply demonstrating as ever the even torque delivery of the 3-litre Essex V6. Recorded in overdrive, the mean lap speed of a banked circuit was exactly 100mph, with a best 103.3mph being seen along the most favourable straight. All of this was accompanied by an overall fuel consumption of 21.0mpg, and 24mpg when being cruised in overdrive at 70mph – excellent figures, both, for such a powerful and heavy estate car. In all, this was the most impressive test report of the Mk 4 so far, and that *Motor's* testers had generally enjoyed their spell with this car could be detected in parts of the report. This perhaps indicated that the attention given to further development since its introduction meant that the

179

The Executive, in turn, had additional walnut interior trim for 1970/71, including door cappings.

Mk 4 was now maturing into something like the car it should have been from the start.

The effects of inflationary economic policies were now being felt in Britain, with the motor industry being affected to the extent of a 20% drop in new car sales over the first half of 1969 by comparison with the same period the previous year. Sales figures showed the Mk 4 at number 17 in the 'top twenty' chart, its 8,639 sales for the six months putting it slightly ahead of its Ford Corsair stablemate (8,221 sales) and the Triumph 2000/2500 range which had found 7,702 buyers over the same six months. Vauxhall's similarly sized rivals to the big Fords, the PC Cresta and Viscount, with 5,352 sales, were just outside the top twenty league.

Although it was already undercut in the price lists by Vauxhall's Cresta and luxury Viscount, Ford had sufficient confidence in the Mk 4 to plan some further refinements for the 1970 models which would necessitate increases in the order of 5% to the prices being asked. The accent was to be on more comfort and luxury. Further enhancing the ride qualities were slightly softer rear springs, whilst an even quieter ride was being assured now by improved door seals designed to reduce wind noise. Better side support on the individual front seats of the De Luxe Zephyrs was achieved by changes to the padding of both cushions and squabs, and on all the Zephyrs a heated rear window became an optional extra item. On the Zodiac and Executive the heated rear window was being introduced as standard equipment, and inside these cars the Zodiac had acquired the Executive-style walnut instrument panel, whilst on the Executive the polished walnut treatment had been extended to include the passenger side of the facia and door cappings throughout. Exclusive to the Zodiac and Executive was the introduction of a bright metal rubbing strip along the full length of the car and bright metal wheelarch cappings, which served to identify these latest editions of the two top Fords.

Announced in October 1969, these changes were accompanied by price rises ranging from £52 to £81, which resulted in list prices for the Mk 4 saloons of £1,027 and £1,115 for the four-cylinder model in its standard and De Luxe guises; £1,110 and £1,197 for the corresponding

180

Zephyr V6 cars; and £1,477 and £1,795 for the Zodiac and Executive. Estate cars could be purchased in any of the foregoing configurations except Executive form, and added £457 to the price of the corresponding saloon. By comparison, Vauxhall's Cresta and Cresta De Luxe saloons were listed at £1,107 and £1,196, at which they approximated very closely to the V6 Zephyrs in equipment level but thanks to their 3.3-litre engines offered rather more speed and acceleration than did the 2½-litre Fords, although they were still unable quite to match a Zodiac in terms of performance. As its price suggests, at £1,573 the Vauxhall Viscount came somewhere between the Zodiac and Executive in equipment level, and included automatic transmission and power steering as standard. Front seat belts were included in the Vauxhall prices now, whereas these were only standard as yet on the Executive; Ford remained, however, the only manufacturer to include delivery in the list price of its cars. BMC had relinquished much of their share of the market for big sixes the previous year, having replaced the Austin A110 Westminster and its plushy Wolseley 6/110 derivative with the completely new but ill-conceived Austin 3-litre which had lost all the 'class' of its predecessors and which, at £1,507 and £1,592 in standard and De Luxe variations, was struggling for survival.

In day to day usage there were really only a couple of irritations now remaining in the Mk 4's make-up, these being the inconsistency of the automatic choke on some cars, and the fact that the handbrake was often inoperative because of the ingress of dirt into the mechanism of the

1971 Ford Executive: the end of the line as far as all-British big Fords were concerned. Future models would be very definitely Ford of Europe projects.

swinging calipers. It was a pity, though, that Dagenham had not seen fit to redesign the engine's timing gear, as the fibre wheel was a definite weakness which could and still occasionally did result in the sudden disintegration of a healthy engine due to the stripping of the fibre teeth. Even so, whilst not generally matching the reliability and longevity of the earlier big Fords, the Mk 4 was just as reliable as the next car in 1970, and better in this respect now than many. And its specification was still remarkably advanced for a four-year old model. Several hundred pounds more were required to buy into the Jaguar XJ6 or Rover V8 league, so at their prices the Zodiac and Executive were very tempting cars and were indeed now earning some esteem as prestige models. The Mk 4 range as a whole was well placed to take the healthiest share of the big-car market in Britain for the forseeable future.

Some consideration was given to a further revision of the rear suspension, on which the restricted movement of the swinging link, which has already been mentioned, remained the eventual limiting factor in the car's cornering behaviour. Designed to replace this link was a large diameter bush, voided each side of its centre in the horizontal plane to allow the wishbone the full desired fore-and-aft movement, but solid above and below its centre. This attachment would have been immune from the effects of weight transfer and should, it would seem, have realised the full potential of this Ford independent rear suspension, but in the event it was not adopted. The changes already introduced, such as the shorter bump stops, the revised camber angles particularly, and even the more recent slightly softer rear springs, had combined to improve the car's capabilities to the extent that the cornering speeds at which it became unpredictable were now rather higher than most would care to use on the road anyway with such a large and comfortably sprung car. Also, the Mk 4 was getting towards the end of its production run, and its replacement was to be a somewhat different car of which much of the design work was being carried out elsewhere than at Dagenham.

In November 1971 came the Zephyr Special, a limited edition model of just 1,000 examples marking the end of a production run for the Mk 4 range which had lasted almost six years. Based on the Zephyr V6 De Luxe saloon, this Special had additional equipment comprising a heated rear window, push-button radio, fabric upholstery, rear centre armrest, overriders, and wing mirrors. Finished in a unique Uranium Blue paint, which was a rich metallic blue, with a parchment-coloured vinyl covering for the roof and rear quarter panels, and Zodiac style wheeltrims, the Zephyr Special was a most distinctive 'last of the line'.

By this time Ford of Britain had lost its autonomy as a design and manufacturing unit, and was on its way quickly to becoming a totally integrated part of the Ford Europe organization which had come into being in 1968, in which the ideas emanating from both Dagenham and Ford of Germany in Cologne would be pooled to provide European, rather than both British and German Fords in the future. The Mk 4's replacement, therefore, the first of the Granadas, whilst featuring the Essex V power units for the British market, was otherwise a rather Teutonic affair; it even had wishbone front suspension rather than MacPherson struts!

CHAPTER 6

Racing and rallying

The big Fords in competition

Henry Ford always felt that car racing successes were good publicity, and around the turn of the century he built and successfully raced cars of his own design in an effort to interest potential investors in his ideas. In January 1904, when the Ford Motor Company was only six months old, he announced that he was going to break the world speed record for the flying mile, in order to put the name of his products into the record books and, hopefully, boost the sales of the infant Ford Motor Company. The record attempt was to take place on the frozen Lake St Clair, which was situated just to the north east of Detroit, and cinders from a nearby power station were strewn across the perfectly flat ice surface so that the tyres would have something to grip. On the bitterly cold morning of January 12, at the wheel of one of his 'home made' racers which he had built two years previously, Henry Ford covered the one-mile course in 39 seconds to set a new world speed record for the distance at 91.4mph.

In 1909, a transcontinental endurance race from New York to Seattle, a distance of 4,106 miles, was being widely publicized, and Henry Ford could not resist the temptation to enter the recently introduced Model T. The cars left the starting line in New York on June 1, and 22 days later the Model T crossed the finishing line in Seattle 17 hours ahead of the second-place car, to be greeted by a smiling Henry Ford.

In the years between the two world wars, Fords, or Ford-engined 'specials' of a variety of descriptions, could be seen contesting virtually every kind of motoring event from the Indianapolis 500 to the Monte Carlo Rally. In Britain, club trials were a popular activity for the sporting motorist in the inter-war years, and this kind of competition eventually gave birth to the famous Ford V8-based Allard cars. In the late 1940s, while the planners at Dagenham were working in secrecy on the new Consul and Zephyr Six, the familiar side-valve-engined Fords were back in action at both local and international level. In the hands of Ken Wharton, an export model 10hp Anglia scored outright victory in the 1949 Dutch International Tulip Rally, and the following year Wharton repeated the achievement, this time at the wheel of a V8 Pilot.

With this sort of background it was inevitable that once production was under way the new Consul and Zephyr Six would soon find themselves on the starting grid, and indeed, on the weekend of March 3, 1951, in the North Staffordshire Motor Club's Burnham-on-Sea Rally, a Consul in the

Ken Wharton brings his Consul into the pits at Zandvoort, having just won the 1952 Tulip Rally.

hands of P. J. Collins won the saloon car class in what appears to have been the model's competition debut. Later in the year a Zephyr Six driven by J. R. Smith won the up-to-3,000cc closed car category in the *Daily Express* National Rally.

The entry list for the 1952 Monte Carlo Rally included several Zephyr Sixes, one of which was entered by the experienced Ken Wharton. However, Wharton's Monte came to an abrupt end when the Zephyr left the road and rolled over four-and-a-half times down an embankment before coming to rest upside-down on top of a Citroen, which itself was on top of a Simca. Meanwhile, R. Nelleman, in another Zephyr, kept going well to finish 20th overall in what proved to be a tough event with more than half of the 328 starters failing to finish. Happily, Ken Wharton and his crew were unhurt, and in April Wharton was back in action looking for his third Tulip Rally win. The engine capacity classes and the handicaps imposed on these classes varied considerably from one event to another, and often from year to year, whilst generally being biased in favour of the smaller-engined cars. One of the categories in the 1952 Tulip was up-to-1,600cc and Wharton entered the 1,508cc Consul in this class. The road section of the Tulip was punctuated with special stages on which much higher average speeds were imposed, and additional tests in which bonus marks could be earned and used to offset penalties incurred for lateness on the road or special stages, the final test being a 10-lap race for each class on the Zandvoort Grand Prix circuit. The first of the tests on the 1952 Tulip was a 5-mile mountain hill-climb abounding with hairpin bends, and Ken Wharton took the Consul up in an excellent 8 minutes 26 seconds. Another test, held on the perimeter track at Schipol Airport, involved zig-zagging in and out of pylons in top gear all the way, with an observer sitting beside the driver and holding a rope around the clutch pedal, and so the Consul engine's flexibility was particularly useful here. At the end of the road section the Consul still had a clean sheet plus 18 bonus marks, and needed maximum bonus points in the final race to score outright victory in

The Gatsonides/Worledge car under preparation for the 1953 Monte. The rear seat was removed for the rally to allow the passenger seat to recline into a comfortable sleeping position.

the rally. This entailed being in the lead at the half-way (5 laps) stage and continuing to win. Ken Wharton made a great start, by the half-way stage had the whole of the finishing straight to himself, and when the Consul took the chequered flag to win the beautiful silver Tulip Trophy, it had actually lapped some of the tail-end cars.

Following up Ken Wharton's success, the Ford Motor Company established a small Competitions Department, with E. A. 'Edgy' Fabris as Competitions Manager, and headquarters at the premises of Lincoln Cars (a Dagenham subsidiary which imported American Fords into Britain) on the Great West Road at Brentford, where a small team of mechanics would now prepare works rally entries. Well-known trials driver T. C. 'Cuth'

The Gatsonides/Worledge Zephyr on the final mountain circuit above Monte Carlo.

185

Harrison took a works Zephyr on the Lisbon Rally in November, and although not gaining an award on this occasion, the name of Harrison was nevertheless to become almost synonymous with competition Zephyrs in future years. The experienced Dutch rally driver, Maurice Gatsonides, with eight Monte Carlo Rallies already behind him, including a second place overall in 1950, felt that the Zephyr would be an ideal choice for the tough mountain circuit final stage that so often decided the Monte Carlo winner, and so he approached Ford about the possibility of a works drive in the 1953 event. At this time the Monte regulations did not allow any changes whatsoever in the mechanical specification which would improve the performance, handling or braking, so the modifications incorporated in the works Zephyrs were restricted to those directly affecting crew comfort and convenience. In the interest of weight saving, 'Gatso' decided on just a two-man crew instead of the three which were more normal for the Monte in those days, and so the Zephyr's front bench seat was replaced with bucket seats, the one for the passenger being fully reclining so as to enable Gatsonides and co-driver Peter Worledge to get plenty of sleep and remain fatigue-free on the five-day-long event. A comprehensively-equipped additional instrument panel was mounted centrally on the dashboard to keep the crew informed of engine oil pressure, oil and water temperature and so on. Special snow tyres, supplied by retreading experts Tyresoles, of Wembley, were fitted to the rear wheels. These tyres featured a very bold lugged tread pattern with a central groove around the periphery into which a motorcycle chain could be fitted in a matter of a minute or so if necessary for driving on ice, although, as these tyres were moulded in a softer than standard rubber compound, adhesion on ice proved to be excellent and the chains were not in fact used on the rally. The spare wheel was also equipped with a snow tyre, whereas the front rims were fitted with a pair of

standard Tyresoles retreads. A large adjustable anti-glare shield, designed by Gatsonides himself, was fitted over the twin fog lamps, and this completed the rally specification.

On Tuesday, January 20, 404 competitors left seven different starting points across Britain, Scandinavia and Europe, and headed for Monte Carlo. 'Gatso' had chosen the Monte Carlo starting point, and the Zephyr

★ **1953**

★ **MONTE**

★ **CARLO**

★ **RALLY**

★ **WINNER**

The outright win by the exciting Zephyr-Six in the Monte Carlo Rally gives the most convincing proof of its reliability, safety, comfort and outstanding performance. The Zephyr-Six is a car with style, a responsiveness, that very few cars in the world can give you . . . and certainly no cars in *this* price range

ZEPHYR-SIX **£532** PLUS PURCHASE TAX **£297.1.1**

Ford **'FIVE-STAR' MOTORING**

THE BEST AT LOWEST COST

Opposite: Ford advertising made the most of the 1953 Monte win. Above: Nancy Mitchell prepares to start the 1953 Tulip Rally, but no awards were won by the Zephyrs on this occasion. Later in the year driving the same car, Mrs Mitchell finished sixth overall and won the Ladies' Cup on the Lisbon Rally. Left: another good result in 1953 was outright victory in the Norwegian Viking Rally for this Zephyr driven by Carsten Johansson, seen here in the final tests, the car having already been cleaned by the jubilant driver in anticipation of his win. Another Zephyr finished third overall and three more were in the top 25 out of 79 entrants and 59 finishers.

first crossed the Alpes Maritimes and the Dauphin Alpes on its way to the Geneva control, from where the route led through Luxembourg, Holland, Belgium and France. Conditions deteriorated after leaving Paris, and the route between St fleur, Le Puy and Valence was covered with old, hard-packed, frozen snow. Commenting on this stage after the rally, co-driver Worledge said: 'Conditions were really bad. It was an ever-twisting road for 150 kilometres and "Gatso" had to drive like mad. Rounding one bend we saw a tractor towing a load of straw over a narrow bridge. The driver turned his tractor into a ditch and the man with him threw himself on top of the load. We shot past but grazed the nearside of the car along the bridge parapet'. The Zephyr arrived at Valence with just 3 minutes to spare, and from there motored on to arrive at Monte Carlo unpenalized. The final mountain circuit stage was 47 miles long and broken into six sections, all of which had to be covered at precisely the same average speed so that time could not be gained on an 'easy' section to compensate for losses on some of the hairpin bend stages, where the timing was almost impossible. In the event, 'Gatso' drove almost to perfection in the mountains, his total time error over the 47 miles being just 2 seconds, and so the Zephyr Six was the winner of the 1953 Monte Carlo Rally. Very close behind in second place was the famed Ian Appleyard in a Mk VII Jaguar, and a little further down the list in 12th place overall was another works Zephyr, in the hands of Cuth Harrison.

In contrast, in the RAC Rally in March, the Zephyrs finished well down the field, and this was followed only a month later by a disastrous Tulip Rally for the Ford team. With just the 10 laps of the Zandvoort circuit to complete, the works Zephyrs were vying with the works Sunbeam-Talbots for the team prize, and Nancy Mitchell was in the lead for the Ladies' Cup in

her Zephyr. However, at the pre-race scrutineering the Zephyrs and the Sunbeams were disqualified on technical grounds as the Zephyrs were fitted with non-standard oil filters, and the Sunbeams with modified brake drums. This was apparently due to nothing more than misinterpretation of the regulations, and the disqualifications were in no way an attempt to deny the British entries the major awards, as in fact they handed the team prize to the Jowett Javelins, one of which was also the outright winner of the rally.

Cuth Harrison on his way to winning the saloon car category in the 1954 RAC Rally. Many contemporary cars, and indeed some much later models, would lift the inside rear wheel well clear of the ground at cornering forces such as these, and were thus far less controllable than the Zephyr in extreme circumstances. Photo from the Edward Harrison collection.

The regulations for the 1954 Monte allowed modified engines for the first time in this event, although additional handicapping was imposed on those cars so equipped. The works Zephyrs were entered in the modified category, running with a high-compression cylinder head and triple SU carburettors. The routes from all starting points finally converged on Valence, from where the competitors continued to the control at Gap. The final 164 miles from Gap to Monte Carlo formed a tightly timed regularity test, the most difficult section being the ascent and descent of the loose gravel-surfaced Col des Leques. The Zephyrs were apparently the most spectacular cars on the Col, according to *The Autocar's* report: 'The Zephyrs particularly travelled faster than any ordinary motorist would dare attempt. T. C. Harrison was typical of this Zephyr contingent, going into a corner just after the summit at what seemed an impossible speed. However, he was checked by a Daimler being driven more slowly and must have been almost blinded by the dust. Sydney Henson's Zephyr was also baulked, this time by a Sunbeam-Talbot'. The regularity section was in place of the previous year's mountain circuit, and the final stage at Monte Carlo this year was five timed laps round the Monaco Grand Prix circuit for the highest placed 100 cars. Seven Zephyrs, including some private entries, were in the top 100, the best placed being the works-entered cars of Jack Reece (14th) and Cuth Harrison (15th). In the speed test Harrison put up the fifth fastest lap of the 100 competitors, and this performance lifted him to 13th overall in the final reckoning. For the RAC British Rally in

March, Cuth Harrison was at the wheel of the same Zephyr, XNO 496, although it was now with a standard cylinder head and single carburettor, as modified cars were not eligible for this event in 1954. Harrison put up an excellent show, winning the saloon car category outright and gaining third place overall behind two Triumph TR2s. The Zephyr was also a member of the winning team, sharing this award with the works-entered Anglias of Jack Reece and Nancy Mitchell.

Both Consuls and Zephyrs featured in the entry list of the 1954 Dutch International Tulip Rally. Cuth Harrison, once again in XNO 496, with his son Edward as co-driver, built up an early lead in the up-to-2,600cc class, whilst a Jowett Javelin held the two Consuls of Jack Reece and W. Fleetwood at bay in the 1,600cc category. By the half-way stage Harrison was in fourth place overall behind an Alfa Romeo, a Porsche and a Jaguar, when he 'lost' the Zephyr on an apparently unexpected icy patch in the Ardennes and the car ended up in a snowbank. The Zephyr was undamaged, but the time lost was sufficient to put the Harrison duo out of the running for major awards, and the renowned Sheila Van Damm now led the 2,600cc class in her works Sunbeam-Talbot. By the end of the road section, the two Consuls had pulled ahead of the Javelin and in fact were now so far in front in this class that their 10-lap race at Zandvoort was just a formality to see which of them would win the class — in the event it was Jack Reece. Reg Philips had brought his Zephyr up to share the 2,600cc class lead with Sheila Van Damm, although with the cars running in standard form it was generally thought that the faster Sunbeam-Talbot would beat the Zephyr at Zandvoort. Philips handed over the Zephyr to his co-driver Denis Scott for the all important race. As expected, Sheila Van Damm took an early lead, but what the Sunbeam could gain on the straights the Zephyr could pull back in the turns, and Scott was giving a masterly display of the Zephyr's superb handling qualities, sometimes bringing the Zephyr within striking distance of the faster car out in front. Then, right at the end of the 26-mile race, almost incredibly it emerged that Scott had been keeping something in reserve, and he brought the Zephyr

192

Cuth and Edward Harrison with their wire-wheel Zephyr on the 1954 Alpine Rally. Photo from the Edward Harrison collection.

through beautifully on the last turn to take the chequered flag literally by inches, to win the class for Ford. Denis Scott's display completed a brilliant hat-trick for Ford in this event, for in addition to Jack Reece's class win in the Consul, Maurice Gatsonides had taken the 1,300cc GT category with a twin-carburettor Anglia.

Unfortunately, the Ford works cars were unable to contest every major event at this time, as the Competitions Department was running on an extremely tight budget. Whilst competition successes certainly added

Jack Reiss swings his Zephyr Six round a pylon in the final test on the 1954 RAC Morecambe Rally. RNW 2 featured a fully-modified engine, with high-compression cylinder head and single-piece copper gasket, double valve springs, triple SU carburettors, and six-branch exhaust system. It was a regular sight at northern rallies, races and sprints for a number of years during the 1950s. Photo from the Jack Reiss collection.

prestige to the Company's name, these same successes could not result in an increase in overall sales at a time when Ford agents everywhere had waiting lists of customers for every model in the range, and so Dagenham simply could not justify a large expenditure on ventures which, even though successful, meant no financial gain whatsoever. This situation certainly did not make things easy for Edgy Fabris and his team at Lincoln Cars, or for the works drivers, who were not always getting the back-up which some other competitors enjoyed. The results gained so far were all the more creditable when related to the limited finances available.

One important event which had not been contested so far by the works team was the famous Alpine Rally, although motoring journalist Bill McKenzie had done well with a Zephyr in the early stages of this event in 1952, before retiring following a crash as a result of braking problems. Cuth Harrison borrowed a Zephyr, XNO 496 again, from the Competitions Department and entered it privately for the 1954 Alpine. One of the biggest problems facing drivers in this event was the almost inevitable brake fade which occurred as a result of the succession of high-speed descents of Alpine passes, and Cuth Harrison sought to overcome this problem by converting the hubs on XNO 496 to take wire wheels, which would allow more cooling air around the brake drums. However, the wheels chosen did not stand up well to the violent cornering tactics employed on the rally by Cuth and Edward Harrison, and with broken spokes becoming a problem the Zephyr was pulled out of the event in the Dolomites.

In August, Nancy Mitchell borrowed another works Zephyr and entered it privately in the tough Liège-Rome-Liège. There were only four British entries in the 99-strong field, and the almost impossible schedule laid down managed to reduce the number of finishers to just 34, one of which was the lone Zephyr in 28th position. Whilst Nancy Mitchell was pressing the Zephyr hard across Europe, another Zephyr put up a remarkable performance in the 12-hour American endurance race held at Linden New Jersey Airport on August 22. The Zephyr, a 1952 model purchased secondhand by Bob Bathhurst only a few weeks before the race, was the only Ford in the field of 39, which was made up of an assortment including 18 Jaguars, several Austin-Healeys, Porsches and MGs and an Aston Martin. The Zephyr ran trouble-free, making only five pit stops for fuel and oil/water checks during the 12-hour stint. Only 20 cars lasted the 12 hours, and at the end the Zephyr was placed fourth overall behind three surviving Jaguars.

The list of starters for the 1955 Monte revealed that 22 of the big Fords were bidding for honours, 19 of which were the six-cylinder Zephyrs and Zodiacs. A strong works contingent was included in this number with the now familiar names of Cuth Harrison, Denis Scott, Jack Reece and Reg Philips in modified Zephyrs, and the well-known competition driver Sydney Allard with a standard Zodiac. BBC commentator Raymond Baxter was covering the rally from Reg Philips' Zephyr. Notable amongst the private entries was G. N. 'Gerry' Burgess. In the previous year's event he had participated as co-driver in J. Risk's Zephyr, and had been suitably impressed with both the event and the excellent performance of the car. Soon after this he purchased a brand new Zephyr himself, and it was this car which he entered for the 1955 rally, with the experienced Ian Walker as his co-driver. The Zephyr was running in the standard category, and as a private entry did not qualify for any works support. Preparation was limited to little more than a thorough routine-type service so as to ensure that the car was in optimum standard condition. Two spare wheels, shod with snow tyres, were carried in addition to the car's four Michelin Xs which Gerry Burgess favoured for normal use. At almost the very last moment, co-driver Ian Walker was forced to withdraw and he suggested Peter Easton as substitute. Burgess had chosen Monte Carlo as his starting point, and on the way to Dover he picked up Peter Easton, whom he was meeting for the first time. Road conditions in Kent were bad, with snow falling in blizzard proportions, and abandoned vehicles were causing serious obstructions in many parts. Easton took over in order to familiarize himself with the Zephyr under adverse conditions and was desperately unlucky to be confronted with an unlit vehicle which had been abandoned by its driver. In the collision that ensued the Zephyr sustained extensive front end damage and was in no condition to continue to the start. The Ford Agents, Haynes of Ashford, did a wonderful 'instant' front-end repair job, and later the next day the Zephyr and its crew were once more on the way to Dover, and then to Monte Carlo for the start.

As the rally got under way, bad weather conditions in Britain and across Europe ensured that whichever starting point had been chosen, no competitor would have an easy run. Secret checks along the route were an added hazard, and as the cars began to converge on Monte Carlo at the end of the 2,000-mile-long road section not one had escaped incurring penalty points. Cars in the 'modified' category had to make up an 8% penalty over their standard counterparts on the timed sections, and this had generally proved to be too much to ask on the hard-packed snow and ice which had prevailed over much of the route. Consequently, it was the standard models which were occupying the leading positions at this stage. The Burgess/Easton Zephyr had had a good run and on arrival at Monte

Gerry Burgess on the final five-lap speed test at Monte Carlo in 1955. Photo by The Motor.

Carlo Gerry Burgess found himself leading the rally. The 100 highest placed cars had still to contest the mountain circuit, and those who survived the gruelling 180-mile course which had been chosen this year would then have to complete a five-lap timed race on the Monaco Grand Prix circuit before the overall results could be decided. An unsuspected secret check had been placed on the road section south of Grenoble at the end of a long fast stretch and many competitors had been caught out here, including the Aston Martin of Monte Carlo veteran Maurice Gatsonides and the green Ford Zephyr of Gerry Burgess. An alleged 7 minutes early at this check added 70 penalty points to the Zephyr's total, and Gerry Burgess now found himself back in 10th position. Conditions for the mountain test were atrocious, hard-packed snow covered virtually the entire 180 miles, sleet and snow was falling in the hills, and the clouds were clinging to the mountain sides, giving foggy conditions along many sections of the route.

The 100 qualifying cars left Monte Carlo at 1-minute intervals and headed into the mountains. Burgess pressed on at an incredible pace, passing many of the competitors who had started out from Monte Carlo ahead of the Zephyr before reaching the Col de Turini. On the twisting climb to the summit of the Col, after more than 100 miles of punishment, the Zephyr's brake fluid boiled and the pedal sank to the floor. Until the brakes had cooled, slowing down for the hairpin bends on the long descent was accomplished by slamming the Zephyr into first gear and putting it sideways on the hard-packed snow to scrub off excess speed. The brakes eventually came back, but the punishment taken by the gearbox in the meantime had now resulted in the loss of top gear completely. Nevertheless, Burgess pressed on regardless, screaming the Zephyr along in second gear, and by the time it swept back into Monte Carlo it had climbed from 10th to fourth place overall, thanks to a magnificent drive. The next best placed Ford was the Zodiac of Sydney Allard, now in 13th place overall after another spectacular mountain drive which had been such as to excite *The Autocar* reporter to comment: 'The prize for the most daring descent might well go to Sydney Allard, who slid his Zodiac around

Best of British. Gerry Burgess (left) and Peter Easton display the Stuart Trophy which was awarded to the highest placed British car/crew combination at Monte Carlo. Their privately-entered Zephyr had finished fourth overall on this, the 1955 event. Photo by The Motor.

with fantastic abandon'. All that now remained were the five-lap races around the Grand Prix circuit, and unless someone failed to finish their particular race it was unlikely that any drivers could improve on the positions they now held. Leading the rally was Norwegian Per Malling in a Sunbeam; he, too, had put up an excellent display in the mountains, having climbed from fourth to first, but at the expense of the Sunbeam's engine, which was now described as 'distinctly rough', and doubt was being expressed in some quarters as to whether it would last out its five-lap race. In the event it did, just, Malling actually being lapped at the end, but

Vic Preston and D. P. Marwaha after winning outright the East African Safari in 1955. This win, coupled with Gatsonides' 1953 Monte Carlo success, gave the Mk 1 Zephyr a rallying double which it shares only with the Mercedes 220.

finishing at all was sufficient for him to hang on to his hard-earned lead.

Gerry Burgess removed the snow tyres from the 'two-speed' Zephyr and put it back on Michelin Xs all round, inflated to 48psi for the 'round the houses' race. He recalled recently: 'I was due to run in one of the last races, so that I knew before I started that I had to achieve a lap time 4 seconds faster than the best of the Ford team had done. I did it, in second gear, and the recording of Raymond Baxter's commentary where he refers to "Gerry's 10,000-revs Ford" has always been a favourite memory'.

Real winter weather conditions in March gave the entrants in the 1955 RAC Rally a tough time throughout the event, and on the first night, in Wales, more than a fifth of the field retired. The works Zephyrs kept going well, although Sydney Allard hit a wall in Wales, and later a bridge parapet in the Lake District, which did extensive damage to the Zephyr. Cuth and Edward Harrison had a good run all the way in spite of the bad conditions, and drove their Zephyr to a class win. Allard kept the damaged Zephyr going to take second whilst Jack Reece came in third to complete a Zephyr hat-trick in the 2,600cc GT saloon category.

In the Tulip Rally, in May, Cuth Harrison took yet another class win, this time with a Zephyr equipped with a Laycock overdrive. According to the regulations for the event the overdrive was considered to be a modification, and the Fords so equipped were given an additional handicap by being placed in the up-to-3,500cc category. The handicap for this class was the same as for some of the sports classes, and for the final test at Zandvoort Cuth Harrison found himself sharing the starting grid with cars like Austin-Healeys and Triumph TR2s. Nevertheless, at the end of the 26-mile race the Zephyr crossed the line in third place, only 15 seconds behind the winner and $2\frac{1}{2}$ seconds behind the second place car, both Triumph TR2s, a performance which earned Cuth Harrison a well-deserved standing ovation from the grandstand crowd. Earlier, Sydney Allard, in a standard Zodiac, had also given the Zandvoort crowd something to cheer about in his race when he had lapped the entire field except for another Zodiac driven by Ralph Sleigh, although as both these cars had incurred many penalties on the earlier stages they were out of the running for awards.

In the *Daily Express* Trophy meeting at Silverstone, in 1955, one of the races was for Production Touring Cars. All the entries in this 25-lap (75-miles) event had modified engines, and the lone Zephyr in the field, although being driven by Ken Wharton, was in fact owned by none other than Raymond Mays. Two Consuls, one modified by Laystall and the other by Derrington, were also amongst the 27 starters. The C Type-engined Mk VII Jaguars inevitably took an early lead, whilst Ken Wharton found himself in the midst of a tangle of Riley Pathfinders. Unfortunately the Consuls fared badly, the Derrington car going out early on with a burst radiator hose and the Laystall car finishing well down amongst the tailenders. The Zephyr finally shook off the Pathfinders on lap 5 and Ken Wharton then settled down to finish comfortably in fourth place behind the three Jaguars, with the Zephyr's average speed for the race of 76.18mph comparing very well against Mike Hawthorn's 78.92mph in the winning Jaguar.

In sharp contrast to the major European rallies was the East African Safari. In the 1955 event, 57 strictly standard cars left the start in Nairobi to follow a 2,490-mile route which would take them across Kenya, Uganda and Tanganyika before eventually leading back to Nairobi, along rocky dirt 'roads' which, according to the *Mombasa Times,* 'would deter a tank'. On the first stage, a Zephyr driven by Vic Preston and D. P. Marwaha hit a vulture and as a consequence suffered a broken windscreen, but the crew pressed on and later on, with some time in hand, they had a replacement screen fitted. After the first 1,000 miles Preston's Zephyr was one of the few cars still unpenalized, but after that, conditions worsened considerably and only 20 cars made it to the finish in Nairobi. Three Zephyrs were amongst the surviving number, with one driven by Mary Wright winning the Lady McMillan Memorial Trophy (Ladies' prize) and that of Vic Preston being the outright winner of the rally. Vic Preston's Safari, coupled with Gatsonides' Monte Carlo and Ken Wharton's Tulip, had given the Mk 1

Ken Wharton at Silverstone in Raymond Mays' Zephyr in 1955.

model a hat-trick of outright wins at the highest level in three widely differing events, which served more than anything else to underline the remarkable competence and versatility which it had shown as a competition car.

The new Mk 2 Zephyr made its international rallying debut in the Alpine Rally in 1956. As its title suggests, the Alpine is almost wholly a mountain rally, consisting of ascents and descents of numerous mountain passes at an 'impossible' schedule which was set so as to virtually ensure that no competitor would be unpenalized at the end of the road section (on top of penalties incurred on the special stages). Those who did occasionally manage to beat the road schedule and finish unpenalized were awarded a Coupe des Alpes (Alpine Cup) irrespective of their final position as decided on the special stages. Modified engines were allowed in each category in the 1956 event and the three works Zephyrs were fitted with triple Zenith carburettors. The new Mk 2 cars went so well that Edward

Harrison, who was co-driving once again for his father, recalled recently that the only problem which occurred was when he suddenly thought he had left the road book at the previous control point; the Zephyr was turned round and headed back to the control when the book was found behind the sun visor. Cuth Harrison brought his Zephyr in to win the up-to-2,600cc class, with Denis Scott's similar car taking second place, and as both had clean sheets on the road the Mk 2 Zephyr had won two Alpine Cups at its very first attempt. Driving the third Zephyr in the works team in this event was Mrs Anne Hall. After co-driving for Sheila Van Damm in the works Sunbeams for the previous four years, Anne Hall had found herself suddenly without a works drive after the retirement of Miss Van Damm and so had moved over to Ford. Although just failing to gain a Coupe des Alpes, her first Zephyr drive was nevertheless very impressive, and she had motored up the snaking Izoard Pass special stage faster than any other competitor in the rally, a performance which earned her a special trophy and the unofficial title 'Queen of the Izoard'. Anne Hall still remembers another incident on that particular Alpine. At one of the overnight stops, as the crews were having supper, she mentioned that her hands were badly blistered. Cuth Harrison suggested that as the Zephyr was appreciably larger and heavier than the Sunbeam perhaps she ought to wear driving gloves until becoming more familiar with the new car. The following morning, before the dawn start, Anne Hall found a pair of new, soft leather gloves at her place at the breakfast table. After the others had retired the night before, Cuth Harrison had been out to the village and persuaded a shopkeeper to open up and sell him a pair of gloves.

The fuel shortages caused by the Suez crisis led to the cancellation of several major rallies in 1957, the Monte Carlo, RAC and Alpine all being victims. The Tulip Rally was unaffected, and a strong works Zephyr contingent was amongst the starters with Gerry Burgess having his first works drive. Unfortunately Burgess went out with a fuel starvation problem, but the remainder of the Zephyrs had a trouble-free run with Anne Hall winning the Ladies' Cup and the three cars of Denis Scott, Cuth Harrison and Ronnie Adams combining to win the Team Trophy, which was normally awarded to the three cars of the same model with the lowest aggregate penalties.

In August, Anne Hall took a works Zephyr on the Liège-Rome-Liège, although as a private entry without works support, and Gerry Burgess

The Mk 2 Zephyrs display their trophies at the finish of the 1956 Alpine Rally. Left to right are Anne Hall and Miss Jackson, Cuth and Edward Harrison, Denis Scott and Stan Astbury. Amongst the trophies can be seen the Coupes des Alpes awarded for an unpenalized road run to the Harrison and Scott cars. Anne Hall was very unlucky not to gain such an Alpine Cup: her Zephyr lost almost half an hour by refusing to restart at a control. A faulty coil was eventually diagnosed and with this replaced Anne did make up some of the lost time, recording the fastest time of the day over the Izoard pass. With three Zenith carburettors, a raised compression ratio and larger valves, these Mk 2s would exceed 100mph. Photo from the Denis Scott collection.

entered his own Mk 2 Zephyr, with an 11:1 compression ratio engine specially prepared by Raymond Mays for this almost racing rally. All went well on the first stage, but after leaving Munich, Anne Hall's Zephyr developed wheel bearing trouble, and with no support at the control points this meant leaving the route to find a suitable garage. Almost an hour was lost having this trouble rectified, but with some spectacularly fast driving, Anne Hall made up all but 3 minutes of the loss by the next control. After over 1,300 miles were completed her Zephyr was hit hard by an Army lorry in northern Italy, the driver of which had totally ignored the car's priority position on a narrow bridge, and more time was lost lashing together the stoved-in nearside doors with the tow rope. Despite this damage, and the

fact that the collision had left the exhaust system trailing on the road, Anne Hall took the Zephyr up the 6,900ft Passo de Giau special stage in the third fastest time of any competitor. But making up so much time after these setbacks had punished the brakes so severely that the linings were well and truly cooked, and the brakes simply would not recover. Before there would be any opportunity to have the brake shoes replaced Anne Hall was faced with the descent of the Stelvio Pass. She almost made it, negotiating more than 30 hairpin bends using only the gearbox as a brake before her luck finally ran out on the third hairpin from the bottom, where the Zephyr hit the retaining wall, so bringing a magnificent drive to an end. Anne Hall's performance so impressed John Gott, the BMC team captain on the Liège, that he wrote to the Ford Motor Company praising her effort, and concluded: 'I do feel, however, and this you may feel impertinent, that it was not really fair to send out a lady driver of this class without some support. The male drivers had been able to change their brake shoes, but Anne had not and it was trying to make up time to get into a garage that was one of the factors resulting in her crash.'

Meanwhile, Gerry Burgess' Mays-tuned Zephyr had no trouble at all keeping up with the leaders, but unfortunately, after his spare supplies of 100-octane fuel had run out in Jugoslavia, he had been forced to fill up with the local 'brew', which at an 80-octane rating was totally unsuitable for the 11:1 compression ratio engine. Eventually, as a result of the sustained detonation which had inevitably taken place, the piston crowns began to break up, and the Zephyr came to rest only 150 miles from the finish. Close behind was another competitor, Schlesser, in a Mercedes 300SL, and as he had some time in hand he very sportingly towed the stricken Zephyr to a

Facia panel of an early Mk 2 Zephyr rally car. In front of the navigator are two stopwatches, whilst the oblong instrument with the two faces, mounted next to the steering column, is the Halda Speed Pilot, which, once set with the distance to be covered and the time allowed, informed the crew whether they were ahead of, or behind time at any stage on the route. Photo from the Norman Masters collection.

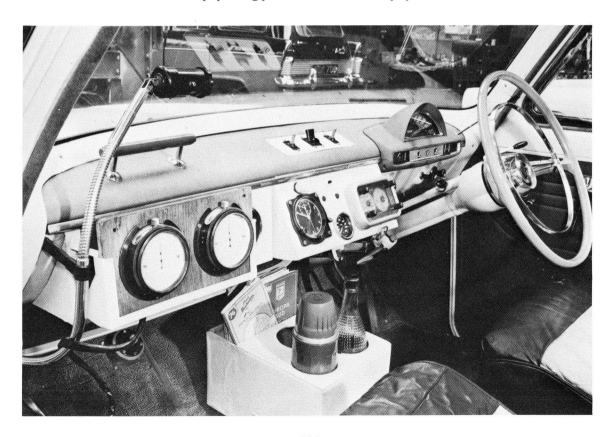

203

nearby garage before continuing on his way to take second overall in his privately-entered Mercedes. Bits of broken piston were retrieved through three of the plug holes, and the Zephyr was then push-started down a nearby slope. On the three remaining cylinders it pulled quite well, and Gerry Burgess pressed on towards the finish. On the descent overlooking the finishing point a fourth piston broke up and seized the engine, but it was downhill all the way and the Zephyr coasted over the line in 12th place overall, the highest British finisher.

Seven works Zephyrs contested the 1958 Monte Carlo Rally, three of them running with modified engines featuring triple carburettors and cylinder capacities increased to 2,648cc by reboring 60-thou oversize. On the night of January 21/22, 303 starters left the eight different starting points and headed for Monte Carlo and into conditions which at the end were generally reckoned to have been the worst ever for this event. As usual the Monte attracted many private entrants, one of which was Eric Jackson, from Barnsley, starting out from Glasgow in a recently acquired secondhand Mk 2 Zephyr. The first of the Glasgow contingent left at 3.40am, and as the Jackson/Boardman Zephyr made its way out of Stranraer at dawn the gearbox failed. By sheer luck the failure occurred near a Ford dealership, and only two hours after waking up the proprietor, the secondhand Zephyr was heading south with a new gearbox 'borrowed' from a Zodiac in the dealer's showroom. As anything over an hour late at the major control points meant automatic exclusion on the Monte, Jackson had a hectic drive south in the wintry conditions and succeeded in pulling back an hour or so of the time lost, clocking in at Dover 59 minutes late, just 1 minute inside exclusion time.

The 85 Paris starters got away in clear weather, but soon met with adverse conditions. Snow began to fall with such intensity that at times it was like a white fog, and competitors were soon dropping out at an amazing rate. Despite the conditions, Denis Scott made good time with his modified Zephyr in the early stages. Running on Pallas snow tyres, Scott was able to keep the Zephyr going well enough to come up really close behind slower moving competitors who were holding him up, and so intimidate them into going too fast into turns and consequently leave a gap which he would then take the Zephyr through. 'We worked our way through an awful lot of vehicles in this way', said his navigator Ken Armstrong recently. However, a lorry completely blocking the road brought their rally to a premature end. Further in front, Edward Harrison was making good progress in another of the modified Zephyrs, and talking about the event recently, he said: 'I remember at one point I didn't leave the driving seat for nearly 20 hours during the drive through the Jura mountains and the Massif Central. We saw an awful lot of cars upside-down, on their sides, in ditches and fields; and then we seemed to motor on for quite a long time without seeing another car, which was quite disconcerting. At one point we put one of the spare wheels with snow chains on the offside front to help steer in the slippery conditions. This was OK until we got on to some tarmac and the friction heated the chain up, which then burnt into the tyre. Fortunately we discovered this before it went right through. I would, of course, like to pay tribute to my crew — Dick Habershon and Jim Furse. How their nerves stood up to it I will never know.' Edward Harrison and his crew made it to Monte Carlo, their Zephyr being the only one of the 85 Paris starters to get through.

The privately entered Jackson/Boardman Zephyr was also amongst the 59 finishers, after managing to pull back more time across Europe and

build up a safer margin than the slender minute with which it had left Boulogne — a particularly good effort, this, in conditions which finally eliminated more than 75% of the entry. The highest placed of the four surviving big Fords was another private entry, a Zodiac which had started out from Rome in the hands of R. Nelleman and M. Skarring, who brought it in to win the over-2,000cc Touring Car class and gain 10th place overall.

Denis Scott drifts an early Mk 2 Zephyr at speed during a production car race. The Zephyr is running on Michelin X tyres, inflated in this instance to around 60psi. Photo from the Denis Scott collection.

In March, Arctic conditions in Britain embraced almost all of the 1,800-mile route chosen for the RAC Rally. Amongst the Ford entries, Denis Scott and Ken Armstrong were in the modified Zephyr which they had used in the Monte, and on the second night, in Wales, they were still unpenalized when the Zephyr came to rest, having run out of petrol as the result of a most unfortunate miscalculation. Nevertheless, when the starters left Blackpool on the Wednesday night for the snowbound northern section of the rally, Scott was still well placed in the GT class despite the time lost in Wales. The snow was thick in the north, but with Firestone Town and Country tyres on the rear, and a set of chains for the really difficult sections, the Scott/Armstrong Zephyr continued to make good time. Then, coming over the brow of a hill at about 80mph at the end of a long straight stretch of road in Cumberland, Denis Scott was confronted with a bend which was far tighter and much nearer the brow than it appeared on the map. There was no way the Zephyr would get round, and at the turn it left the road, ran up the verge and became airborne. The ground fell away after the verge, and the Zephyr went through the top of a hedge and completely cleared an adjacent fence before landing all square in a snow-covered field. 'It was just like Becher's Brook' said Scott when recalling the incident. Further along the fence over which the Zephyr had just flown was a gateway on to the road, and so within minutes Scott was back on course. Only a mile or so further along, the temperature gauge needle was off the scale, and Ken Armstrong guessed correctly that the radiator tap must have been turned open as the car went through the top of the hedge. Attempts to replenish the cooling system with snow only resulted in huge clouds of steam; however, the provisions on board included several bottles of Lucozade, and with these emptied into the radiator the Zephyr was back in action. With no more

'excursions' — 'I only allowed him one excursion per rally' says Ken Armstrong — Denis Scott brought the Zephyr in to the finish to win the over-2,000cc GT category ahead of Lyndon Sims' Aston Martin and B. Mitton's 3.4 Jaguar.

The major manufacturers did not yet officially contest the East African Safari, the line-up being made of locally entered cars, some of which were sponsored by a garage dealing in the make concerned, but with many being simply private entries. The 1958 event was split into three categories — Impala, Leopard and Lion class — which were decided on price, but nevertheless came out conveniently as small, medium and large. Several Zephyrs were in the Lion class, with the principal opposition coming from

the Mercedes 219/220 series and a team of Jaguars. At the end of the 2,900-mile event, the leading Zephyr, crewed by the Kopperud brothers, had lost just 3 minutes on its schedule and so incurred 150 penalty points, which appeared to give it the joint outright win with the leading Leopard class car, a German DKW, also with 150 penalties. The Zephyrs were first, third, fifth and sixth in their class, with Mercedes occupying second and fourth positions, and with the three leading Zephyrs' total penalties of 6,050 being less than any other three-car combination the Team Prize also looked secure according to the provisional results. However, when the final results were posted, the leading Zephyr was shown as second in the Lion class, with an additional 1,000 penalty points handed out at the scrutineering for a broken shock absorber seal. The Impala class-winning Anglia had been given an extra 2,000 penalties for the same reason, putting it behind four Volkswagens, three of which were awarded the team prize, apparently because of their now 1,2,3 position in the Impala class, despite the fact that their total penalties of 7,850 were still higher than the Zephyrs' 'new' total of 7,050. So, what at first had looked to be a Ford-dominated event suddenly became an almost wholly German affair, although Mrs Mary Wright's Ladies' Cup-winning performance in her Zephyr was confirmed. The seals at the centre of the disputed penalties were those of the wire and lead variety fixed to certain components by the organizers at the beginning of the rally, and some of these had simply worked loose or been broken by the pounding on the 3,000-mile route. As can be imagined, protests followed, and since it was obvious that the Kopperuds' Zephyr had not had any components changed it was reinstated as the Lion class winner.

The Zephyr's previous Tulip successes were not repeated in the 1958 event. The three cars of Denis Scott, Cuth Harrison (now with younger son John as co-driver since Edward had graduated to being a works driver in his own right) and Edward Harrison, vied with each other for the 2,600cc class lead in the early stages before both the Harrisons went out with fuel starvation. Although foreign matter was found in the petrol in both cases it appears to have been sheer coincidence that it had afflicted just the Harrison-manned cars. The Scott/Armstrong car lost the class lead when it

Jeff Uren battles with Doc Grace's Riley Pathfinder in 1958. Photo from the Jeff Uren collection.

followed another competitor's tail-lights round a wrong turning on a foggy mountain climb and was late at the next control. This mistake handed the 2,600cc class to the Morley brothers in a 2.4-litre Jaguar. Although being held in late April, the Tulip route still usually featured snow and ice in the hilly regions, and it was normal on this event for the Zephyrs to take two spare wheels shod with snow tyres, usually the Firestone Town and Country cross-ply type. As the other four tyres were almost always the radial-ply Michelin X type, this resulted in the Zephyrs often running on a front radial/rear cross-ply combination, a mix which is illegal in Britain today and yet which apparently worked well on the Zephyr. Denis Scott won his race at Zandvoort at the end of the 1958 Tulip on this combination, as one of his X tyres had been punctured on the road section.

Three of the six Zephyrs amongst the 58 starters in the Alpine Rally in July had disc brakes on the front wheels for the first time. In the event, however, it was the standard Zephyr of Edward Harrison which put up the best Ford display in what proved to be the toughest Alpine Rally yet, with only 25 of the original 58 who set out actually making it to the finish. Edward Harrison finished fifth overall behind three Alfa Romeos and a Triumph TR3, and just ahead of a shoal of Austin-Healey 100s. This class-winning performance also added the third Coupe des Alpes to the Zephyr's total.

Although already very familiar with the Mk 2 Zephyr as a racing saloon, Jeff Uren had his first works Zephyr drive in the 1959 Monte, and brought the car in 13th overall at the finish, the highest placed of the big Fords at Monte Carlo on this occasion. In March that year, Denis Scott and Edward Harrison, accompanied by Competitions Manager Edgy Fabris and mechanic Jack Welch, flew to Nairobi as the first-ever works contingent in the East African Safari Rally. One of the three Zephyrs entered by the works was to be crewed by local drivers, whilst Scott and Harrison would each team up with a local co-driver whose knowledge would be an essential asset at this stage as no suitable maps of the area existed. The 63 entrants left Nairobi on Good Friday and headed out on the southern loop. The Scott/Davies car first hit trouble approaching Mbulu, after the Zephyr had been bottoming almost continuously on a tight section with a 41mph average; when Scott braked for a turn the pedal just sank to the floor. The Zephyr made it round after hitting the bank on the outside of the corner and was pulled up on the handbrake. One of the brake pipes had been knocked loose, but fortunately not broken, although some time was now lost refilling and bleeding the system. The next section was 46 miles of

Jeff Uren holds a slight lead over Jack Sears at Brands Hatch in 1958 in one of several dices the pair had that year. More than 20 years later, Jeff Uren still rates the Jack Sears/Austin Westminster combination as one of the finest ever in saloon car racing. Photo from the Jeff Uren collection.

The start of the great adventure. The privately entered Zodiac of Lawrence 'Tommy' Handley and Dacre Harvey sets out for Monte Carlo in 1959. NBL 666 was of early 1956 vintage. This photo and the following two from the Dacre Harvey collection.

En route and going well. The Handley/Harvey Zodiac on snowy roads in France.

They made it! Dacre Harvey (left) with Mr and Mrs Handley just after having checked in at the finish of the 1959 Monte Carlo Rally.

Another of the big Fords arrives in the Principality in 1959, this time the works-entered Zephyr driven by Anne Hall. An interesting fitment visible on this car is the speedometer drive taken from the front hub, replacing the usual drive from the gearbox and thus eliminating inaccuracies caused by rear wheel spin. Photo from the Anne Hall collection.

unmade track at a 42mph average, and all went well until 7 miles from the end when, just after overtaking a slower-moving competitor, the Zephyr went into a huge pothole. Denis Scott remembers: 'I thought we would turn completely over, but the car somehow bounced out. During the quick stop to see what damage had been done the car we had just passed came by, the crew laughing their heads off; however, 5 miles further on we had the last laugh as we came across them with the sump of their car firmly embedded on a large rock.' A bent track rod was the only apparent damage, and the Zephyr arrived at Dabil exactly on schedule. The 'road' improved slightly between Dabil and Banga, 37 miles away, and the average was stepped up to 50mph. Even so, some time was made up, and with a few precious minutes to spare the Zephyr was stopped in Banga for a quick check-over by the crew and had the fuel tank replenished from the jerrycans on board. The 50mph average continued for the next 38 miles, but conditions worsened and the Scott/Davies Zephyr was a minute late at the Kolo control. Denis Scott put in a terrific effort over the next 110-mile stage to Dodoma, gaining enough time to take the Zephyr into the Ford agents there and have the brakes properly bled and the track readjusted in an effort to lessen the excessive tyre wear being caused by the bent track rod. By the time Scott reached Nairobi and the end of the southern loop he had lost 12 minutes on the schedule and was lying third overall; with Edward Harrison in fifth place and several other Zephyrs still going well, the team prize at least looked a possibility.

After leaving Nairobi once more for the northern stage, Scott made up about 10 minutes to the control at Thika, where exactly 20 minutes was taken to replace the bent track rod at the Ford garage. This loss was made up over the next 50 miles and the Scott/Davies car pulled into the Kangondi control on time. The pace had now taken its toll, almost half the competitors were out, and Edward Harrison had moved up into fourth place after the Mercedes lying between himself and Denis Scott had retired

A considerable drop over the edge of the road does not stop Denis Scott from hanging the tail out as he hurries to Monte Carlo in 1959. Photo from the Denis Scott collection.

with mechanical failure, although Mercedes were still holding first and second overall. With just 100 miles of the 3,200-mile route left to cover, the second-placed Mercedes went out with brake failure, so handing the team prize to the Zephyrs. Denis Scott and Edward Harrison had taken second and third place overall at their first attempt in the world's toughest rally, and had combined with the locally entered Zodiac of W.F.C. Young and L. Baillon to take the team prize for Ford.

In view of the Safari entry at Easter, the Competitions Department did not support the Tulip Rally later in April, although several Zephyrs were there, in some cases with works drivers. At the end of the 2,000-mile run, which had taken them as far south as Avignon before turning north towards the eventual finish in Noordwijk, the Zephyr of Peter Riley had taken third place overall behind a 3.4-litre Jaguar and a Triumph TR3, had won the 2,600cc class from Schock's Mercedes 220, and had combined with the Zephyrs of Cuth and John Harrison and of Gerry Burgess and Sam Croft-Pearson to give the Zephyr its second major team award in a month.

A full works Zephyr entry contested the Alpine Rally in June. The classifications had been changed for this year's event, with all cars over 2,000cc being in the same class, but with each capacity class divided into Touring (saloons), or Grand Touring (sports cars). Out of the 58 starters, only 27 survived to finish, and the Zephyrs continued their recent successes with the cars of Riley/Pitts, Harrison/Harrison and Harrison/Fleetwood coming in first, second and third in the over-2,000cc Touring class. This performance also gave the Zephyr its third consecutive team award in a major international event and added three more of the coveted Alpine Cups to the Zephyr's total. Anne Hall was particularly unlucky in this event, being deprived of the Ladies Cup almost right at the end when her Zephyr went out with mechanical trouble. None of the other ladies had survived as far as Anne Hall in this tough event, and the organizers presented her with a special trophy, for 'Courage, endurance and tenacity of purpose'. The severity of an event such as the Alpine can best be imaged

when it is realized that many of the passes were gravel-surfaced, often too narrow for overtaking, and some of the seemingly endless succession of hairpin bends were tighter than the turning circle of cars like the Zephyr. The technique used to get the Zephyrs round these particular hairpins was known as 'kicking it round'; first gear would be engaged on the approach and the tail end deliberately broken away with a wide throttle opening at the apex of the corner, then the car would be 'caught' by the driver as it

The camera catches Denis Scott's Zephyr as it dives into a huge pothole on the 1959 Safari whilst on its way to second place overall. Photo from the Denis Scott collection.

213

lined up for the exit. When talking about this method, recently, Gerry Burgess remembered an incident when, at one control point, all the Zephyrs were featuring a similar dent in one of the rear doors, after they had all collided with the same piece of rock jutting out from the rock face at the exit from one hairpin.

Saloon car racing was by now a popular part of the motor racing scene, and having been elevated to championship status the previous year it was also now being taken very seriously. To chart the Mk 2 Zephyr's success in this sphere of competition it is necessary to go back to 1957. Jeff Uren was successfully racing an Anglia that year, and he approached the Ford Competitions Department about the possibility of driving a works Zephyr in these events, a request which was turned down as there were already enough works drivers, and in any case, although competing in some of these races, the Competitions Department were concentrating far more on rallying. Although he didn't own a Zephyr at this stage, Jeff Uren nevertheless entered one for the saloon car race at Silverstone in September, and once the entry was accepted he bought a brand new example. The engine was immediately stripped down, and the individual components balanced before reassembly. A single $1\frac{3}{4}$in SU carburettor was adapted to operate as a downdraught instrument and replaced the standard Zenith. The Zephyr was run-in by driving from London to Exeter and back twice in one night the week before the race, and at the weekend, with just 700 miles on the clock, it took its place on the starting grid. In the practice session Jeff had lapped consistently slower than the works

214

Zephyrs, which were also competing that day, but in the race itself he comfortably led them home, being beaten only by the 3.4-litre Jaguars.

In 1958, Jeff Uren contested the BRSCC Saloon Car Championship as a private entrant, but was beaten on several occasions by Jack Sears in the BMC works-prepared Austin Westminster, which proved itself to be a faster car than the Uren Zephyr, although the pair did have some memorable dices that year, including one at Silverstone in May, when they lapped just feet apart for almost the entire distance and the Zephyr's superior handling qualities got it to the flag ahead of the faster car. Not far behind this particular struggle were three works Zephyrs with standard engines and automatic transmissions which were having a private dice of their own, eventually won by Denis Scott. The automatic Zephyrs had been entered at the suggestion of Borg-Warner, and in fact went remarkably well, their performance at Silverstone that day earning much favourable comment in the motoring press. Jack Sears went on to win the championship that year, with Jeff Uren runner-up.

Jeff was confident that he could win the championship with some works support, and he approached Ford once again. This time his approach paid off, and he was given facilities at Lincoln Cars and some financial support from the experimental engineering budget with which to prepare a racing Zephyr for the 1959 season. A Raymond Mays light-alloy cylinder head, with a compression ratio of 10:1, was used as a basis for the increased power output being sought. Three twin-choke Weber carburettors and twin fuel pumps, one AC mechanical and one SU electrical, supplied the mixture, whilst a Servais six-branch/twin-tailpipe exhaust system was chosen to complete the top-end arrangements. The engine was fully blueprinted, and an increased capacity sump incorporating cooling tubes ensured adequate lubrication at sustained racing speeds. These modifications resulted in 168bhp at 5,800rpm, and this was transmitted to the rear axle via the standard clutch and three-speed gearbox, and a heavy-duty propeller shaft with special high-torque universal joints. An alternative set of straight-cut higher ratio first and second gears was also available, as were several axle ratios from elsewhere in the Ford range, although the standard 3.9:1 was most used. The suspension was lowered all

BMC Competition Manager Marcus Chambers presents Jeff Uren with the Bonneville Trophy, which was donated by BMC for the BRSCC Saloon Car Championship. The scene here is at Brands Hatch after the final race in the 1959 series. Photo from the Jeff Uren collection.

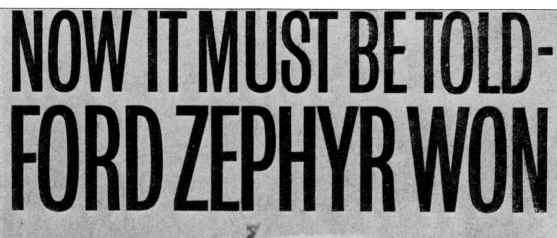

NOW IT MUST BE TOLD – FORD ZEPHYR WON

THE R.A.C. RALLY

An appeal against the final placings in this year's R.A.C. British International Rally has been dismissed by stewards of the Royal Automobile Club. The British driver G. N. Burgess (Ford Zephyr) remains, therefore, the provisional winner—subject to final confirmation by the International Automobile Federation.

OUTRIGHT WINNER
1st
ZEPHYR
(G. N. BURGESS)

Self-explanatory Ford advertisement after the 1959 RAC Rally. The company was never slow to publicize its competition achievements.

Back again. The Handley/Harvey Zodiac tackles the 1960 Monte: this time their efforts were rewarded by a win in the over-2,000cc GT class, no mean feat for a privateer. Photos from the Dacre Harvey collection.

Jeff Uren's Championship-winning Zephyr at the BRSCC Racing Car Show in January 1960. Photo from the Jeff Uren collection.

Jeff Uren demonstrates the cornering capabilities of another of his racing Zephyrs. Photo from the Jeff Uren collection.

Team Prize winners in the 1960 Safari. Left to right, Cuth Harrison and Peter Davies, Denis Scott, John Harrison and Vic Preston. Photo from the Denis Scott collection.

round by 1½in, with uprated Armstrong front struts 40% stiffer than standard embraced by 20% uprated springs. An extra leaf was incorporated in the rear springs, and Armstrong adjustable shock absorbers replaced the originals, with the rear axle additionally located by an anti-tramp bracket. The steering gear ratio was raised to 12.5:1, and the braking system was the servo-assisted Girling front disc/rear drum arrangement already used on the Alpine Rally Zephyrs. As there were no 13in racing tyres available, standard-size Michelin Xs running at 50-55psi on the standard Zephyr rims were used. Additional instrumentation, lightweight bucket seats, safety harness and perspex side and rear windows were the only bodywork/interior modifications. This proved to be a championship-winning combination, with six class wins and one second in the eight-race championship series, with class lap records at Aintree (2min 32.4sec), Goodwod (1min 53sec), Snetterton (2min 06.6sec) and Brands Hatch (1min 10.2sec). The final race in the series was at Brands Hatch on August 29, and Les Leston's Riley 1.5 could in fact still draw level, although only if Jeff Uren failed to finish and Leston won his class and set fastest class lap. However, it was Leston who fell back, while Jeff Uren completed an immaculate season to take the Bonneville Trophy which went with the BRSCC Saloon Car Championship and record yet another notable success in the competition career of the Mk 2 Zephyr.

Following this performance, Jeff Uren joined the Ford Competitions Department as Team Manager, with responsibility for looking after the driver's interests 'on the spot' during the events, a move which relieved some of the pressure from Edgy Fabris, who would now have more time to tackle the surprising amount of administration involed in organizing works participation in the major international competitions.

Additional fuel capacity was allowed on cars competing in the Modified or Grand Touring category. In order to enable the standard fuel tank, with its filler in the back panel behind the number-plate, to be filled from a jerrycan single-handedly, the Mk 2 rally cars carried a funnel with a hook which fitted over the lip of the back panel.

The last major event in 1959 was the RAC Rally, scheduled that year for November rather than its previous stagings in March. The new 105E Anglia was making its rallying debut in this event alongside the established Zephyrs, one of the latter being driven by racing ace Graham Hill, and another appearing in the hands of the regular pairing of Gerry Burgess and Sam Croft-Pearson. Winter arrived early in Scotland and the RAC Rally got well and truly caught up in the adverse conditions. From the control at Nairn the route led to Braemar, via the Tomintoul Pass, and now Gerry Burgess takes up the story: 'Arriving at Tomintoul we and the rest of the runners found the road hopelessly blocked by snowdrifts. Approaching there, we met many cars already going back the way we had come. It was fairly obvious that some of the cars had turned back even before reaching the block, and most we could see were turning west to come right round back to Braemar via the main road. I decided to turn east and whilst making as good time as possible Sam worked out our route through Dufftown, Ballater and into Braemar from the right direction. As soon as I began to get figures from him I saw it was possible to make the control

Anne Hall's Zephyr after an incredible high-speed loop on the Acropolis Rally in 1960. The Zephyr had run into a roadside quarry and climbed a vertical rock face before falling over backwards. Photos from the Norman Masters collection.

before exclusion time and I got down to hurrying. In my memory, we flew; the Zephyr's wheels didn't touch the road again and we finally reached the control a few minutes late only, and a few minutes quicker than Levy, who was the fastest round the main road way. When I was told later that I was leading the rally it was hard to believe, but I was.' Gerry Burgess held on to his lead, despite a collision almost right at the end when the Zephyr hit a competing Aston Martin which was inexplicably coming the wrong way. Unfortunately, the German entrant Levy protested at the Zephyr's win, and asked for the Braemar stage to be deleted from the rally as many competitors had missed it out altogether. Sir Hartley Shawcross was appointed to hear the protest, and after listening to Levy and Ford Team Manager Jeff Uren he dismissed the German's argument and awarded Gerry Burgess his rightful victory.

After the successes of 1959 there were high hopes of a Zephyr victory at Monte Carlo in 1960, and at the end of the 2,000-mile road section the works-entered cars of Cuth Harrison, Edward Harrison and Denis Scott

Unfortunately the original NBL 666 was wrecked in a road accident during 1960 when the driver of a Green Line bus suddenly decided on an unscheduled change of direction. A brand new NBL 666 therefore appeared on the 1961 Monte, fitted with the modified engine parts salvaged from the earlier car, and distinguished itself when the Handley/Harvey duo again carried off the over-2,000cc GT class winner's prize. The car is seen here high up in the mountains above Monte Carlo and later on the final speed test around the Grand Prix circuit. Beautifully prepared, the new car also won the Comfort and Safety Cup on this event. Photos from the Dacre Harvey collection.

WHEN EXPERTS MEET
-SO DO ZEPHYRS

Competitor and spectator alike are proud to own Ford's splendid Zephyr. For this is a *motorist's* car, brilliantly designed and brilliantly built to give any-road any-conditions satisfaction. The sturdy 6-cylinder engine, with or without automatic transmission, gives reassuring acceleration and a steady drive at all speeds from traffic-jam creep to an open-road gallop that tops 90 mph. The finely furnished interior promises luxury motoring for six without squashing or squeezing: power disc brakes are now standard.

ZEPHYR FROM **FORD** OF BRITAIN

A lovely period advertisement seeking to capitalize on the sporting image conferred by the big Mk 2's many competition successes.

were amongst the 10 unpenalized survivors, and had booked their place amongst those which would contest the final mountain circuit. However, in the mountains Edward Harrison went out when his Zephyr sustained a fractured brake pipe, Denis Scott left the road and Cuth Harrison surprisingly lost time. Meanwhile, the factory-entered Mercedes team, which, with typical German thoroughness, had spent the previous three months practising in the mountains above Monte Carlo, swept in to the finish for an impressive first, second and third overall. It was two privately entered Fords, the standard Zephyr of Mike Sutcliffe, who finished sixth overall, and the modified Zodiac of Handley, who won the over-2,000cc GT category, which kept the Ford flag flying at the end. After the disappointment at Monte Carlo, consolation came at Easter when the three works Zephyrs of Vic Preston/John Harrison, Cuth Harrison/P. Davies and Denis Scott/L. Baillon took the team award once again in what proved to be the toughest East African Safari yet, with only 25 cars out of the 84 starters completing the 3,200-mile course. Although Mercedes had again won the event outright, this was nevertheless a good rally for Ford, as in addition to the Zephyr's team prize the new Anglias had come first, second, third and fifth in the small car category.

The Harrison family had a keen interest in the 1960 Alpine Rally; with two consecutive Alpine Cups to his credit, Edward Harrison was in line to win one of the extremely rare Gold Cups, which were awarded for a third successive unpenalized run, and his father, Cuth, with two non-consecutive Cups, would win a Silver Cup if he, too, could finish unpenalized on the road this year. However, new 'coefficient' regulations, based on engine capacity and weight, had been introduced. According to Team Manager Jeff Uren, they were 'totally anomalous', being biased heavily against the Zephyr, and they made the 'impossible' schedule on this event just that as far as the Zephyr was concerned. Edward Harrison, particularly, made a terrific effort to beat the handicap, but just failed to do so and, although four Zephyrs finished, a brilliant run in this competition had been brought to an end. As if this were not enough, new regulations for the 1961 Monte Carlo Rally included a 'factor of comparison' which made a complete mockery of the event that year, and was seemingly introduced to ensure that no matter how well a car performed in the rally, if it were not a small-

Anne Hall on her way to a magnificent third place overall and the Ladies Cup on her first Safari. Photo from the Anne Hall collection.

224

engined French model it would not figure high in the final placings. Nevertheless, the few big Fords which entered went well, with Lawrence Handley's Zodiac, the lone works Zephyr of Gerry Burgess and Eric Jackson's Zephyr taking first, second and third places respectively in the over-2,000cc GT category.

The East African Safari was not affected by such things as 'coefficients' and 'factors of comparison'; it was a case of survival of the fittest in a straight fight in which the terrain itself was the 'handicap' which ensured that many would not finish. Although a team of Anglias was entered once again for the 1961 event, Anne Hall, who already had three Ladies' Cups to her credit in the new Anglia, was back at the wheel of a Zephyr for this, her first Safari. Soon after arriving in Nairobi, Anne Hall, with her local co-driver Lucille Cardwell, was out on a reconnaissance of the southern loop when the Zephyr hit a deep drift at speed, ripping off both front wheels and bringing the car sliding to a stop on the remains of its front suspension. The hazard had quite probably been deepened by the local natives, who liked to see cars crash, and would then offer 'protection' of the vehicle on the payment of a few shillings whilst the driver went for help. The protection was necessary, otherwise such things as tyres would be cut up for sandals and many other items from the car would be put to all sorts of uses which the manufacturer had never dreamed of. This incident highlighted the value of a local co-driver for the British entries, as Lucille Cardwell could speak some Swahili and soon 'organized' things with the natives, including the loan of a bicycle. Seven miles of pedalling brought Anne Hall and Lucille Cardwell to a large village, from where they were able to hitch a ride to a town and eventually arrange for transport back to Nairobi and the recovery of the Zephyr. Now without a recce car of her own, Anne Hall went over the northern loop with Jeff Uren in one of the Anglias. On the rally itself, the southern loop didn't give Anne Hall any trouble; she did lose some time, but so did everybody else, and many were already dropping out. As the survivors returned towards Nairobi for an overnight rest before tackling the northern loop, the familiar Safari Mercedes-versus-Zephyr picture was emerging once again.

At Nairobi, two past winners, local drivers Manussis and Fritschy, were lying first and second in their Mercedes 220SEs, being 22.86 and 26.58

For the fourth year running, three Mk 2 Zephyrs had the lowest aggregate penalties of any three-car combination on the Safari. Here the 1961 Team Prize winners line up. Anne Hall (sunglasses), here with her co-driver Lucille Cardwell, rates this as her best-ever achievement in a rallying career which brought her many awards at International level. In the centre is veteran motoring correspondent Tom Wisdom with his local co-driver and, on the left, Cuth Harrison and Peter Davies, who were sharing in the Team Prize for the second year running. Photo from the Anne Hall collection.

minutes late, with Anne Hall in third place having lost 35.52 minutes. With the Zephyrs of Cuth Harrison and veteran motoring correspondent Tommy Wisdom being close behind with 41.84 and 44.20 minutes lost, the big Fords were once again well placed for the team award, although anything could still happen on the 1,300-mile northern loop. After an overnight rest, the rally was underway again. The tightest section of all on the northern loop was a special stage from Rondo to Timboroa, 55.2 miles of rough mountainous road which would take the competitors through several small villages with 30mph speed limits, enforced by a secret check in one of the villages. Any time over an hour taken on this section would mean more penalty points, and recalling this stage recently Anne Hall remembered: 'We put crash hats on and set off; it was a case of driving like lunatics.' On one of the very few bits of decent 'road' on this section, sharp stones had been strewn across the road by the local natives and Anne Hall's Zephyr sustained a puncture. The car was quickly surrounded by grinning natives who simply lifted the offending corner of the car clear of the ground while the crew did a record-breaking wheel change without the need of a jack. The Zephyr covered this stage almost exactly on time. Anne Hall didn't give either Manussis or Fritschy a chance to ease up at all, and was herself being pushed hard by a Humber Super Snipe close behind in fourth place, which was also going extremely well. Towards the end of the rally, coming over the brow of a hill at over 70mph, Anne Hall was faced with a right-angle turn over a narrow bridge which was much nearer the brow than she remembered from the recce. 'Luckily, I had practised handbrake turns', she remembers, and the Zephyr arrived sideways at the bridge scattering a group of reporters gathered there. The story goes that when the Zephyr appeared at speed over the hill, a chorus of 'She'll never make it' went up from the assembled scribes. One of them, however, who had seen her in action in Europe, quickly replied 'I'll bet everybody here £10 that she does.' She did, but whether the opportunist gambler ever collected his winnings is not recorded. She kept going hard to finish third overall and win the Ladies' Cup in her first Safari, coming in 13 minutes and 7 minutes behind the first and second place Mercedes. Tom Wisdom and Cuth Harrison came in sixth and seventh overall, and this, coupled with Anne Hall's performance, gave the Mk 2 Zephyr yet another team prize in the world's toughest rally.

After this, the Competitions Department turned its attention more to the Anglia for the immediate future, as the Mk 2 Zephyr was, of course, well into its last year of production. The big Fords had completed a remarkable run in international rallying, having contested, as far as can be ascertained, 50 events, many as private entrants only, which had resulted in five outright wins, six team prizes, six Alpine Cups, five Ladies' Cups, and 16 class wins, in addition to their disputed win and team award in the 1958 Safari. This was a record second to none throughout the period, and the Zephyrs particularly had proved themselves to be at least the equal in ruggedness and durability of cars like the Mercedes 220, which was selling at three times the price, and was considered by many to be the yardstick by which medium/large six-cylinder saloons were judged. That all of this was achieved on what amounted to a shoestring budget does the greatest credit not only to the cars themselves, but also to Edgy Fabris, Jeff Uren and the team of mechanics at Lincoln Cars and, of course, to the skill of the drivers to whom the Zephyr had endeared itself.

As competition saloons, therefore, the Mk 1 and Mk 2 Zephyr and Zodiac were a hard act to follow, and so it caused considerable interest when Ford announced that six of the brand new Mk 3 Zodiacs would contest the 1962 East African Safari Rally, which was taking place within a few days of the model's public announcement.

Pre-release secrecy surrounding the new model resulted in the crews doing much of their reconnaissance in Mk 2 cars, second-hand examples acquired locally by the Ford dealership, Hughes of Nairobi, and only one Mk 3 was made available for any practice. Gerry Burgess and his local co-driver, Beau Younghusband, were the first to take this car out, after dark because of the secrecy, and, as was so often the case with the Safari, they ran into their fair share of drama even before the rally proper began, as Gerry recalls:

'When we were near Kilimanjaro, we turned off for a special stage circuit of the mountain. Pitch dark, raining, I began to get with the new car – throwing it about, power slides and all, down unmade-up tracks through the bundu. Then suddenly I was confronted with a great black expanse, glistening in the rain, which we were crossing at 80 or 90mph and I couldn't see the track ahead! Then I saw a small plank bridge over a 30ft-wide river. No chance of stopping, the wet black lava was like sheet ice. I only got my offside wheels on the plank and we turned over into the river.'

A soaking wet Younghusband went off into the night in the direction of Ol Donyo Sambu to enlist some help, leaving an equally soaked Gerry Burgess to some hours of apprehension listening to the assorted grunts and

On Safari in 1962 with the new Mk 3 Zodiac. Competitions Manager Edgy Fabris (left) and some of the Ford drivers discuss the route. Veteran rally driver and motoring journalist Tom Wisdom stands between Lucille Cardwell and Anne Hall. With sunglasses is Gerry Burgess, who was to bring the Zodiac in to a class win on this Safari. Photo from the Anne Hall collection.

snorts of the African wildlife while he supposedly guarded the car. Dawn eventually broke, and with it came some light relief when a couple of natives wearing army-surplus greatcoats and footwear by Firestone passed by the marooned Burgess and had a good laugh, with the elder underlining his powers of observation by exclaiming 'Motoren kaput!' Actually, it was not, and was back in action by lunchtime, having been hauled out of the river with only minor damage.

In addition to the Burgess-Younghusband pairing were Anne Hall and Lucille Cardwell, Edward Harrison and David Markham, Vic Preston and Leon Baillon, Eric Jackson and Gregor Grant, and Tommy Wisdom sharing a Zodiac with Peter Walker. Competition Department mechanics Jack Welch and Norman Masters were supervising a team of local mechanics from the Hughes Ford dealership, and Competitions Manager Edgy Fabris had a light aeroplane at his disposal in order to monitor the event. This was, therefore, by quite a considerable margin Dagenham's most serious attempt so far to clean-up on the Safari Rally. However, revised rally regulations, plus a changing set of circumstances beyond anyone's control, which occurred as the cars contested the second (southern) loop, were to combine and make it virtually impossible for any of the large-car entries to win the Safari this year.

The big-engined cars were now divided into two capacity classes, 2,000cc to 2,500cc, and over 2,500cc, with the big Fords of course being just inside the largest capacity class alongside teams of Rover 3-litres and Humber Super Snipes. In the smaller of these two classes were the ever-present Mercedes 220s, the Fiat 2300s, a team of Australian Ford Falcons, and a number of General Motors Holden cars. Starting at three-minute intervals, the 107 cars were to leave Nairobi in numerical and class order, with the smallest class first, and therefore more than five hours would separate the first and last cars at the beginning of the event. With all the time-control points along the route this year to remain open for only seven hours after the first car to clock-in, this gave the earliest starting, smallest models more than six hours lateness before exclusion, with the safety margins reducing up through the entire entry until the last car away, number 107, had a margin of only 1 hour 40 minutes lateness to stay in the rally. Also, at the time controls, at which the cars were allowed a three-minute stop to attend to things like cleaning the windscreen and lamp glasses, if any two cars arrived within one minute of each other that with the lowest rally number had to restart first. Thus, a faster car which had overtaken a slower one within the previous few miles could find itself back behind the overtaken car again when leaving the control. These measures had been introduced specifically to even up the sheer performance differences between the large and the small cars, and now meant that the usually dominant Mercedes and big Fords were facing their toughest Safari yet; all the more so this time as they also had to contend with the equally rugged Rover 3-litre models which were making their Safari debut.

With an evening start for the rally, it was well after dark when the big Fords left Nairobi to tackle the northern loop around five hours after car number 1, Erik Carlsson's little Saab, had got away. The first 40 miles or so were on tarmac, and the Zodiacs were settled down to an easy 80-85mph cruising gait over this distance, before turning off onto the rough tracks which would take them to the first control at Kandongi. Unmade roads after dark are treacherous, and even before reaching that first control point the Ford team were dealt a devastating double blow when the Zodiacs of Anne Hall and Edward Harrison went out. Both cars hit the

ZODIAC Mk III WINS CLASS 8 (GROUPS 1 & 2)
IN THE COUPE DES ALPES

TOURING CARS (OVER 2,500 C.C.) —1ST FORD ZODIAC Mk III *(Vinatier & Charon)*

CLASS 8–GROUPS 1 & 2—2ND FORD ZODIAC Mk III *(Greder & Hazard)*

GENERAL CLASSIFICATION
TOURING CARS–GROUPS 1 & 2—2ND FORD ZODIAC Mk III *(Vinatier & Charon)*

same 3ft-deep washaway at high speed; whilst miraculously the suspension and steering gear survived, the tremendous impact had in both cases caused the heavy engines to move forward momentarily on their flexible mountings and smash the fan blades into the radiator.

'Tail-end Charlie', car number 107, was the Zodiac crewed by Eric Jackson and Gregor Grant, and they got into Kandongi without trouble only to find themselves at the end of a long queue because the organisers had mounted a spot check on the cars, including a compression test on the engine to detect an illegal high-compression head. A 45-minute delay was the result for number 107, and Jackson set about recovering some of this despite the unmade roads, but, like the other three Zodiac crews, sensibly resisted the temptation to take a known short-cut off the route which would

Contemporary advertisement records another class win for the Mk 3 Zodiac second time out, in the hands of a French crew on the 1962 Alpine Rally.

229

have saved some time getting into the next control at Chuka. Some crews did take the short-cut but were found out and penalized an extra 50 minutes (50 penalty points).

Running beautifully, the surviving Zodiacs were holding their own well, and confidence in this brand-new model was high. The Jackson/Grant car was being held at 100mph on the straighter sections of unmade road between Nakaru and Londiani, systematically picking off the earlier starters despite the dangers of overtaking through the huge dust clouds generated by every car. The big Fords did lose some time however on the stiff eight-mile climb of the Nandi Hill escarpment, with fuel vaporization slowing the cars near the 9,000ft summit. Vaporization again afflicted the Zodiacs on Mount Elgar, costing a few more precious minutes, but a bigger handicap was the blanket speed limit of 55mph which had to be observed once the cars entered Uganda. A much needed short rest period was alllowed at Kampala before the cars headed out of speed-limited Uganda, back towards Nairobi and completion of the northern loop. Of the 83

Anne Hall swings the Zodiac into a hairpin on the Liege-Sophia-Liege Rally in September 1962 whilst co-driver Val Domleo admires the scenic splendour. Photo from the Anne Hall collection.

surviving entries the Mercedes 220s of Lead/Cardwell and Coniglio/ Jacobz were in first and second places overall, having lost just 29 minutes and 42 minutes, respectively, on·their schedule. Bad news for Mercedes though was that the 220 model of former winner Bill Fritschy had not made it back, having sustained a broken half-shaft. A Fiat 2300 was in third place with 44 minutes lost, whilst Vic Preston, with 54 minutes lost, was the best placed of the Zodiacs in joint ninth position. Gerry Burgess had 56 penalties and was lying 11th overall, and with Tommy Wisdom's and Eric Jackson's Zodiacs also still in, some pundits who had forecast the elimination of all six Zodiacs on the northern loop were forced to eat their words. Even so, the Zodiacs were headed in the over-2,500cc class by the Rover 3-litre in which Ronnie Adams had had an excellent drive so far, having completed the northern loop with a loss of only 48 minutes.

There were 14 hours of rest at Nairobi, with the cars locked away in parc ferme, following which the 83 survivors, again in original numerical order, headed south into the night for Tanganyika on the 1,600-mile southern loop. 120 miles of reasonable dirt roads were covered by the big cars at 80mph or so before the rally turned off into the treacherous, muddy, rock-strewn tracks at the foot of Kilimanjaro. The high set averages proved impossible to keep here, and more penalties were being incurred by all. Away from Kilimanjaro the route eased for a while, but fate now took a hand in the proceedings.

As the smaller classes were getting clear of the Magara-Mbulu section the heavens opened, and torrential rain greeted the first of the big cars to reach the climb over the Magara escarpment. The rally was won and lost right there. As the smaller cars continued on ahead, the escarpment was becoming littered with bogged-down big cars. Much pushing and mutual assistance got some of them going, but the time lost for many was too much for them to beat the closing-time rule at the next checkpoint, several who reached Mbulu finding it already closed. Back-marker Eric Jackson squeezed his Zodiac past many stranded cars but it was damaged underneath, having been grounded when violent evasive action was necessary to avoid a Rover 3-litre attempting to reverse itself out of the morass. Keeping going nevertheless, the Jackson/Grant car managed it

The 1962 Liege-Sophia-Liege again, with Edward and John Harrison seen at the finish with their travel-stained Zodiac. Suspension problems befell the big Fords in this event and the Harrisons' Zodiac was the only one to finish. Photo from the Edward Harrison collection.

almost to the top, only to find there a small queue of cars behind a Mercedes which was completely blocking the road. With everyone lending a hand the Mercedes was freed, but when it came to the Zodiac's turn to restart it wouldn't move; that grounding further back had damaged the clutch mechanism. Tommy Wisdom's Zodiac, too, was out, firmly stuck in what someone said was 'the biggest hole in Africa', and four of the five Ford Falcons had also succumbed.

Both big-car classes had in fact been decimated, and for the few who had somehow made it to Mbulu just within exclusion time there remained of course more than another 1,000 miles of East African terrain – and with hardly a minute to spare. Among them, the Ronnie Adams Rover eventually went out with broken steering, whilst the remaining Humber Super Snipe was eliminated when its sump was holed. Yet, incredibly, a handful of these cars emerged from the drama almost unscathed. A Fiat 2300 survived and just beat the Lead/Cardwell Mercedes 220 in the 2,000cc to 2,500cc class, whilst the Zodiacs of Burgess/Younghusband and Preston/Baillon got back to take first and second respectively in the over-2,500cc class ahead of two Rover 3-litres which had also survived to the end. Naturally pleased with his class win, Gerry Burgess recently recalled: 'They took my car, scrubbed it, polished it until it was in showroom condition for the prize presentation – and then there was a cable from London saying that they (Ford) wanted the car for a special display in the Regent Street showroom, but it had to be exactly as it finished the rally! So I had to go out and find some flooded roads to get it really soiled again.'

As he was now moving to another position within the Ford Motor Company, this Safari had been the last occasion on which the Ford team had been under the managership of Edgy Fabris. He could look back with much satisfaction. Syd Henson, formerly with Ferodo, was now taking on the responsibility of managing Ford's competition programme.

Other interests had resulted in Jeff Uren relinquishing his position within the Competitions Department some time earlier, but he was still available to drive and was at the wheel of a works Zodiac for the Mk 3's racing debut at Silverstone on May 12. This was to be a very serious attempt by the company to explore the Mk 3's racing potential, as additional to Jeff's car were works entries for racing drivers Stirling Moss and Innes Ireland, and a fourth Zodiac for David Haynes who had previously raced a Mk 2 Zephyr as a privateer. However, on the preceding Easter Monday at Goodwood the accident which was to cut short the brilliant racing career of Stirling Moss intervened, and Ford hurriedly signed Continental racing driver Maurice Trintignant as replacement. In practice at Silverstone Jeff Uren was the fastest of the Ford team, but in the race itself his Zodiac developed a misfire during the first lap which persisted throughout to keep him out of contention. Whilst doing battle with John Whitmore's Austin Mini-Cooper, Innes Ireland's Zodiac spun on the 10th lap of the 12-lap event, but rejoined the race still ahead of the other three Zodiacs which were not faring well. Inevitably, the 3.8 Jaguar Mk 2 contingent led everybody home, but it was a disappointment that at the finish Ireland's Zodiac was also headed by the Mini-Coopers two works Sunbeam Rapiers.

The next event contested by Ford was the Alpine Rally, with a four-car team. Anne Hall in an Anglia and newcomer Henry Taylor with a Zodiac were both entered by Ford of Britain, whilst Ford France borrowed two of the Zodiacs from Lincoln Cars and entered these with French crews. This Alpine was divided into Grand Touring (sports car) and Touring (saloon)

Gerry Burgess and Ian Walker head for Monte Carlo in 1963, the weather at low altitude looking anything but wintry.

categories, with separate capacity classes within these two, and the Zodiacs were in the unlimited, over-2,500cc class. Starting from Marseilles, the 2,400-mile route was split into three sections of approximately equal mileage, with the first leg taking the 48 starters north into the mountains before turning east for Brescia and an overnight stop. This section included 10 special stages over mountain passes, and after negotiating these the Greder/Hazzard Zodiac was lying in third place in the Touring Car class behind the Mercedes 220SE of Harris/Ickx and class leader Rene Trautmann's Citroen DS. Leaving Brescia at dawn the following morning the cars headed for the Monza racing circuit where each was to be timed over 20 flat-out laps. Here, the Zodiac came into its own, taking over the class lead from the Citroen and the Harris/Ickx Mercedes, the latter car in fact going out of the rally when its independent rear suspension disintegrated on the rough Monza track. Another contender in the over-2,500cc class was also eliminated here, when the engine of the privately entered 3.8-litre Jaguar Mk 2 of Humble and Dixon suffered a holed piston on the ninth lap. This middle section of the rally was a loop of Northern Italy, taking in many mountain passes, and it was on one of these that the Taylor/Melia Zodiac went out with damaged front suspension after hitting a rock on an unmade stretch. Back at Brescia, the position in the Touring Car category was now Zodiac (Greder/Hazzard), Citroen (Trautmann/Chopin), and Zodiac (Vinatier/Charon), with plenty of opposition to these still remaining in the form of BMW saloons, Mini-Coopers, and a surviving Mercedes 220.

Heading back into Northern Italy on the final section, the rally had to be diverted as, even in June that year, the mighty Stelvio Pass was still blocked by snow. Not affected by snow but nevertheless very treacherous was the Col du Vivione, a gravel-surfaced pass abounding with hairpin bends and unguarded drops. A 31mph average was set for the climb and descent of this, with only two of the GT class, a Porsche and the Morley twins' Austin-Healey 3000 managing this speed to stay clean and, incredibly,

Trautmann's Citroen was also unpenalized over the pass. This fine display put Trautmann back in the lead in the Touring Car category, but some equally fine driving by Greder eventually saw the Zodiac in front again as they headed for the finish at Cannes. Then, right at the end, Greder's Zodiac came to rest with a fuel system failure, so handing the Touring Car category back to the Citroen, with Vinatier's Zodiac runner-up. These two had finished a most creditable fifth and sixth overall in the general classification, behind two of the big Healeys, a Porsche and a Triumph TR4, and ahead of another Austin-Healey 3000 and a couple of TR4s amongst others. With some penalties on the road, however, Vinatier had just failed to win an Alpine Cup, but had won the over-2,500cc Touring class for Ford, whilst Greder had managed to get his Zodiac going again in time to finish in second place in this class.

A formidable-looking works Zodiac entry contested the Liege-Sophia-Liege rally in September, crewed by Anne Hall/Val Domleo, Gerry Burgess/Jeff Uren, Edward and John Harrison, and a fourth car for the Taylor/Melia duo. This line up certainly had potential, but unfortunately the Zodiacs all had front suspension problems because of being fitted with faulty struts in which the rebound stop tubes were too long and punched out the top glands. This problem apparently showed up on the recce, as replacements were sent out for the service crews to fit but did not arrive in time for the start. Although some struts were replaced on the event, the time lost put the cars out of contention. Anne Hall was in sixth place overall when she went out, and the Harrisons were lying fifth overall near the finish when their car succumbed to the problem; but this resourceful pair succeeded in persuading a French photographer working for Ford to 'lend' them the struts from his Zephyr and they changed them over themselves at the roadside in remarkably quick time to get going again and still finish a respectable 11th overall.

The Harrison's car on the Liege, KOO 48, was in action again three weeks later, this time in the hands of Jeff Uren and David Haynes in *The Motor* six-hour saloon car race at Brands Hatch on October 6. Although a works car, this and another Zodiac (COO 10, which had already done the Safari) for Paul Hawkins and Brian Johnstone, were being prepared by Jeff in conjunction with the Ian Walker racing team with whom Hawkins

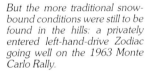

But the more traditional snow-bound conditions were still to be found in the hills: a privately entered left-hand-drive Zodiac going well on the 1963 Monte Carlo Rally.

and Johnstone were sports-car racing drivers. All the entries were permitted to run with modifications within the FIA's Group 2 regulations which, broadly speaking, allowed reworking of the original standard components, but disallowed substituting a light-alloy cylinder head, for example, for the original cast-iron item, and there could be no multiple carburettor arrangements in place of a standard single instrument. Even so, Jeff was able to extract more than 140bhp from the Zodiac engine, achieved principally by gas-flowing and opening up the porting in the standard head, rejetting the carburettor, and reprofiling the camshaft to give more 'bite' above 3,500rpm; changes to the ignition advance curve, and a baffle-less silencer also helped. The lower axle ratio of the Zephyr 4 (3.9:1) was permitted, as was the floor gearchange scheduled, although not yet released, as an option on the standard Mk 3s. A stiffened anti-roll bar at the front and flattened rear leaf springs were used in conjunction with revised damper settings giving a harder action on compression but softer on rebound. Tyre pressures of 46psi front and 42psi rear were used to lessen the Mk 3's normally prodigious understeering characteristics.

With six individually entered 3.8-litre Mk 2 Jaguars amongst the 35 starters, no other model was expected to win outright, but the competition in the other classes was extremely varied and promised considerable interest. Against the Zodiacs in the 1,600cc to 3,000cc class were a pair of 2½-litre V6 Lancia Flaminia Coupes and a trio of Mercedes 220SE saloons, although Mercedes withdraw two of these at the last minute as they were said not to be fully fit, having already been rallied. The Zodiacs started well, proving early on to be faster than the Lancias and the lone Mercedes, with the Hawkins/Johnstone car leading the class at the end of the first hour. Pit stops for fuel and tyre replacements however put them behind the Lancias at the two-hour stage, but after three hours (half way) the Uren/Haynes Zodiac was back leading the class with 80 laps completed, and in close contention with the Harper/Proctor Sunbeam Rapier and the Mini-Cooper of Hulme/Aley both of which had also completed 80 laps. Heavy tyre wear was to be the Zodiac's undoing, with the several pit stops for replacements being made worse by the fact that unlike most other teams the Fords did not have the benefit of a pneumatic jack, and so wheel changing was costing a lap and a half or so each time and was more than offsetting their slightly faster lap times than the two Lancias. Ford had intended to use a pneumatic jack made specially for the Zodiac, but for some reason had not been able to get it ready in time. Running on their standard Michelin X tyres, the Lancias required only one stop throughout for replacements, and even then for the front wheels only, and whilst one of the Italian cars was delayed badly due to an electrical fault, the other finished its six hours stint on 161 laps, having covered two more laps than the best-placed Zodiac of Jeff Uren and David Haynes which took second place in this class.

Jaguars had taken first and second overall with 171 and 167 laps, and the Hulme/Aley Mini-Cooper had covered 164 laps to take an excellent third overall ahead of a Sunbeam Rapier and the Frescobaldi/Fiorio Lancia Flaminia in fifth place. The Zodiacs had finished in eighth and 17th overall, and so far as the Uren/Haynes car is concerned this was a disappointment, as a better equipped pit could have easily resulted in a gain of two, and possibly three full laps.

A team of three works-entered Zodiacs contested the Monte Carlo Rally in January 1963, with the car of Peter Riley finishing quite well placed although not getting amongst the award winners. This proved to be the last works entry of the big Mk 3 Fords, which whilst obviously competitive were nevertheless now recognized as simply not possessing the enormous sporting potential of the company's new mid-range Cortina, of which both Ford's own high-performance GT version and the rather specialized Lotus derivative appeared early in 1963. These were to take over not just from the Zodiac, but also from the Anglia in so far as Ford's own competition programme was concerned, and with the benefit at last of a big-budget approach to competition would be honed into very fine racing and rallying machines which were to bring many honours to the company.

By the time the Mk 4 Zephyr/Zodiac models appeared, Cortina supremacy was widespread indeed in motor sport, and there was certainly no necessity to develop the latest big-car range at all in this respect. Whilst not therefore figuring prominently at all as a competition car, the Mk 4 did nevertheless have its moments, and in fact within a month of its introduction was driven into the record books.

In conjunction with Castrol, who were looking for a spectacular debut for their new 'Liquid Tungsten' motor oil, Ford embarked upon an attempt to set new FIA International speed and endurance records for cars with an engine of up to 3,000cc, in which class the present records were held by Austin-Healey (97mph over four days) and Citroen with an average speed of 86mph for seven days. The venue was to be Monza's banked 2.65-mile oval track, and the target for the Zodiac was to achieve a 100mph average over a full week.

Modifications were allowed under the rules for these attempts, which were open to any types of car, including single-seaters, and therefore several changes were made to the Zodiac which it was hoped would guarantee success. The porting in the cylinder heads was improved, in conjunction with new free-flow manifolds and exhaust system, but the carburation remained the model's standard Weber, and the bowl-in-piston combustion chambers were unchanged. Specially hardened valves were fitted in order to reduce the possibility of valves burning out at sustained full throttle over many hours, but otherwise the engine remained standard from the mechanical point of view, although it was without a cooling fan. In conjunction with the normal four-speed gearbox, a special rear axle assembly of 3.1:1 ratio, with the standard tyre rolling-radius, gave 24mph/1,000rpm without the complication of an overdrive. The tyres however did

Although the factory Competitions Department abandoned the big sixes on the advent of the smaller but quite potent Cortina GT early in 1963, the Zodiac was still popular amongst local private entrants in the East African Safari, and one such car is seen here raising the dust. In British saloon car racing David Haynes continued to race a Zodiac for a while, and Edward Harrison shared one with John Mannussis to score a second in class behind a Volvo 122S in the 1963 Motor six-hour event at Brands Hatch.

pose a problem. The standard 6.70 x 13 cross-ply type could not really be relied upon to withstand a sustained 100mph-plus over several hours, particularly on the rough Monza track which had a reputation for destroying tyres, not to mention breaking suspension systems. The available 13in radials were all of much too small rolling radius, but after having been asked to help at short notice Goodyear came up with a special high-profile radial tyre suitable for the Ford 4½in-wide rim. A set of heavy-duty export road springs were also fitted.

Whilst the bodywork remained standard, a useful aid to streamlining was complete underbody plating enclosing the mechanicals. Changes inside the car involved removing all seating but the driver's, with a 40-gallon fuel tank residing transversely in the rear compartment and stowage space alongside the driver for spare parts and service items, as any parts required throughout the attempt, including the tools, had to be carried inside the car. Major assemblies such as the engine, transmission and suspension units cannot be changed on these record attempts, so mechanical reliability is essential. With 40 gallons on board, plus well-filled tool boxes and numerous spares, the Zodiac was weighing-in substantially heavier than normal, but with its increased tune and underbody streamlining was able to build up to well over 100mph. Practice sessions the week before the attempt determined fuel consumption rates and realistic lap times, and also, thanks to the car being equipped with much additional instrumentation, showed up an alarming tendency for the gearbox and axle oils to overheat. This was due to the underbody shroud, and so it was now partly cut away in the vicinity of the gearbox and final drive to ensure adequate cooling of these parts. Suspension damage occurred too, largely due to a ridge several inches high where one of the concrete sections had become badly misplaced. This in fact had to be broken up by some of the Ford crew before the attempt proper began, but even then the Monza circuit remained like 'a permanent special stage' according to driver Eric Jackson.

In addition to Jackson were drivers Ken Chambers, John Bekaert, John Maclay and Michael Bowler, who drove in shifts on a three hours on twelve hours off basis. Watched anxiously by the small team of mechanics, amongst whom was present-day Ford Press Garage Manager, Lionel Sangster, Zodiac OWC 500D began its attempt at midday, Saturday, May 7. All went well until 11 o'clock on Sunday morning when gloom descended over the watching crew as the Zodiac came to a stand out on the track. Fuel starvation was suspected, and this could perhaps be easily rectified. But as the regulations stipulated that no assistance could be given whilst the car was on the track, there was the difficulty now of getting it back under its own, or the driver's steam, for it was that individual alone who was permitted by the rules to push the car. Solving this problem resulted in the curious sight of a dozen or so helpers in line astern apparently pushing each other, with only the leader, the driver, actually pushing the car! They need not have bothered however, as the trouble lay in the standard carburettor settings which were too lean for the modified car's maximum speed, and the overheating in the combustion chambers caused by the weak mixture had resulted in a melted piston. That record attempt was all over. But there was nothing which barred starting the whole seven-day attempt again – and there was a company hack Zodiac in the pits, with a perfectly healthy engine.

It took Ford mechanics Lionel Sangster, Alf Belson, Dudley Moore and Ernie Pittock, and Castrol's Ron Stacey, less than six hours to get OWC 500D going again with a 'new' engine built up from the two. The block, pistons, connecting rods and crankshaft of the hack engine were used, with new crankshaft bearings. Married to this assembly were the cylinder heads, valve gear, manifolding and fuel system from the damaged engine, the carburettor now fitted with appreciably richer jets.

There was time for some initial running-in, followed by a complete service, before the record attempt started all over again at precisely midnight when John Bekaert embarked upon the first three-hour stint. It was all systems go, with the Zodiac soon settling down to a consistent 106mph lap speed and the whole operation getting into the planned routine. Pit stops occupied little time as everyone swung into action. It took only 12 seconds to replenish the 40-gallon fuel tank by simple gravity feed from a large overhead drum arrangement; there was a filler neck on each side of the car, both of which were opened for the refill, with one taking the nozzle whilst the other instantly discharged the large quantity of displaced air. Other routine checks were carried out under the bonnet, and such was the glow from the almost white-hot exhaust manifolds that no underbonnet lighting was needed when checking the car during the hours of darkness. Changing the spark plugs, which on the V6 are right alongside these manifolds, was a tricky job under these conditions: 'It was one job I wished I hadn't drawn,' remembers Lionel Sangster.

The old records started to fall as the Zodiac began replacing them with altogether more impressive figures: 15,000kms at 105.27mph; 10,000mls at 105.36mph; and 4 days at 105.31mph. But there was anxiety now: the ridged surface construction of the Monza track was taking its toll on the tyres which already had the quite formidable job of coping with over $1\frac{1}{2}$ tons of laden Zodiac at a constant 100mph or more. Tyre wear was rapid, and with a small number having to be discarded early due to chunking, the stock of 36 of these special covers was dwindling faster than had been anticipated. Quick response by Goodyear with more tyres however alleviated the problem. It was the front outside which took the worst hammering of all, with three tyres here losing pieces of their tread; but none of these deflated, nor did a fourth tyre which later lost the whole of its tread whilst on the rear, and this speaks volumes for the soundness of their carcass construction. A broken rear spring was the only other casualty, but it had little adverse effect on the car and was left in position.

With the V6 engine never missing a beat, the record for 20,000kms was taken at 104.73mph, and that for five days at an almost identical speed of 104.72mph. There was a problem ahead now not connected with the car itself at all: Ford had originally booked the track for the week finishing on the Saturday which would have been the final day of the originally planned attempt. Now it would be needed until midnight Sunday, but someone else had already booked it for that day. Delicate negotiations quite literally 'saved the day', and so the white Zodiac pounded on into the early hours of Sunday morning, by this time having added the 15,000mls and six-days records to its growing total, both at an average of 104.43mph.

Eric Jackson took this Zodiac on the Monte Carlo Rally in 1970. A relatively heavy car, fitted with snow tyres and having good suspension geometry, the Mk 4 had excellent traction in slippery going, but unfortunately this attempt was hampered by a frozen fuel system resulting from water-contaminated petrol.

Speed could now be eased a little, as only 95mph or so over the final day would be sufficient to keep both the 25,000kms and seven-day averages comfortably over the three-figure mark. The 25,000kms record was in fact taken at 104.12mph, and when midnight came the Zodiac had completed the seven days at an overall 103.04mph and had covered 17,311 miles. Petrol had been consumed at the rate of 11mpg, whilst consumption of Castrol's new oil had been a modest 1,000 miles-plus per pint. All that had been attempted – nine world records – had been achieved, and all at over 100mph. Total success, and none were more jubilant than those five mechanics whose astonishing makeshift engine had enabled an outstanding victory to be snatched from the very jaws of defeat.

Ford didn't disregard the Mk 4 completely in respect of direct competition work, and one unlikely branch of motor sport in which a works Zodiac proved to be competitive was rallycross, where a subtly modified example gave some remarkable displays in the hands of the versatile Barry Lee. Estate car springs were fitted to this saloon, and at the front were a pair of MacPherson struts specially uprated by Armstrongs. A stiffer anti-roll bar was used, this being of appreciably greater diameter than the original but ground down to standard thickness around the middle of its centre portion. Slightly longer, fabricated track control arms were used in conjunction with a slight negative camber angle adopted for the front wheels. The front-end bodywork was also stiffened with additional welding of the flitch plates and crossmembers, whilst engine movement was restricted by modified mounts.

At the rear were larger bushes at the wishbone's swinging link attachment point, and geometry which now included appreciable rear wheel toe-in in the static condition, and greater negative camber, with the latter angle being calculated to eliminate any of the tuck-under which sometimes afflicted the standard cars. Although seemingly extensive in number these changes were in no way fundamental, but rather refinements for specific use, and were to prove sufficient to make this Zodiac handle in a manner quite appropriate to a competition saloon. It remained, of course, a very large and heavy car, but proved agile enough for Barry Lee to put up some creditable rallycross displays, often in the thick of it with the nimbler smaller models. An outright victory was gained in one autocross event, and Barry also took the Zodiac through a series of driving tests to take first prize at a Plessey Auto Club meeting.

Although it would perhaps have been unreasonable to expect the Mk 4 to gain any top-level rally awards, in an effort to boost the model's image somewhat the Zodiac did make a couple of international rally appearances, the first of these being the Three Cities Rally (Munich-Vienna-Budapest) in 1969. Prepared to Group 2 standards, and driven by Roger Clark of Ford Cortina and Escort fame, the Zodiac finished 16th overall and won its class on this event. The other entry was in the 1970 Monte Carlo Rally on which Eric Jackson took a virtually standard Zodiac. Unfortunately, time was lost on the Continent due to ice in the fuel system after having taken on some water-contaminated petrol, and this spoilt any chances the car might have had of finishing highly-placed in its class. It was perhaps a rather downbeat end for the international competition career of the big British Fords, but nothing could detract from those remarkable performances in the earlier years.

CHAPTER 7

A very special Zephyr

Case history of Peter Scott's car

Amongst the many surviving examples of the big Fords which have come to light in recent years since the formation of the owners' clubs there is surely none more remarkable than RUR 5, which has been owned by Peter Scott, of Barnet in Hertfordshire, ever since it was new. Riding in a friend's model T Ford in the early-1920s had triggered off in Peter Scott an interest in Fords that would continue to grow enthusiastically over the years. As his own motoring experiences broadened he began to visualize a car that would suit his particular requirements right down to the last detail. A succession of Fords, which had included one of the original Y-type Populars, and a secondhand 1935 10hp model still affectionately remembered as 'Barrel Billy', had given him good service, and being a gifted amateur engineer himself he had always appreciated their sound technical features and the quality of the workmanship and materials which had gone into their construction. So it was becoming evident that the 'ideal' car that he had in mind would inevitably be based on a Dagenham product.

What he envisaged was a high-performance saloon that would easily swallow up two people, a large inflatable boat complete with its outboard motor, and all the other luggage and paraphernalia that would be needed on long continental tours. A maximum speed of 100mph would be desirable so that even with all the gear on board an easy 80mph cruise could be maintained along the German autobahns, and acceleration, hill-climbing and handling would have to be good enough to allow Alpine passes to be stormed in something very close to rallying style. At the £1,000 or so which he had available in 1953 there was nothing in the showrooms to fit the bill exactly, but the well-proven, Monte Carlo Rally-winning Zephyr Six, at a tax paid price of £754, certainly did seem to have the potential.

An order was placed with Dagenham Motors, and in March 1954 a brand new Zephyr Six, registration number RUR 5, was collected from their London garage and driven home through a heavy thunderstorm to Barnet. The first stage in achieving that 100mph capability was now begun. It would have been relatively easy to have bought some extra performance by purchasing a tuning conversion, such as those offered by Raymond Mays or Laystall, but Peter was keen to do the cylinder head work himself. The standard head was first exchanged for the optional 7.5:1 compression

ratio Zodiac fitting; this was then gas-flowed by Peter himself in the home workshop at Barnet. The valve ports were carefully opened out and polished, and on reassembly the original valve springs were replaced with Terrys Aero double springs. To get the gases away a complete Servais exhaust system was fitted, comprising a six-branch manifold, a 'straight through' cylindrical silencer 4ft long by 6in diameter, and a large-bore tail-pipe. To give a fatter spark at high rpm a Lucas Sports coil was substituted for the original. An auxiliary electric fan was added to the cooling system along with an automatic tube and bottle radiator replenishing system, whilst warming up was to be assisted by a radiator blind mechanically operated by a crank handle beneath the dashboard in front of the driver.

In view of the heavy loads and high speeds anticipated, Firestone Nylon Sports tyres of the standard 6.40 × 13 size were chosen. Uprated front springs, obtained from the Ford Competitions Department, and Thames van rear shock absorbers were also fitted to help to take care of the load, whilst axle tramp was eliminated by Scott-designed and made nylon-bushed anti-tramp bars.

A very large, heavy-duty Exide battery was found a home in the luggage boot on the opposite side to the spare wheel. All the electrical circuits were individually earthed and fused, the fuseboard being situated on the interior side of the dashboard. The radio aerial, fuel filler cap and windscreen washers are all electrically operated, the washers in particular reflecting Peter Scott's ingenuity; the water line runs inside the windscreen rubber beading to two outlets that are directly above the wipers, and thus allow the water to flow downwards over the screen and on to the wiper blades. A well-stocked instrument panel, designed and made by Peter himself, and carrying fuel gauge, ammeter, combined oil pressure and water temperature gauge, rev-counter, speedometer and clock, sits neatly on top of the steering column shroud in place of the original Ford speedometer housing.

Before running-in was commenced, attention was turned to protecting the bodywork. All the body joints and seams were treated with Dum Dum

waterproof putty, accessibility for this operation being made easy by the bolt-on construction of the front panel and all four wings. The entire under-surfaces were then coated with a home-made mix of lead paint and rubber solution. By now some £200 had been spent on the various bits and pieces, in addition to around 600 hours' work, and RUR 5 was ready for the road. Part of the running-in procedure was accomplished by going from Barnet to Land's End and back on two consecutive weekends.

At this stage, RUR 5 was already considerably quicker than a standard Zephyr, and the suspension modifications ensured that handling and road clinging could match the extra urge. With the brakes, however, it was a somewhat different story, and stopping the Zephyr at an all-up weight with the boat on board of around 3,500lb from speeds approaching 90mph would be a dicey business. The only modifications to the braking system so far had been the introduction of automatic brake bleeders to make fluid changes a simple, one-man operation and thus ease the servicing situation. A set of Ferodo/Girling bonded shoes with a harder than standard grade of lining material, aided by a servo unit which was salvaged from a crashed Connaught racing car, were then installed, and thereafter RUR 5 could stop as well as it could go. The servo unit fitted neatly under the bonnet in the space that had been vacated by the battery.

In the quest for more speed, experiments were carried out with both twin and triple SU carburettor arrangements, but Peter has always had a preference for the simplicity of a single instrument, and a modified and rejetted Zenith, aided by a forward-facing air intake situated under the front of the car and feeding directly into the air cleaner, was found to give very satisfactory results.

In 1957, two further modifications were carried out which put RUR 5 into the genuine 100mph category; the standard crownwheel-and-pinion assembly of 4.444:1 ratio was replaced by a 3.90:1 unit obtained from the Ford Competitions Department, and a Laycock de Normanville overdrive was fitted to the standard three-speed gearbox. The electrically-operated overdrive is controlled by a switch in the top of the gearlever, which is floor-mounted on RUR 5, and is yet another example of Peter Scott's skill, being designed, manufactured and fitted in the home garage in Barnet while the gearbox was out of the car for the installation of the overdrive unit. RUR 5 could now manage just over 100mph in overdrive top and would give a fuel consumption of 22-23mpg cruising at 80mph. In this form the car was

243

taken on a 4,800-mile tour of central Europe during the 1957 summer.

By 1960, the engine, and indeed the whole car, were in peak form, and in June of that year, with some 70,000 miles already behind it, RUR 5 was pounding across Thetford Heath, in Norfolk, in a gale-force wind that was following precisely the same direction. The speedometer quickly left the 100mph scale and settled against the stop, whilst the rev-counter carried on enthusiastically to 6,800rpm which, even allowing for some optimism in the instrument, equated to a speed in excess of 120mph.

The long continental tours each summer, at high speeds and with a heavy load on board, inevitably took their toll, and at 110,000 miles Peter decided that wear in the engine was sufficient to warrant a complete overhaul. The unit was removed from the car and dismantled. The cylinder block was rebored, and the new pistons that were to be fitted were carefully balanced before reassembly. The reground crankshaft was balanced by Alexander, the tuning specialists, and the cylinder head was skimmed to raise the compression ratio still further, the new figure of 9.7:1 being about the limit that can be achieved with the original cylinder head. The power output of the engine has never been measured, but taking into account the original modifications, coupled with the balanced rebuild, a figure of 95bhp would seem to be a reasonable assumption at this stage in the career of RUR 5. In 1966, after a particularly fierce 'pass storming' holiday in the Alps, which had involved much full-throttle first and second gear work, some trouble arose with the gearbox; as the mileage had by now exceeded 120,000, an overhaul of this unit seemed wise and was undertaken by Peter himself.

In 1989, more than 35 years after first taking to the road, and with some 320,000 miles having passed beneath its wheels, RUR 5 still runs as well as ever. There have inevitably been some other repairs and replacements along the way. The car is now on its third clutch assembly, and its fourth Servais 'straight through' silencer was fitted in 1980. The fuel pump and water pump are both replacement items, in 1970 the radiator was reconditioned, and more recently the starter motor was overhauled. A new brake master cylinder has been fitted, and all the brake wheel cylinder seals have been renewed. Brake lining wear has been moderate, thanks no doubt to the harder grade material, and the car is on only its third set of shoes.

Balancing the engine components at the rebuild has certainly paid dividends; in the 200,000-plus miles that have since been covered the only engine replacements have been the timing chain and another set of valve springs. Oil changes at 2,500-mile intervals have also played their part in the low rate of engine wear. Castrol is always used — XXL in the early days and latterly GTX. The benefits gained from regular attention with a grease gun, loaded in this case with Duckhams Laminoid, are amply demonstrated by the fact that apart from a new idler arm assembly, fitted in 1979, the steering gear is still original, and the universal joints on the propeller shaft have also survived from new.

Tyre pressures of 30psi front and 26psi rear, fully loaded (two people and boat on board), or 2psi less all round solo, have always been meticulously maintained, with the result that RUR 5 is only now on its fifth set of covers. The home-made underseal has been periodically inspected and reapplied wherever and whenever necessary, and consequently the whole structure of the car is still virtually perfect. Regular washing and a twice-yearly polishing of the paintwork and chrome-plating with 'old fashioned' Simoniz have endowed RUR 5 today with a remarkably well

kept appearance, although the pleasing Opal colour does seem to have faded a little in places, perhaps because of all those hours of exposure to the brilliant continental sunshine.

Naturally enough, in a life of more than 300,000 miles that has taken RUR 5 across France, West Germany, Holland, Belgium, Denmark, Italy, Monaco, Switzerland and Austria, many times over, there have been some incidents, but fortunately no major accidents. Collision with a pheasant, which was taken home and served for dinner, necessitated the fitting of a new windscreen. Far more alarming was the occasion when both front tyres blew out almost simultaneously at high speed on the autobahn. 'It was a very anxious few moments, but no real disaster', recalls Peter. The German ADAC, an organization similar to the RAC in Britain, came to the rescue on this occasion with a pair of suitable tyres obtained in Munich. In France in 1972, RUR 5 was brought to another involuntary stop after being filled up with petrol that proved to be contaminated with water, and a considerable delay ensued while the fuel lines were disconnected and the system drained and replenished. The comprehensive tool kit that is stowed permanently in RUR 5 was brought into service this time. Peter also remembers, with some amusement, being stopped by Police in Italy for theoretical non-observance of local overtaking rules on an autostrada, and having a furious row when offering a 10,000-lire note for a 2,000-lire fine — they had no change!

Peter Scott will never sell RUR 5; instead, when he, to use his own phrase, 'stops living', the old Zephyr will also return to its makers under the provisions of a clause already included in his will — 'To the Ford Motor Company, for their museum, my Mark 1 Zephyr car, RUR 5, chassis and engine number 80,508, as some appreciation of its excellence and the pleasure it has given me'.

The additional brake fluid reservoir, six-branch manifold and brake servo in the nearside front are all evident in these views. Chrome-plated rocker cover and air cleaner enhance the underbonnet scene. Photos by Peter Scott.

CHAPTER 8

Ahead of its time

The Ferguson Formula Zephyr

Amongst upmarket cars in Britain during the 1960s, one which stood out was the Chrysler V8-powered Jensen FF, which incorporated both the 'Ferguson Formula' four-wheel-drive system of Harry Ferguson Research Ltd and Dunlop's Maxaret anti-lock brakes in its unique specification. The fact that in 1967 these sophisticated transmission and braking arrangements accounted for more than £1,500 of the Jensen FF's tax-paid price of £5,340 was quite enough to indicate that four-wheel-drive would remain out of the reach of most motorists for some considerable time to come. Nevertheless, having successfully converted an American Ford Mustang as a one-off venture during 1967, the Ferguson concern then turned its attention to the possibility of producing four-wheel-drive Mk 4 Zephyrs for which there existed quite a large potential market in the shape of the numerous police forces who already ran Zephyrs and in whose hands the benefits of four-wheel-drive could well be able to justify the extra cost. A successful approach to the Home Office resulted in the Government becoming involved, with orders being placed by the Ministry of Technology for a trial batch of 25 four-wheel-drive Zephyrs with automatic transmission, otherwise to police specification, plus 25 normal-drive automatic Zephyrs also to police specification for direct comparative purposes.

Being of large build, the Mk 4 was a relatively easy car to convert but even so it needed floorpan changes in order to accommodate the transfer gearbox, and a slight realigning of the engine off-centre towards the left-hand-side of the car whilst also being raised very slightly was necessary in order to achieve an ideal front-drive run. Two quite different layouts were initially under consideration, with Scheme A being in effect a mirror-image of the left-hand-drive Mustang conversion, whilst an alternative Scheme B suggested the positioning of the transfer box at the rear of the car immediately ahead of the axle rather than just behind the gearbox as on the Mustang. This would have improved the weight distribution, but introduced a further complication in that an extremely long two-piece propeller shaft back from the transfer box to the front-drive unit would have been needed, and in the event it was the Scheme A layout that was proceeded with. All the changes therefore would be concentrated towards the front of the car; in so far as the drive to the rear wheels was concerned, the only difference would be a shorter propeller shaft because the transfer box was longer than the standard gearbox extension. With a 37% front/ 63% rear power split calculated to retain the feel of a normal car, the transfer box utilized chain drive to a differential within the same casing, from where a short propeller shaft ran forward to another differential for the front-wheel drive. The casing for this front differential was included in the side of a new sump of cast aluminium construction; although integral with the sump, the differential housing contained a separate oil supply from that of the engine. One output shaft ran through the sump to emerge at the nearside. The pair of driveshafts to the front wheels had Rotoflex 'doughnut' couplings at their inner ends, with Hardy Spicer outer joints of the type used on BMC's front-wheel-drive Austin 1800.

Redesigned front suspension was necessary to allow the front wheels to be driven, and this involved the deletion of the MacPherson struts. The anti-roll bar and track-control arms were retained in the role of lower wishbones, with Mustang upper wishbones being introduced. Coil springs embracing telescopic shock absorbers were situated above the upper wishbones, and these arrangements necessitated considerable alterations to the Mk 4's inner wing.

A dual-line braking system was used, with the added refinement of anti-lock operation. Situated at the rear of the transfer box and driven from an idler shaft therein, the Dunlop Maxaret anti-lock unit was essentially a rotating mechanical sensing device which operated an electrical switch should rotation of a driveshaft suddenly almost cease due to imminent wheel-lock. The switch was connected to a solenoid-operated double-diaphragm servo control valve incorporated in the braking system. This could instantly relieve the pressure being applied, and re-apply it as necessary, causing the brake pedal to kick back in a pulsating manner under the driver's foot whenever the car was being braked hard enough to induce wheel locking.

In all, this conversion added 240lbs to the weight of the Mk 4 Zephyr, but although this was concentrated on the front wheels, the provision of power steering as standard meant no extra effort for the driver. This extra weight however, coupled with the greater power losses through the more complicated drive, inevitably resulted in a performance decrease, with rather less lively acceleration and a maximum speed down by some 5 or 6mph. Whilst this could be seen as a slight disadvantage on motorway patrol work, particularly under perfectly dry weather conditions, it was of little consequence otherwise and in fact under give-and-take conditions was almost always more than compensated for by the vastly improved traction, especially of course in wet conditions.

An extensive evaluation programme was carried out by numerous police forces, in many cases with one Ferguson Zephyr and one standard model operating strictly in pairs. Fitted with tachographs, and with their allotted drivers alternating on a shift, or even call-out basis, between the Ferguson and the standard car, both Zephyrs would attend the same incident/emergency calls. Unlike routine patrol work, these call-outs were of course always 'full chat' operations, and so an extremely accurate assessment of these cars' capabilities could be made, with the four-wheel-drive models displaying varying degrees of superiority depending upon the distances involved and the prevailing weather conditions. Comments such as 'uncannilly surefooted' and even 'it was King of the road' amongst the reminiscences of police drivers involved at the time, serve to indicate that the roadability of these Ferguson Zephyrs was of the highest order.

From the mechanical viewpoint also the Ferguson system appears to

247

have been a success, seemingly little in the way of serious trouble being encountered with the four-wheel-drive arrangements, although unfortunately these same Zephyrs were not always trouble-free in other respects. Being at the time the only two Zephyrs on their force, the Ferguson car and its standard model companion evaluated by the Leeds City Police are well remembered by police mechanic Peter Tindall, whose job it was to look after these two cars. Big-end failure at only 3,000 miles on the engine of the Ferguson car was an unfortunate occurrence not characteristic of the Mk 4, but in this case it created difficulties when the local Ford agency claimed that the Ferguson sump had invalidated the Ford warranty. It had not in fact, and Ford sorted out the situation. Another engine rebuild following a stripped fibre timing gear and failure of the Ford C4 automatic gearbox are recalled by Peter as two more blemishes on the record of this pair of cars; but in respect of both the four-wheel-drive arrangements as such and the outstanding roadholding they conferred upon the Mk 4, he remains full of praise. Almost nonchalantly climbing an extremely steep snowbound hill which had defeated all attempts by other traffic is remembered, as are some high-speed laps of the Mintex test track at Sherburn, in Yorkshire, where both the Leeds Zephyrs were checked out during some testing of brake pad materials. Here, whereas the normal Zephyr negotiated a tight dumbell section at one end of the track at impressively high speed, but with a series of somewhat untidy tail-end hops, the Ferguson Zephyr went round appreciably faster, leaning hard but never suggesting that it might put a wheel out of place.

A Ferguson Zephyr was also acquired by the Ministry of Defence, although for what purpose is not stated, whilst a similar car, again to police specification, was in use during 1970 with the British School of Motoring's High Performance Course fleet which was based at the Brands Hatch racing circuit. And, not surprisingly, there were one or two other four-wheel-drive Mk 4s, including a Zodiac estate car driven by one of Ferguson's top management.

By this time the police cars had built up considerable mileages, and the official police report to the Home Office following the lengthy evaluation period is known to have been very highly complimentary indeed. The report was classified information at the time and unfortunately does not appear to have survived; a recent search through their records by the archives branch of the Home Office failed to find any trace, and so it is assumed to have been disposed of during the intervening years. Nevertheless, from talking to those involved who had to use and maintain these cars, it can be established beyond doubt that in 1968 the Ferguson company, who remain in business today under the name FF Developments Ltd, were offering a four-wheel-drive system which twenty years later would have been close to 'state-of-the-art'.

The cost of the Ferguson conversion on the Zephyr was approximately £1,000 per car for the limited numbers involved, but reducing to an estimated £400 each on a batch of 5,000 similar models. In relation to what the car had to offer it was a reasonable figure: but at a time when many forces were being directed to buy cheap cars in the interests of economy, it was too much. Despite the enthusiasm of many policemen for the Ferguson Zephyr, the project was doomed to go no further.

APPENDIX A: Technical specifications

CONSUL (Mk 1)
Engine: 4-cylinder in-line, overhead valves. Bore × stroke 79.37mm × 76.2mm, capacity 1,508cc. Compression ratio 6.8:1. Maximum power 47bhp (nett) at 4,400rpm. Maximum torque 72lb/ft (nett) at 2,400rpm.
Transmission: 3-speed manual gearbox. Axle ratio 4.625:1 (4.556:1 from November 1952). Mph/1,000rpm with 4.625:1 axle: 1st 5.24, 2nd 9.06, top 14.9; with 4.556:1 axle: 1st 5.38*, 2nd 9.3*, top 15.3 (*lower 1st and 2nd gear ratios fitted between November 1952 and April 1953 giving 4.67 and 9.04mph/1,000rpm, respectively).
Tyres: Cross-ply, 5.90 × 13, pressure 28psi. When 165 × 13 radial-ply tyres fitted, overall gearing is reduced to 14.6mph/1,000rpm.
Brakes: Lining area 121sq in.
Steering: Ratio 13.6:1, 2½ turns lock to lock. Turning circle 40ft 6in.
Dimensions: Length 13ft 10in, width 5ft 4in, height 5ft 0¾in, wheelbase 8ft 4in, ground clearance 6½in, track 4ft 2in front, 4ft 1in rear.
Weight: 21¾cwt unladen.

ZEPHYR SIX and ZODIAC (Mk 1)
Engine: 6-cylinder in-line, overhead valves. Bore × stroke 79.37mm × 76.2mm, capacity 2,262cc. Compression ratio 6.8:1 (Zodiac 7.5:1). Maximum power 68bhp (nett) at 4,000rpm (Zodiac 71bhp at 4,200rpm). Maximum torque 108lb/ft (nett) at 2,000rpm (Zodiac 112lb/ft at 2,000rpm).
Transmission: 3-speed manual gearbox. Axle ratio 4.375:1 (4.444:1 from November 1952). Mph/1,000rpm with 4.375:1 axle: 1st 5.75, 2nd 9.95, top 16.35; with 4.444:1 axle: 1st 5.68*, 2nd 9.83*, top 16.15 (*lower 1st and 2nd gear ratios fitted between November 1952 and April 1953 giving 4.93 and 9.55mph/1,000rpm, respectively). Mph/1000rpm with 4.444:1 axle and Borg-Warner overdrive: 2nd 14.2, top 23.0; with Laycock overdrive: 2nd 12.8, top 20.7.
Tyres: Cross-ply, 6.40 × 13, pressure 24psi. When 175×13 radial-ply tyres fitted, overall gearing is reduced to 15.4mph/1,000rpm.
Brakes: Lining area 121sq in.
Steering: Ratio 13.6:1, 2½ turns lock to lock. Turning circle 41ft 6in.
Dimensions: Length 14ft 3¾in, width 5ft 4in, height 5ft 0¾in, wheelbase 8ft 8in, ground clearance 7in, track 4ft 2in front, 4ft 1in rear.
Weight: 23¼cwt (Zodiac 23¾) unladen.

CONSUL (Mk 2)
Engine: 4-cylinder in-line, overhead valves. Bore × stroke 82.55mm × 79.5mm, capacity 1,703cc. Compression ratio 7.8:1 (6.9:1 optional). Maximum power 59bhp (nett) at 4,400rpm (55bhp at 4,400rpm with 6.9:1 CR). Maximum torque 91lb/ft (nett) at 2,300rpm (87lb/ft at 2,300rpm with 6.9:1 CR).
Transmission: 3-speed manual gearbox. Axle ratio 4.11:1. Mph/1,000rpm: 1st 5.95, 2nd 10.2, top 16.9.
Tyres: Cross-ply, 5.90 × 13, pressure 28psi. When 165 × 13 radial-ply tyres fitted, overall gearing is reduced to 16.2mph/1,000rpm.
Brakes: Lining area 147sq in. With disc/drum system, swept area 299sq in.

Steering: Ratio 16.8:1, 3¼ turns lock to lock (ratio 18.1:1, 3½ turns lock to lock, from October 1957). Turning circle 34ft.
Dimensions: Length 14ft 4in (14ft 6½in from February 1959), width 5ft 9in, height 5ft 2in (5ft 0½in from February 1959), wheelbase 8ft 8½in, ground clearance 6¼in, track 4ft 5in front, 4ft 4in rear.
Weight: 22¼cwt unladen.

ZEPHYR and ZODIAC (Mk 2)
Engine: 6-cylinder in-line, overhead valves. Bore × stroke 82.55mm × 79.5mm, capacity 2,553cc. Compression ratio 7.8:1 (6.9:1 optional). Maximum power 85bhp (nett) at 4,400rpm (81bhp at 4,400rpm with 6.9:1 CR). Maximum torque 133lb/ft (nett) at 2,000rpm (127lb/ft at 2,000rpm with 6.9:1 CR).
Transmission: 3-speed manual gearbox (automatic transmission optional extra). Axle ratio 3.90:1. Mph/1,000rpm: 1st 6.5, 2nd 11.27, top 18.5. With Borg-Warner overdrive: 1st 9.2, 2nd 16.1, top 26.42. With Laycock overdrive: 2nd 14.52, top 23.99.
Tyres: Cross-ply, 6.40 × 13 (6.70 × 13 for estate car and with automatic transmission), pressure 24psi. When 175 × 13 radial-ply tyres fitted, overall gearing is reduced to 17.5mph/1,000rpm. 6.70 × 13 tyres (estates and automatics) raise overall gearing to 19.1mph/1,000rpm.
Brakes: Lining area 147sq in. With disc/drum system swept area 299sq in.
Steering: Ratio 16.8:1, 3¼ turns lock to lock (ratio 18.1:1, 3½ turns lock to lock, from October 1957). Turning circle 36ft.
Dimensions: Length 14ft 10½in (Zodiac 15ft 0½in) prior to February 1959, 14ft 11in (Zodiac 15ft 0½in) from February 1959, width 5ft 9in, height 5ft 2in (5ft 0½in from February 1959), wheelbase 8ft 11in, ground clearance 6¼in, track 4ft 5in front, 4ft 4in rear.
Weight: 24cwt (Zodiac 24½cwt) unladen.

ZEPHYR 4 (Mk 3)
Engine: 4-cylinder in-line; overhead valves. Bore × stroke 82.55mm × 79.5mm, capacity 1,703cc. Compression ratio 8.3:1 (7.0:1 optional). Maximum power 68bhp (nett) at 4,800rpm. Maximum torque 93.5lb/ft (nett) at 3,000rpm.
Transmission: 4-speed manual gearbox. Axle ratio 3.90:1. Mph/1,000rpm: 1st 4.91, 2nd 7.86, 3rd 12.29, top 18.5. With optional overdrive and 4.11:1 axle ratio: top 17.55, overdrive top 22.79. With optional automatic transmission and 3.545:1 axle ratio: top 20.3.
Tyres: Cross-ply, 6.40 × 13, pressure 22psi. When 175 × 13 radial-ply tyres fitted, overall gearing is reduced to 17.5mph/1,000rpm with standard 3.90:1 axle.
Brakes: Front disc/rear drum, swept area 299sq in.
Steering: Ratio 18.6:1, 4¼ turns lock to lock. Turning circle 36ft.
Dimensions: Length 15ft 0½in, width 5ft 9in, height 4ft 9½in, wheelbase 8ft 11in, ground clearance 6in, track 4ft 5in front, 4ft 4in rear (4ft 5½in rear track from October 1962.
Weight: 23cwt unladen.

ZEPHYR 6 and ZODIAC (Mk 3)

Engine: 6-cylinder in-line, overhead valves. Bore × stroke 82.55mm × 79.5mm, capacity 2,553cc. Compression ratio 8.3:1 (7.0:1 optional). Maximum power 98bhp (nett) at 4,750rpm (Zodiac 109bhp at 4,800rpm). Maximum torque 134lb/ft (nett) at 2,000rpm (Zodiac 137lb/ft at 2,400rpm).

Transmission: 4-speed manual gearbox (overdrive or 3-speed automatic transmission optional extras). Axle ratio 3.545:1 Mph/1,000rpm: 1st 6.23, 2nd 9.15, 3rd 14.35, top 20.3 (overdrive top 26.4).

Tyres: Cross-ply, 6.40 × 13, pressure 22psi (Zodiac 24psi). When 175 × 13 radial-ply tyres fitted, overall gearing is reduced to 19.2mph/1,000rpm.

Brakes: Front disc/rear drum, swept area 330sq in.

Steering: Ratio 18.6:1, 4¼ turns lock to lock. Turning circle 36ft.

Dimensions: Length 15ft 0½in (Zodiac 15ft 2½in incl. overriders), width 5ft 9in, height 4ft 9½in, wheelbase 8ft 11in, ground clearance 6in, track 4ft 5in front, 4ft 4in rear (4ft 5½in rear track from October 1962).

Weight: 24½cwt unladen (Zodiac 25¼cwt).

ZEPHYR (Mk 4)

Engine: 4-cylinder in 60-degree V formation, overhead valves. Bore × stroke 93.7mm × 72.4mm, capacity 1,996cc. Compression ratio 8.9:1. Maximum power 88bhp (nett) at 4,750rpm. Maximum torque 116lb/ft (nett) at 2,750rpm.

Transmission: 4-speed manual gearbox (3-speed automatic transmission optional extra). Axle ratio 3.70:1. Mph/1,000rpm, standard model with 6.40 × 13 tyres: 1st 4.4, 2nd 8.24, 3rd 12.9, top 19.4.

Tyres: Cross-ply, 6.40 × 13, pressure 24psi. Radial-ply (De Luxe), 185 × 14, pressures 24psi front, 28psi rear.

Brakes: 4-wheel discs, swept area 336sq in.

Steering: Ratio 20.6:1, 5 turns lock to lock (ratio 23.5:1, 6 turns lock to lock, from October 1967). Power steering ratio 18.4:1, 4½ turns lock to lock. Turning circle 36ft.

Dimensions: Length 15ft 5in, width 5ft 11in, height 4ft 10½in, wheelbase 9ft 7in, ground clearance 6½in, track 4ft 9in front, 4ft 10in rear.

Weight: 25¼cwt unladen.

ZEPHYR V6 (Mk 4)

Engine: 6-cylinder in 60-degree V formation, overhead valves. Bore × stroke 93.7mm × 60.3mm, capacity 2,495cc. Compression ratio 9.1:1. Maximum power 112bhp (nett) at 4,750rpm. Maximum torque 137lb/ft (nett) at 3,000rpm.

Transmission: 4-speed manual gearbox (overdrive or 3-speed automatic transmission optional extras). Axle ratio 3.90:1. Mph/1,000rpm, standard model with 6.70 × 13 tyres: 1st 6.03, 2nd 8.62, 3rd 13.52, top 19.1 (overdrive top 23.3).

Tyres: Cross-ply, 6.70 × 13, pressure 24psi. Radial-ply (De Luxe) 185 × 14, pressures 24psi front, 28psi rear.

Brakes, steering, dimensions: as 4-cylinder car.

Weight: 25¾cwt unladen.

ZODIAC (Mk 4)

Engine: 6-cylinder in 60-degree V formation, overhead valves. Bore × stroke 93.7mm × 72.4mm, capacity 2,993cc. Compression ratio 8.9:1. Maximum power 136bhp (nett) at 4,750rpm. Maximum torque 181lb/ft (nett) at 3,000rpm.

Transmission: 4-speed manual gearbox (overdrive or 3-speed automatic transmission optional extras). Axle ratio 3.70:1. Mph/1,000rpm, with 185 × 14 radial-ply tyres, 1st 6.22, 2nd 8.89, 3rd 13.95, top 19.7 (overdrive top 24.0). Early models with 6.70 × 13 tyres, top 20.0, overdrive top 24.4.

Tyres: Cross-ply, 6.70 × 13, pressure 24psi. From October 1967, radial-ply, 185 × 14, pressures 24psi front, 28psi rear.

Brakes: 4-wheel discs, swept area 336sq in.

Steering: Ratio 20.6:1, 5 turns lock to lock. Power steering standard from October 1967, ratio 18.4:1, 4½ turns lock to lock. Turning circle 36ft.

Dimensions: Length 15ft 5½in, width 5ft 11½in, height 4ft 10½in, wheelbase 9ft 7in, ground clearance 6in, track 4ft 9in front, 4ft 10in rear.

Weight: 26cwt unladen.

APPENDIX B: Colour schemes

The following information on paint colours and combinations for Mk 1, 2, 3 and 4 cars has been gathered from Ford Motor Company parts manuals, passenger car colour guides and brochures.

Mk 1 CONSUL and ZEPHYR SIX
Saloons

Winchester Blue, Westminster Blue, Channel Green, Deep Carriage Green, Edinburgh Green, Lichfield Green, Canterbury Green, Dorchester Grey, Bristol Fawn, Ivory*, Metallic Light Blue**, Metallic Light Olive**, Metallic Light Coral**, Opal Blue**, Essex Blue**, Honey Beige**

Convertibles

Westminster Blue, Winchester Blue, Canterbury Green, Dorchester Grey, Black, Mandarin Red*, Ivory*.

MK 1 ZODIAC
Saloons (two-tone)

Dorchester Grey/Bristol Fawn, Dorchester Grey/Canterbury Green, Dorchester Grey/Winchester Blue. (All black to special order.)

*Export only
**Australia/NZ only

Coronation Blue was a colour listed for the Consul and Zephyr Six convertibles during 1953 only. From late 1954 the Zephyr Zodiac was available on request in any current Zephyr Six single-tone paint scheme.

Mk 2 CONSUL, ZEPHYR and ZODIAC
All models February 1956 to October 1957

Black, Ivory, Wells Fawn, Sarum Blue, Carlisle Blue, Hereford Green, Warwick Green, Corfe Grey.

Mk 2 CONSUL De Luxe
Single colours as standard models, or two-tone, body/roof:
Kenilworth Blue/Black, Pembroke Coral/White, Dover White/Ludlow Green, Durham Beige/Pembroke Coral, Norwich Blue/Brecon Grey, Conway Yellow/Black, Pompadour Blue/Black, Sunburst Yellow/Black, Shark Blue/Cirrus White, Cirrus White/Monza Red, Imperial Maroon/Smoke Grey, Black/Smoke Grey, Sapphire Blue/Pompadour Blue, Linden Green/Ermine White, Imperial Maroon/Chateau Grey, Ambassador Blue/Pompadour Blue, Ermine White/Linden Green.

Mk 2 ZODIAC
Single colours as Zephyr, or two-tone, main body/lower side:
Hereford Green/Ivory, Carlisle Blue/Wells Fawn, Ivory/Black, Warwick Green/Carlisle Blue, Corfe Grey/Norwich Blue, Pembroke Coral/Arundel Grey, Newark Grey/Pembroke Coral, Kenilworth Blue/Newark Grey, Dover White/Ludlow Green, Black/Guildford Blue, Ludlow Green/Arundel Grey, Durham Beige/Newark Grey, Norwich Blue/Brecon Grey, Conway Yellow/Newark Grey, Black/Norwich Blue, Sunburst Yellow/Cirrus White, Black/Smoke Grey, Smoke Grey/Pompadour Blue, Vulcan Grey/Smoke Grey, Monza Red/Cirrus White, Cirrus White/Lichen Green, Imperial Maroon/Smoke Grey, Shark Blue/Pompadour Blue, Ming Yellow/Ermine White, Imperial Maroon/Chateau Grey, Ambassador Blue/Pompadour Blue, Ermine White/Linden Green, Lime Green/Regency Grey, Caribbean Turquoise/Ermine White, Ermine White/Pompadour Blue, Lime Green/Linden Green, Windsor Grey/Ascot Grey, Ermine White/Ascot Grey, Rougemont Red/Brecon Grey.

Mk 2 CONSUL, ZEPHYR and ZODIAC
Convertibles: single colours from October 1957
Black, Dover White, Kenilworth Blue, Pembroke Coral, Arundel Grey, Harlech Green*, Guildford Blue, Conway Yellow, Rougemont Red, Brecon Grey, Pompadour Blue, Shark Blue, Ambassador Blue, Smoke Grey, Cirrus White, Lichen Green, Sunburst Yellow, Monza Red, Imperial Maroon, Chateau Grey, Ming Yellow, Regency Grey, Ermine White, Lime Green, Caribbean Turquoise.
Harlech Green unique to convertibles

Mk 2 ZODIAC Convertibles
Two-tone from October 1957, upper/lower:
Conway Yellow/Dover White, Conway Yellow/Black, Arundel Grey/Black, Pembroke Coral/Dover White, Guildford Blue/Arundel Grey, Harlech Green/Arundel Grey, Imperial Maroon/Smoke Grey, Monza Red/Cirrus White, Lichen Green/Cirrus White, Ambassador Blue/Smoke Grey, Sunburst Yellow/Cirrus White, Arundel Lilac/Black, Guildford Blue/Arundel Lilac, Harlech Green/Arundel Lilac, Ermine White/Pompadour Blue, Ming Yellow/Ermine White, Imperial Maroon/Chateau Grey, Regency Grey/Chateau Grey, Ambassader Blue/Pompadour Blue, Lime Green/Regency Grey, Caribbean Turquoise/Ermine White.

Mk 2 ESTATE CARS
October 1956 to October 1957: as saloons.
October 1957 to mid-1959: as saloons, plus two-tone on Consul and Zephyr.
From mid-1959: all black, or two-tone, upper/lower:
Ludlow Green/Dover White, Newark Grey/Kenilworth Blue, Dover White/Newark Grey, Kenilworth Blue/Norwich Blue, Durham Beige/Ludlow Green, Dover White/Durham Beige, Dover White/Conway Yellow, Brecon Grey/Rougement Red, Norwich Blue/Brecon Grey, Ludlow Green/Arundel Lilac, Vulcan Grey/Pompadour Blue, Smoke Grey/Shark Blue, Pompadour Blue/Ambassador Blue, Ambassador Blue/Smoke Grey, Smoke Grey/Vulcan Grey, Monza Red/Cirrus White, Smoke Grey/Lichen Green, Lichen Green/Morocco Beige, Smoke Grey/Sunburst Yellow, Smoke Grey/Monza Red, Smoke Grey/Imperial Maroon, Pompadour Blue/Ermine White**, Regency Grey/Lime Green**, Ermine White/Ming Yellow, Linden Green/Lime Green**, Chateau Grey/Imperial Maroon, Ermine White/Linden Green, Chateau Grey/Regency Grey, Ermine White/Caribbean Turquoise**, Linden Green/Ermine White, Pompadour Blue/Sapphire Blue*.
Consul and Zephyr only
**Zodiac only*

Two-tone 'sandwich' schemes, Zodiac only
Main colour/sandwiched colour:
Newark Grey/Kenilworth Blue, Newark Grey/Durham Beige, Ludlow Green/Dover White, Brecon Grey/Norwich Blue, Newark Grey/Conway Yellow, Norwich Blue/Black, Ambassador Blue/Smoke Grey, Pompadour Blue/Smoke Grey, Smoke Grey/Vulcan Grey, Lichen Green/Cirrus White, Smoke Grey/Imperial Maroon, Pompadour Blue/Shark Blue, Ermine White/Ming Yellow, Chateau Grey/Imperial Maroon, Chateau Grey/Regency Grey, Pompadour Blue/Ambassador Blue, Regency Grey/Lime Green, Ermine White/Caribbean Turquoise, Pompadour Blue/Ermine White, Linden Green/Lime Green, Linden Green/Ermine White.

Colours introduced from October 1957 onwards were identified by code letters on the vehicle trim identification plate:
A Black, AA Richmond Blue, AB Pembroke Coral, AC Newark Grey, AD Ludlow Green, AE Durham Beige, AF Arundel Lilac†, AG Guildford Blue, AH Conway Yellow†, AN Rougement Red†, AP Cirrus White, AQ Morocco Beige, AR Pompadour Blue, AS Lichen Green, AU Smoke Grey, AV Shark Blue, AX Vulcan Grey, AZ Imperial Maroon, BA Ermine White, BB Regency Grey, BC Lime Green, BD Ming Yellow, BE Chateau Grey, BH Caribbean Turquoise, BJ Linden Green, BL Ascot Grey, BM Windsor Grey, BN Sapphire Blue, BP Panama Yellow, BR Goodwood Green, BS Monaco Red, E Dorchester Grey, M Norwich Blue, N Ambassador Blue, W Brecon Grey, X Rialto Red, Y Dover White, Z Kenilworth Blue.
(† code AF later changed to Arundel Grey; AH to Sunburst Yellow; AN to Monza Red)

MK 3 ZEPHYR 4, ZEPHYR 6 and ZODIAC
Saloons and estate cars
Caribbean Turquoise, Sapphire Blue, Savoy Black, Ermine White, Ascot Grey, Ambassador Blue, Imperial Maroon, Windsor Grey, Goodwood Green, Lime Green, Monaco Red, Platinum Grey, Aqua Blue, Tuscan Yellow*, Spruce Green, Panama Yellow, Purbeck Grey, Light Blue* Velvet Blue, Alpina Green, Black Cherry, Ebony, Midnight Blue**, Sable**, Alcuda Blue metallic**, Malabu Gold metallic**.
*Zephyr 4 and 6 only
**Zodiac only

Mk 3 EXECUTIVE
Alcuda Blue metallic, Malabu Gold metallic, Sable, Midnight Blue, Ebony, Ermine White, Purbeck Grey, Spruce Green, Velvet Blue, Aqua Blue, Black Cherry, Alpina Green.

Mk 4 ZEPHYR, ZEPHYR V6, ZODIAC and EXECUTIVE
Saloons
Ermine White, Purbeck Grey, Alpina Green, Black Cherry, Lagoon Blue, Anchor Blue, Ebony, Spruce Green, Seafoam Blue, Ligfht Blue, Light Green, Light Grey, Red*, Burgundy Red, Beige, Aubergine**, Garnet, Diamond Blue, Marine Blue, Silver Fox metallic, Blue Mink metallic, Venetian Gold metallic**, Saluki Bronze metallic, Amber Gold metallic, Fern Green metallic, Aquatic Jade metallic, Light Orchid metallic**, Tawny metallic, Evergreen metallic, Sapphire metallic, Pacific Blue metallic, Glacier metallic.
*Zephyr and Zephyr V6 only
**Zodiac and Executive only

Estate cars
Ermine White, Alpina Green, Lagoon Blue, Purbeck Grey, Diamond Blue, Garnet, Anchor Blue, Silver Fox metallic, Fern Green metallic, Evergreen metallic.

APPENDIX C: Production figures

Mk 1 MODELS

Consul	1951	1952	1953	1954	1955	1956	Total
Built up	19,787	22,611	32,452	34,998	42,186	5,978	158,012
Knocked down	15,880	13,681	15,773	14,895	13,040	200	73,469
Total	35,667	36,292	48,225	49,893	55,226	6,178	231,481

Mk 1 Consul production ran from January 1, 1951 to February 22, 1956.

Zephyr/Zodiac	1951	1952	1953	1954	1955	1956	Total
Built up	2,513	12,656	25,180	27,814	28,075	2,148	98,386
Knocked down	950	11,670	18,950	21,480	22,875	1,000	76,925
Total	3,463	24,326	44,130	49,294	50,950	3,148	175,311

Mk 1 Zephyr/Zodiac production ran from Febraury 12, 1951 to February 22, 1956. Total production was split as follows: Zephyr Six 152,677; Zephyr Zodiac 22,634.
All quoted Mk 1 production figures include convertibles and estate cars, which are believed to account for less than 2% of the total.

Mk 2 MODELS

Consul	1956	1957	1958	1959	1960	1961	1962	Total
Built up	28,054	42,038	58,853	57,038	54,354	44,265	6,349	290,951
Knocked down	11,990	12,890	8,415	11,368	9,660	4,400	570	59,293
Total	40,044	54,928	67,268	68,406	64,014	48,665	6,919	350,244

Mk 2 Consul production ran from February 1956 to April 1962.

Zephyr/Zodiac	1956	1957	1958	1959	1960	1961	1962	Total
Built up	23,233	26,986	26,686	36,386	37,195	23,786	3,313	177,585
Knocked down	15,022	22,360	26,470	27,700	18,820	11,835	1,625	123,832
Total	38,255	49,346	53,156	64,086	56,015	35,621	4,938	301,417

Mk 2 Zephyr/Zodiac production ran from January 26, 1956 to April 1962.
Zodiac models accounted for approximately 80,000 of total Zephyr/Zodiac production.
Both Consul and Zephyr/Zodiac figures include convertibles, which accounted for approximately 2% of total production.

Estate car	1956	1957	1958	1959	1960	1961	1962	Total
Consul/Zephyr/Zodiac								
Built up	119	870	898	1,204	1,475	1,039	38	5,643
Pick-up/Utility								
Built up (Nov 56 – Aug 59)	1	13	21	11	–	–	–	46
Knocked down (June 57 – Jan 61)	–	3,030	5,820	4,650	4,030	50	–	17,580
Station wagon (Australian)								
Knocked down (Mar 59 – Jan 61)	–	–	–	3,880	3,530	60	–	7,470

Figures for pick-up/utility and station wagon are for 4-cylinder and 6-cylinder models combined.

Mk 3 MODELS

Zephyr 4 saloons

	1961	1962	1963	1964	1965	Total
Domestic	–	16,636	23,060	20,828	18,993	79,517
Export built up	–	4,823	2,733	2,444	1,369	11,369
Export knocked down	–	5,465	4,950	2,360	850	13,625
Total	–	26,924	30,743	25,632	21,212	104,511

Zephyr 4 estate cars

	1961	1962	1963	1964	1965	Total
Domestic	–	48	247	231	137	663
Export built up	–	12	21	13	16	62
Total	–	60	268	244	153	725

Zephyr 6 saloons

	1961	1962	1963	1964	1965	Total
Domestic	–	7,255	12,549	12,838	10,603	43,245
Export built up	–	6,481	4,052	3,293	1,982	15,808
Export knocked down	–	10,895	14,995	12,595	7,520	46,005
Total	–	24,631	31,596	28,726	20,105	105,058

Zephyr 6 estate cars

	1961	1962	1963	1964	1965	Total
Domestic	–	54	470	542	558	1,624
Export built up	–	40	107	97	80	324
Total	–	94	577	639	638	1,948

Zodiac saloons

	1961	1962	1963	1964	1965	Total
Domestic	29	11,043	14,901	14,199	11,446	51,618
Export built up	12	4,869	3,063	2,784	1,168	11,896
Export knocked down	–	4,680	3,095	2,705	1,650	12,160
Total	41	20,592	21,059	19,688	14,294	75,674

Zodiac estate cars

	1961	1962	1963	1964	1965	Total
Domestic	–	64	578	520	410	1,572
Export built up	–	4	30	26	17	77
Total	–	68	608	546	427	1,649

Mk 3 Zodiac saloon figures include Executive production.
Mk 3 1966 production: 2,375 vehicles (all models).

Mk 4 MODELS

All versions	1965	1966	1967	1968	1969	1970	1971	Total
	3	49,773	18,406	24,744	19,828	18,925	16,758	148,347

Approximate individual totals:

Zephyr	45,000
Zephyr V6	57,000
Zodiac/Executive	46,000

APPENDIX D: Major competition awards

1952
Dutch International Tulip Rally
  Outright winner   Consul Mk 1   K. Wharton/J. Langalaan

1953
Monte Carlo Rally
  Outright winner   Zephyr Six Mk 1   M. Gatsonides/P. Worledge
Norwegian International Viking Rally
  Outright winner   Zephyr Six Mk 1   C. Johansson/G. Jensen
  3rd overall   Zephyr Six Mk 1   I. Hartley/H. Tillbjorn
Lisbon Rally
  Ladies prize   Zephyr Six Mk 1   Nancy Mitchell

1954
RAC International Rally

3rd overall	Zephyr Six Mk 1	T. C. Harrison/E. Harrison
1st Saloon car category	Zephyr Six Mk 1	T. C. Harrison/E. Harrison

Dutch International Tulip Rally

1st 1,301-1,600cc Touring cars	Consul Mk 1	J. G. Reece/P. Reece
2nd 1,301-1,600cc Touring cars	Consul Mk 1	J. W. Fleetwood/G. Read
1st 1,601-2,600cc Touring cars	Zephyr Six Mk 1	R. W. Philips/D. G. Scott

Scottish International Rally

1st 1,301-1,600cc Touring cars	Consul Mk 1	D. G. Morley/E. Morley
1st 1,601-2,600cc Touring cars	Zephyr Six Mk 1	P. S. Hughes

1955
Monte Carlo Rally

4th Overall	Zephyr Six Mk 1	G. N. Burgess/P. Easton
Stuart Trophy (1st British car/driver)	Zephyr Six Mk 1	G. N. Burgess/P. Easton

RAC International Rally

1st 1,301-2,600cc GT cars	Zephyr Six Mk 1	T. C. Harrison/E. Harrison
2nd 1,301-2,600cc GT cars	Zephyr Six Mk 1	S. H. Allard/T. L. Allard
3rd 1,301-2,600cc GT cars	Zephyr Six Mk 1	J. G. Reece/P. B. Reece

Dutch International Tulip Rally

1st 1,301-3,500cc Special Series	Zephyr Six Mk 1	T. C. Harrison/R. Habershon
2nd 1,301-3,500cc Special Series	Consul Mk 1	J. G. Reece/P. B. Reece
3rd 1,301-3,500cc Special Series	Zephyr Six Mk 1	S. Henson/Weich

East African Safari

1st overall	Zephyr Six Mk 1	V. Preston/D. P. Marwaha
Lady McMillan Trophy (Ladies prize)	Zephyr Six Mk 1	Mary Wright

1956
Alpine Rally

Coupes des Alpes	Zephyr Mk 2	T. C. Harrison/E. Harrison
Coupes des Alpes	Zephyr Mk 2	D. G. Scott/S. Astbury
1st 2,000-2,600cc category	Zephyr Mk 2	T. C. Harrison/E. Harrison
2nd 2,000-2,600cc category	Zephyr Mk 2	D. G. Scott/S. Astbury

1957
Dutch International Tulip Rally

Team prize	Zephyr Mk 2	D. G. Scott/J. D. Irlam
	Zephyr Mk 2	R. J. Adams/E. T. McMillan
	Zephyr Mk 2	T. C. Harrison/J. F. Harrison
Ladies prize.	Zephyr Mk 2	Anne Hall/Mary Hopkinson

1958
Monte Carlo Rally

1st over 2,000cc Touring cars	Zodiac Mk 2	R. Nelleman/M. Skarring

RAC International Rally

1st over 2,000cc GT cars	Zephyr Mk 2	D. G. Scott/K. Armstrong

East African Safari

1st overall (see text)	Zephyr Mk 2	A. T. Kopperud/K. M. Kopperud
Team prize (see text)	Zephyr Mk 2	A. T. Kopperud/K. M. Kopperud
	Zephyr Mk 2	F. Brown/F. Collis
	Zephyr Mk 2	V. Preston/K. Springer
Ladies prize	Zephyr Mk 2	Mary Wright

Scottish International Rally

1st 1,601-2,600cc Touring cars	Zephyr Mk 2	E. Jackson

Alpine Rally

Coupe des Alpes	Zephyr Mk 2	E. Harrison/R. Habershon
1st Over 1,600cc Touring cars	Zephyr Mk 2	E. Harrison/R. Habershon
2nd Over 1,600cc Touring cars	Zephyr Mk 2	T. C. Harrison/J. F. Harrison

1959

East African Safari
2nd overall	Zephyr Mk 2	D. G. Scott/P. R. Davies
3rd overall	Zephyr Mk 2	E. Harrison/D. L. Markham
Team prize	Zephyr Mk 2	D. G. Scott/P. R. Davies
	Zephyr Mk 2	E. Harrison/D. L. Markham
	Zodiac Mk 2	F. C. Young/L. Baillon

Dutch International Tulip Rally
3rd overall	Zephyr Mk 2	P. Riley/R. Bensted-Smith
1st 1,601-2,600cc Touring cars	Zephyr Mk 2	P. Riley/R. Bensted-Smith
3rd 1,601-2,600cc Touring cars	Zephyr Mk 2	T. C. Harrison/J. F. Harrison
Team prize	Zephyr Mk 2	P. Riley/R. Bensted-Smith
	Zephyr Mk 2	T. C. Harrison/J. F. Harrison
	Zephyr Mk 2	G. N. Burgess/S. Croft-Pearson

Alpine Rally
Coupe des Alpes	Zephyr Mk 2	P. Riley/A. Pitts
Coupe des Alpes	Zephyr Mk 2	T. C. Harrison/J. F. Harrison
Coupe des Alpes	Zephyr Mk 2	E. Harrison/W. Fleetwood
1st Over 2,000cc Touring cars	Zephyr Mk 2	P. Riley/A. Pitts
2nd Over 2,000cc Touring cars	Zephyr Mk 2	T. C. Harrison/J. F. Harrison
3rd Over 2,000cc Touring cars	Zephyr Mk 2	E. Harrison/W. Fleetwood
Team prize	Zephyr Mk 2	P. Riley/A. Pitts
	Zephyr Mk 2	T. C. Harrison/J. F. Harrison
	Zephyr Mk 2	E. Harrison/W. Fleetwood

RAC International Rally
Outright winner	Zephyr Mk 2	G. N. Burgess/S. Croft-Pearson

BRSCC Saloon Car Championship
Outright winner	Zephyr Mk 2	J. M. Uren

1960

Monte Carlo Rally
1st Over 2,000cc GT cars	Zodiac Mk 2	L. Handley/D. Harvey

East African Safari
3rd overall	Zephyr Mk 2	V. Preston/J. F. Harrison
Team prize	Zephyr Mk 2	V. Preston/J. F. Harrison
	Zephyr Mk 2	T. C. Harrison/P. Davies
	Zephyr Mk 2	D. G. Scott/L. Baillon

1961

Monte Carlo Rally
1st Over 2,000cc GT cars	Zodiac Mk 2	L. Handley/D. Harvey
2nd Over 2,000cc GT cars	Zephyr Mk 2	G. N. Burgess/S. Croft-Pearson
3rd Over 2,000cc GT cars	Zephyr Mk 2	E. Jackson/J. Foster

East African Safari
3rd overall	Zephyr Mk 2	Anne Hall/Lucille Cardwell
Ladies prize	Zephyr Mk 2	Anne Hall/Lucille Cardwell
Team prize	Zephyr Mk 2	Anne Hall/Lucille Cardwell
	Zephyr Mk 2	T. Wisdom/P. Walker
	Zephyr Mk 2	T. C. Harrison/P. Davies

1962

East African Safari
1st Over 2,500cc category	Zodiac Mk 3	G. N. Burgess/B. Younghusband
2nd Over 2,500cc category	Zodiac Mk 3	V. Preston/L. Baillon

Alpine Rally
2nd Touring Car category	Zodiac Mk 3	J. Vinatier/J. Charon
1st Over 2,500cc Touring Cars	Zodiac Mk 3	J. Vinatier/J. Charon
2nd Over 2,500cc Touring Cars	Zodiac Mk 3	Greder/Hazzard

1966

International Class D (2,000 to 3,000cc) speed and endurance records taken by Zodiac Mk 4 at Monza:
15,000kms at 105.27mph
10,000 miles at 105.36mph
4 days at 105.31mph
20,000kms at 104.73mph
5 days at 104.72mph
15,000 miles at 104.43mph
6 days at 104.43mph
25,000kms at 104.12mph
7 days at 103.04mph
Drivers: E. Jackson, K. Chambers, J. Bekaert, M. Bowler, J. Maclay.

APPENDIX E: Clubs and spares specialists

Owners' Clubs

Five Stars, the Ford Mk 1 Consul Zephyr Zodiac Owners' Club.
Membership Secretary, Neil Tee, 8 Park Farm Close, Shadoxhurst, Ashford, Kent TN26 1LD

Ford Mk 2 Consul Zephyr Zodiac Owners' Club.
Membership Secretary, Wendy Debenham,
170 Conisborough Crescent, Catford, London SE6 2SH

Mk 2 Independent Owners' Club (1959-62 Consul Zephyr Zodiac)
173 Sparrow Farm Drive, Feltham, Middlesex TW14 0DG

Ford Mk 3 Zephyr & Zodiac Owners' Club
Membership Secretary, Chris Bagley, 33 Cambridge Road, Mitcham, Surrey CR4 1DW

Zephyr & Zodiac Mk 4 Owners' Club
94 Claremont Road, Rugby, Warwickshire CV21 3LU

A network of local owners' clubs catering for all Consul Zephyr Zodiac models exists throughout Australia and New Zealand.

Spares Specialists

Ford Fifty Spares: prop. K. Tingey
69 Jolliffe Road, Poole, Dorset BH15 2HA
Tel. 0202 679258

Goldendays Motor Services: prop. J. Blyth
1 St Walstans Road, Taverham, Norwich NR8 6NE
Tel. 0603 881155

Old Ford Spares Service: prop. A. Murrell
24 Marlborough Road, Rugby, Warwickshire CV22 6DD
Tel. 0327 843688

Cotswold Classic Car Services: prop. A. Tutt
Worgans Barn, Folly Lane, Stroud, Glos. GL6 7JS
Tel. 0453 750713

Paul Boothby
68 King Street, Burton-on-Trent, DE14 3EF
Tel. 0283 32954

D. & E. Brown
Hill Crest, Buckstones Road, Grains Bar, Oldham OL1 4SU
Tel. 061 633 3223

Five Star Ford
Unit 12, Industrial Estate, Milkwood Road, London SE24
Tel. 01 326 0306

New Ford Parts Centre
Abbey Mill, Abbey Village, Nr. Chorley, Lancs. PR6 8DN
Tel. 0254 830343

Reg Hewitt
214 Middle Lane, Hornsey, London N8
Tel. 01 340 9001

Ludford Spares
Tel. 0584 5142

Barry's Automobilia: prop. D. Barry
P.O. Box 46, Epping, N.S.W. 2121, Australia
Tel. (International) 612 869 8969